A PANDEMIC OF PC

Over the last decade, the world has watched in shock as populists swept to power in free elections. From Manila to Warsaw, Brasilia to Budapest, the populist tide has shattered illusions of an inexorable march to liberal democracy. Eschewing simplistic notions of a unified global populism, this book unpacks the diversity and plurality of *populisms*. It highlights the variety of constitutional and extraconstitutional strategies that populists have used to undermine the institutional fabric of liberal democracy and investigates how ruling populists responded to the Covid-19 crisis. Outlining the rise of populisms and their governing styles, Wojciech Sadurski focuses on what populists in power *do*, rather than what they *say*. Confronting one of the most pressing concerns of international politics, this book offers a vibrant, contemporary account of modern populisms and, significantly, considers what we can do to fight back.

WOJCIECH SADURSKI is Challis Professor of Jurisprudence at the University of Sydney and Professor at the Centre for Europe at the University of Warsaw, formerly Professor and Head of Department of Law at the European University Institute in Florence. He is author of several books, most recently *Poland's Constitutional Breakdown* (2019) and *Constitutionalism and the Enlargement of Europe* (2012). He regularly teaches, as visiting professor, in top universities around the world, including at Yale and New York Universities.

A PANDEMIC OF POPULISTS

WOJCIECH SADURSKI
University of Sydney
University of Warsaw

CAMBRIDGE
UNIVERSITY PRESS

CAMBRIDGE
UNIVERSITY PRESS

University Printing House, Cambridge CB2 8BS, United Kingdom

One Liberty Plaza, 20th Floor, New York, NY 10006, USA

477 Williamstown Road, Port Melbourne, VIC 3207, Australia

314–321, 3rd Floor, Plot 3, Splendor Forum, Jasola District Centre, New Delhi – 110025, India

103 Penang Road, #05–06/07, Visioncrest Commercial, Singapore 238467

Cambridge University Press is part of the University of Cambridge.

It furthers the University's mission by disseminating knowledge in the pursuit of education, learning, and research at the highest international levels of excellence.

www.cambridge.org
Information on this title: www.cambridge.org/9781009224505
DOI: 10.1017/9781009224543

© Wojciech Sadurski 2022

This publication is in copyright. Subject to statutory exception and to the provisions of relevant collective licensing agreements, no reproduction of any part may take place without the written permission of Cambridge University Press.

First published 2022

A catalogue record for this publication is available from the British Library.

Library of Congress Cataloging-in-Publication Data
Names: Sadurski, Wojciech, 1950– author.
Title: A pandemic of populists / Wojciech Sadurski, University of Warsaw.
Description: Cambridge, United Kingdom ; New York, NY : Cambridge University Press, 2022. | Includes bibliographical references and index.
Identifiers: LCCN 2022001086 (print) | LCCN 2022001087 (ebook) | ISBN 9781009224505 (hardback) | ISBN 9781009224536 (paperback) | ISBN 9781009224543 (epub)
Subjects: LCSH: Law–Political aspects. | Populism.
Classification: LCC K487.P65 S23 2022 (print) | LCC K487.P65 (ebook) | DDC 340/.115–dc23/eng/20220430
LC record available at https://lccn.loc.gov/2022001086
LC ebook record available at https://lccn.loc.gov/2022001087

ISBN 978-1-009-22450-5 Hardback
ISBN 978-1-009-22453-6 Paperback

Cambridge University Press has no responsibility for the persistence or accuracy of URLs for external or third-party internet websites referred to in this publication and does not guarantee that any content on such websites is, or will remain, accurate or appropriate.

In paradise a work week is thirty hours
salaries are higher prices plummet down
manual labor isn't tiring (due to decreased gravity)
chopping wood is equivalent to typing
the social order is stable and the government wise
paradise really is better than any country in sight
(...)

Few see God
God is only for those who are made of pure pneuma
the rest listen to bulletins on deluges and miracles
with time everyone will see God
though no one knows when that will happen

For now every Saturday at noon
sirens sweetly holler
and celestial proletarians exit factories
wings tucked clumsily under their arms like violins

    (Zbigniew Herbert, "Dispatch from Paradise," 1969, excerpt.
                    Transl. Natalia Osiatyńska)

I am very grateful to Natalia Osiatyńska for her kind permission to publish an excerpt of her translation of Zbigniew Herbert's poem. I am also grateful to the holders of copyright to Zbigniew Herbert's works for their generous permission.

CONTENTS

Introduction   1
1   Why Populisms?   17
2   The War on Institutions   48
3   Constitutions: Breaches, Abuses, and Literal Democracy   83
4   Courts: The Least Resilient Branch   106
5   Paranoia   143
6   Democracy Diseased: Populism in the Time of Covid   174
7   Antidotes, Remedies, and Miracles   206

Annex: Country Selection Explanation   222
References   226
Acknowledgments   243
Index   244

Introduction

As anyone who has visited Budapest over the past few decades knows, the best way to get from Liszt Ferenc Airport to a hotel in downtown Budapest is by minibus. Unless, that is, you are rich or a VIP, in which case you would take an overpriced taxi or be provided with a limousine. The road all minibuses take is an ordinary thoroughfare through some decrepit, Stalinist-era city quarters, gradually moving into Üllöi Street with its increasingly beautiful nineteenth-century bourgeois edifices, ultimately revealing the enormous charm of this Austro-Hungarian pearl of a city.

The last time I visited, in mid-April 2018, I noticed something I had not seen in my earlier visits to Budapest. Every 100 meters or so, there were gigantic street-side billboards, each depicting two men. One man – older – was always the same on all billboards. The other – younger – man varied from one billboard to another. But the variations were limited: There were just two or three men, whose faces alternated between each billboard. Although I could not understand the huge text on the billboard (how many non-Hungarians speak Hungarian? I don't), I quickly realized that they were remnants from Hungary's recent electoral campaign. The election had taken place some ten days before, and the billboards hadn't yet been removed. Perhaps they were left up on purpose.

I did not recognize the faces of the middle-aged men, but the older constant character is very well known. His name is George Soros – American billionaire of Hungarian-Jewish origin, financial dealer on a global scale and global philanthropist, too. To make it clear, he was *not* on the ballot box. In a Photoshopped embrace with the *opposition party* leaders, he symbolized everything evil and dangerous according to Viktor Orbán's incumbent Fidesz party: cosmopolitanism, "anti-Hungarism" (whatever that might mean) and, above all, a secret plan to import millions of Muslims to Hungary. Billboards were signed with the logo of Fidesz. And the billboards, along with all the other elements of Orbán's partisan propaganda, worked. Orbán's party won nearly 48 percent of the vote, giving it nearly 67 percent of seats in Hungary's unicameral parliament.

After I settled in my nice hotel in a lively street just a block from the Danube, I met my younger friends, two socio-legal scholars working at a university in Budapest, for dinner. We had known each other from their earlier doctoral research years, when I was their mentor/teacher/friend at the European University Institute (EUI) in Florence. The dinner – including an obligatory, delicious fish soup – had all the promise of a joyful, carefree conversation among friends, including scholarly matters but also the usual gossip: who did what, who married whom, who split up with whom, and so forth. But the joy of the evening was only temporary.

My ex-students, now my friends, had good reason to be concerned about their fates. Their university – the Central European University (CEU), an elite, international, state-of-the-art higher education institution that attracted the very best professors and students from all over the world – was in big trouble, and my friends' professional futures were uncertain. First established in 1991, the university was founded and initially funded by the Orbán government's Public Enemy No. 1. Yes, you guessed it: George Soros. And so Orbán and his people were doing everything they could to banish the university from Hungary's patriotic, Christian soil. The pretext for this could be found in a law on foreign universities passed in April 2017, which was designed specifically to target the CEU. Among other things, the law required foreign universities to have a campus not only in Hungary but also in their home country, which CEU didn't have. CEU officials complied with the terms of the new law by establishing academic programs in New York State. But the Hungarian government refused to sign an agreement, which left CEU deprived of a legal basis to continue to operate normally in Budapest.

Eventually, the university was "evacuated" to Vienna in 2019. One of my dinner companions, a woman, later moved to a good university in the UK; another, a man, continued to work in the CEU, but no longer in Budapest. (In a significant postscript, in 2020, the Hungarian government signed an agreement with the Shanghai-based Fudan University to set up a new campus in Budapest.)

And so, the billboard images and the fates of my friends came together through one link: the figure of George Soros.

There was another story related to my airport-to-city transfer that I was told that night at dinner. A "while we are talking about billboards..." type of segue, but this time not in connection with George Soros.

Founded as early as 1989, a Spanish-Hungarian company called ESMA became the leading outdoor advertiser in Hungary. It was big on what economists call "rent seeking" – in this case, state advertisements. But

ESMA had a major defect in Orbán's eyes: The company was close to his chief political rival, the Socialist Party (MSZP). In fact, it was due to ESMA's proximity to that party – MSZP was the main ruling coalition partner between 2002 and 2010 – that the company was doing really well. However, the combination of its huge profits and "wrong" political colors made it a vulnerable target for a predatory takeover by Orbán's clique. Two major bids by Orbán's main oligarch and economic mastermind, Lajos Simicska, were refused. The second bid, in 2012, belonged to the category of offers you cannot refuse – and yet, despite enduring punitive tax controls in its corporate offices, ESMA had the temerity to resist. Soon after, the Hungarian parliament (safely controlled by a Fidesz majority) prohibited all advertising on sidewalks within five meters off the road. It was necessitated by road safety, you see. There was one little problem, though – the rule would have affected some of Simicska's companies too, including MAHIR, which also owned advertising boards. But this unpleasant effect was quickly eliminated by way of a simple legal exemption for MAHIR. The legislative change meant that ESMA, of course, lost almost all its value overnight. The company once brought in fantastic profits, but in the first year after the legislation was passed, ESMA suffered losses of more than 209 million HUF (EUR 627,000). After a few years of agony, the company was sold in April 2015 to István Garancsi, one of Hungary's richest citizens and Orbán's close friend.

And the billboards, what about the billboards? you might ask. The answer is nothing. The five-meter regulation was repealed in July 2015, immediately after the billboards changed hands. The government discovered that road safety was not such a big problem after all. In fact, a new rationale *for* roadside billboards was found – billboards are of importance in providing information to the people. It is no wonder that under Garancsi's leadership, the company could again operate at full capacity. In the first year that ESMA was in Garancsi's hands, it returned a handsome 117 million HUF in profit (EUR 351,000). And those very billboards that I had seen when transferring from the airport to the city were offered to Fidesz at a 95 percent discount.[1]

*

---

[1] For a short account of the ESMA story see Bálint Magyar, *Post-Communist Mafia State: The Case of Hungary* (Budapest: CEU Press, 2016), pp. 181–182. On a 95 percent discount, see John Woods, "Government-Close Advertising Company Gives 95% Reduction to

Viktor Orbán's Hungary is one example of a new family of political systems often branded as "populist" – and their numbers are rising. They include Poland under Jarosław Kaczyński (the party leader, not head of state or even prime minister, both of whom are under his command), the Philippines under President Rodrigo Duterte, Brazil under Jair Bolsonaro, and many others. This list is nonexhaustive, and scholars disagree over which cases to include. All share some common characteristics, already hinted at in the account of Hungary just given. They are ruled by leaders who use aggressive language about their opponents, and often define an "enemy" (George Soros, Muslims, the liberal left, Jews, atheists, etc.) to demonize. The narratives they develop often draw on conspiracy theories: There are invidious "plans" to harm the people, but these plans are fortunately exposed by the Leader. The discourse used by leaders often deploys familiar tropes that bring it close to fascism: anti-Semitism, religious bigotry, antipathy to rationalism and Enlightenment, xenophobia.

They all have a charismatic leader personifying the regime, and often the name given to the regime carries the name of the Leader. But even if it does not, even if the Leader is not "charismatic" in the conventional sense of the word (attractive, eloquent, able to excite crowds, subject of popular adulation, etc.), indeed even if the Leader is quite ordinary (as is the case of Jarosław Kaczyński), nevertheless he (and very occasionally she, as was Cristina Fernández de Kirchner in Argentina) is viewed by their proponents as absolutely indispensable for the success of the system: There is no feasible alternative to him or her. As a result, these political systems are highly personalized: There is no regular procedure for replacing this particular person with another. (Occasionally, they appear out of nowhere and become suddenly popular thanks to a brilliant "performance," which the electorate turned into audience enjoys. Orbán became well known after his speech in Budapest in 1989 at the reburial of national heroes of the 1956 uprising; the political career of Chávez was initiated by his appearance on television in the aftermath of a failed coup which...he actually had launched.)

In addition to their use of exclusionary discourse and charismatic leadership, those regimes are in many ways "anti-institutional." The institutional tool kit of representative democracy, inherited from their predecessors, is respected only insofar as it suits the new ruling elite. If it

Government Parties," *Daily News Hungary*, February 27, 2018, www.dailynewshungary.com/government-close-advertising-company-gives-95-reduction-government-parties/.

does not – it is disposed of without regret. Sometimes formal constitutional rules are changed, and sometimes (when populists do not hold the power to change the constitution) they remain unchanged – and unused. Formal institutions are viewed by populists as irritants, unnecessarily throwing obstacles on the path of implementing the leadership's will (Chapter 2, below). Populists do not like being straitjacketed by formal rules and institutions: They are impatient and practice "instantaneous" democracy,[2] in which political will is smoothly and quickly transformed into binding policy or new laws – as was the case of Hungary's laws banning roadside advertising.

Populists do not like formal institutions, but they are not averse to using the law whenever it suits them – including to reward their cronies and disadvantage their opponents. "For my friends, everything; for my enemies, the law" – this (in)famous maxim by Peru's General Óscar Benavides is a nice encapsulation of what has become known as "discriminatory legalism."[3] While the law may provide a handy hammer with which to hit your opponent's head, law enforcers in populist systems look the other way when a Leader and his acolytes obviously break the law.

The author of these words has been prosecuted in Poland in three separate defamation cases by its populist rulers (twice by the state TV [TVP] and once by the ruling party, PiS). I was SLAPPed, to use an acronym coined by international NGOs to mean Strategic Litigation Against Public Participation. The slap has so far not been too harsh, and gave me the privilege of practicing, for once, what I had preached for much of my life. As of the time of the writing, all three cases are still pending at different stages of progression through the court system. But while I could see, courtesy of PiS and TVP, the inner workings of a vindictive state, there hasn't been even a *preliminary* investigation into PiS leader Jarosław Kaczyński's active participation in what appear to be clearly corrupt real estate dealings, which were leaked to, and announced by, opposition media. He is heard on tapes deliberating with his acolytes (including the PiS-nominated boss of the major state-run bank) about a multimillion-dollar construction in the center of Warsaw, with every regulatory concession and easy credit so long as PiS is in power. ("Twin Towers": Think of Petronas building in Kuala Lumpur, but with

---

[2] A term coined by Ming-Sung Kuo, "Against Instantaneous Democracy," *International Journal of Constitutional Law*, 17 (2019), 554–575.

[3] See Kurt Weyland, "The Threat from the Populist Left," *Journal of Democracy*, 24/3 (2013), 18–32.

an East European solidity.) It would support the party for rainy days. He even colluded with his collaborators about how to trick an Austrian developer by not paying him for his two years' worth of work on the project. When the desperate Austrian came to Kaczyński's office to claim his money, the party leader cheerfully suggested that the developer sue him in a court of law. (Kaczyński himself has not denied the authenticity of these tapes, and the facts of these dealings.)

The case of the Hungarian billboards points to yet another common characteristic. Each of these "populist" regimes relies on a thoroughly corrupt symbiosis of political power with the economy: Businesses operate thanks to government largesse (privileges in public procurement, special taxes, government contracts – all devices that justify the economist [and former liberal politician] Bálint Magyar calling today's Hungary "a mafia state") while the rulers, for their part, benefit from these businesses' reciprocal generosity. Perhaps the *least* shocking example of this is the practice of acquiring very costly advertisements in pro-government periodicals, even if the expense is not warranted by the circulation of those titles. State advertisements are omitted from weeklies critical of the government, no matter how wide their circulation. Indeed, the wider, the worse. In Poland, for example, the two political weeklies with the highest circulation, 50 percent of readers in that segment, receive the grand total of 0.5 percent of the entire budget given by Poland's state enterprises for ads in print media. It goes without saying that these weeklies are highly critical of PiS.[4] Of course, some degree of corruption exists everywhere, including in unimpeachable liberal democracies – but this type of cozy relationship between politics and business occurs to an extreme that is distinctive of populist regimes.

One may think that all these features are indicative of traditional authoritarianism. Aggressive language and paranoid narratives, a charismatic leader and a cult of personality, a cavalier attitude to formal institutions and to the rule of law, structural corruption...but there is a difference. All the populist regimes discussed in this book involve rulers emerging from (by and large) free and (by and large) fair elections. (The "by and large" clause is necessary because over time, elections tend to be less free and less fair if these rulers are able to entrench themselves for consecutive terms.)

---

[4] This is the statistic for 2018 and the two weeklies are *Polityka* and *Newsweek Polska*. The data are taken from an article by Jakub Bierzyński in the *Rzeczpospolita* (Warsaw) daily, March 3, 2019.

INTRODUCTION

So, in contrast to good old authoritarian tyrants (tanks on the streets, thousands of political prisoners, general violence and fear), populist regimes respect at least one civil right of their citizens: that of participating in free, fair, and regular elections. Populists come to their first term of office by offering policies that are accepted by the majority (and if not the majority, at least by the largest plurality). They stay in power because their mandate is reconfirmed by the electorate. Populists are unlikely to fundamentally abolish free and fair elections because their whole legitimacy relies upon the claim to represent the People. To achieve reelection, they want to be *liked* by people. Hence, much of what populist regimes do between elections can be understood in terms of maximizing their chances of reelection, that is, their popularity. And that is what makes them "populist" in an ordinary, intuitive sense of the word.

Of course, there is a degree of exaggeration in the last point. Populists in power do many *other* things, in addition to endearing themselves to the electorates. They cheat and deceive the population, often through state-run propaganda machines. They conduct non-transparent dealings and, in the process, break the law. They corrupt some businesses and discriminate against others. They buy docile judges and prosecute independent ones. Most significantly, they change the rules of the electoral game in order to reach a result that is optimal for them, including by controlling electoral officials. Irrespective of whether these activities increase the genuine popularity of populists, each targets reelection. We must (and we shall, in this book) be realistic in our perception of populist strategies. And we must always keep in mind that actions speak louder than words, and that it is more important to see what populists *do* than what they *say*. Which, of course, applies to all politicians, populist or non-populist alike.

And yet, we may justifiably say that leaders such as Orbán, Duterte or Bolsonaro *are* liked by large segments of their respective populations, in ways that we cannot say the same about, for instance, Kim Jong-un of North Korea or Bashar al-Assad of Syria – if only for the simple reason that there is no way we can measure the popularity of politicians in North Korea or Syria. Many policies adopted by Orbán, Duterte, or Bolsonaro – but not by Kim Jong-un or Bashar al-Assad – are carefully designed and calibrated to elicit *actual* support from the people, rather than the forced enthusiasm of masses gathered at propagandist rallies. Social welfare and tax policies are meant to generate support from the largest number of voters possible, as is beefing up national pride through a "historical policy" that exaggerates the nation's past virtues and minimizes its past misdeeds, and similarly, by disadvantaging unpopular minorities and hitting hard at unpopular would-be migrants...The conscious pursuit of popularity, reflected also in an obsession with public opinion polls, combined with an electoral pedigree, is what renders populist regimes fundamentally distinct from, and not merely different by degree, "traditional" authoritarianisms or despotisms. This is what makes them populist, and what renders their relationship to democracy so problematic and ambiguous.

Populists claim to be democrats – in fact, they insist that they are even *more* democratic than the much-maligned "liberal democracy" they reject. What they are building now, they say, is a better democratic system – an "illiberal democracy" – which is a concept coined years ago by Fareed Zakharia as a pejorative term,[5] but gladly adopted by Viktor Orbán, among others, not with apologies but with pride. In a speech in 2018, when he renewed his own 2014 endorsement of "illiberal democracy," Orbán derided liberal democracy as strong on liberalism, but weak on democracy: "liberal democracy has undergone a transformation...into liberal non-democracy. The situation in the West is that there is liberalism, but there is no democracy."[6] And even some *antipopulist* scholars who depict democratic deficits in the existing liberal democracies adopt this perspective. "The populist surge is an illiberal democratic response to decades of undemocratic liberal policies" – says Cas Mudde, a leading expert in radical and extremist movements.[7]

An illiberal but *democratic* response...but what sort of democracy do you have if there is no respect for academic freedom, as the CEU example shows? Or freedom to criticize the government? Or checks and balances that prevent the accumulation of all powers in the hands of one person? Or the rule of law, which makes it possible for people to be assured that their grievances will be fairly adjudicated by an independent court? Is it a *variant* of democracy, or rather *deformation* of democracy – to the point at which the absence of the separation of powers and of the rule of law depletes the system of all the reasons why democracy is such a valued ideal in the first place?

---

[5] Fareed Zakaria, "The Rise of Illiberal Democracy," *Foreign Affairs*, 76/6 (1997), 22–43.
[6] Viktor Orban's speech of July 28, 2018, quoted by Kim Lane Scheppele, "The Opportunism of Populists and the Defense of Constitutional Liberalism," *German Law Journal*, 20 (2019), 314–331 at 323.
[7] Cas Mudde, "Europe's Populist Surge," *Foreign Affairs*, 95/6 (2016), 25–30 at 30.

So perhaps the formula adopted by Italian scholar Nadia Urbinati, professor at Columbia University in New York, which holds that populism uses democratic *procedures* for non-democratic *purposes*, better captures the uneasy relationship between populism and democracy?[8] Some democratic procedures, such as free elections, are used for many non-democratic *purposes*, such as the political exclusion of some groups from their common polity. It is true that the initial success of populist movements is a good symptom of democratic deficits of their predecessors ("a mirror in which democracy can contemplate itself"),[9] and that often their diagnosis of democratic deficits of liberal democrats in power is incisive and warranted – but when they are elected into power, the cure is often worse than the disease.

This, at least, will be argued in this book. The steady erosion of democracy in the world over the past two decades is mainly due to populist regimes with weak democratic practices but with an unquestionable electoral pedigree. About two-thirds of all episodes of democratic decline were overseen by democratically elected incumbents, not by military putschists.[10] These incumbents have employed a number of different strategies causing democratic erosion, including restricting media and civil society organizations, sidelining the opposition, and undermining the autonomy of electoral officials.

In the past ten years, the decline of democracy worldwide has been continuous and steep. In 2020, the number of countries that (according to V-Dem Institute of Gothenburg – one of the leading research centers on democracy in the world) were in democratic decline was twenty-five (home to 34 percent of the world's population), while the number of democratizing countries dropped by almost half to sixteen countries (home to a mere 4 percent of the global population). Between 2010 and 2020, the number of liberal democracies diminished from forty-one to thirty-two, with a population share of just 14 percent. The same think tank, when creating the figure of the "average global citizen," estimated

---

[8] Nadia Urbinati, *Me the People: How Populism Transforms Democracy* (Cambridge: Harvard University Press, 2019), p. 94.
[9] Francisco Panizza, "Introduction: Populism and the Mirror of Democracy," in Francisco Panizza (ed.), *Populism and the Mirror of Democracy* (London: 2005), pp. 1–31 p. 30.
[10] Anna Lührmann and Staffan I. Lindberg, "A New Way of Measuring Shifts toward Autocracy," in *Post-Cold War Democratic Declines: The Third Wave of Autocratization*, Carnegie Europe (June 27, 2019). www.carnegieeurope.eu/2019/06/27/post-cold-war-democratic-declines-third-wave-of-autocratization-pub-79378, p. 1.

that in 2020 the level of democracy enjoyed by such a statistical character was down to levels last found around 1990.[11]

And then along came the pandemic.

*

A word about definition: As a starting point, I adopt a working, naïve understanding: I will consider as populist those politicians, parties, and programs usually dubbed populist. (In scholarly jargon, this is a "nominalist" definition.) No prize for originality but a premium for uncomplicatedness, I hope. My main suspects in this story will be, primarily, Poland, Hungary, India, the Philippines, Venezuela, and Brazil (see the Annex, with an important caveat regarding Venezuela). They are countries run by populists who came to power in a (more-or-less) fair and free election, and use the power to consolidate their rule, and in the process try to be liked rather than feared. On the democratic border, they are flanked by genuine liberal democracies, with checks and balances, maintenance of fairness in elections that leads to alternation in power and judicial independence. On the authoritarian side, they are bordered by states in which elections are a meaningless ritual, either because the outcome is predetermined or inconsequential, with a high degree of cruel repression, and utter disregard for what citizens really think and want. The six I have just listed are not the only countries that belong in the category (what about Turkey, South Africa, Trump's United States, Johnson's United Kingdom?), but *any* such taxonomy and selection is always arbitrary to some extent. Consideration of these politicians and parties when they have gained power, and when their programs become official programs of their state, will help reveal the general traits of today's populism in power.

But what is populism a characteristic *of*?

If one considers the current scholarly literature on populism, one can note a fundamental divide between those who locate populism primarily in a politician's *discourse* (rhetoric, narrative, ideology, etc.), and those who see it in the realm of *institutions* (or institutionally structured political strategies). The former understanding, which is dominant in the political sciences, and especially in political theory, refers to the fundamentally *anti-pluralist* rhetoric employed by populist rulers or populist movements who assume the role of true representatives of or the real identity of the people. As Jan-Werner Müller observed, the

---

[11] All these numbers in this paragraph are taken from V-Dem Institute, *Autocratization Turns Viral: Democracy Report 2021*, The University of Gothenburg, March 2021.

"claim to *exclusive* moral representation of the real or authentic people is at the core of populism."[12] Populists, Müller added, attempt "to speak in the name of the people as a whole" and "to morally de-legitimate all those who in turn contest that claim (which is to say: those who contest their involuntary inclusion in a 'We the People'; such resisters to populism are effectively saying: 'not in our name')."[13]

Müller's understanding of populism as a particular type of rhetoric, an understanding he first firmly established in his enormously influential book on populism, which has become canonical in current discussions,[14] has influenced a large number of outstanding scholars. For Cristóbal Rovira Kaltwasser, "populism is conceived of as *a moral discourse*, which by pitting 'the pure people' against 'the corrupt elite' defends the idea that popular sovereignty should be respected by all means."[15] Similarly, for Bart Bonikowski, populism is "a form of political discourse" that can be best "measure[d]...at the level of political speeches, or even speech elements."[16] In a more recent and very important article, Jane Mansbridge and Stephen Macedo conceive of populism as a political discourse in which "the people" are "in a morally charged battle against the elites."[17] Thus, the common conceptual core of populism that they identify is discursive in nature – it comprises anti-elitist tropes that have a moralistic tinge.

But I doubt whether a purely "discursive" account, without more, is sufficiently determinate to distinguish populist from non-populist politicians and governments: Perhaps it focuses too much on what populists *say* as opposed to what they *do*. As Nadia Urbinati noted, in short passage which I am tempted to adopt as my motto in this book:

> [T]o understand the character of a populist democracy, we should not concern ourselves only with what the leader says and the audience echoes.

---

[12] Jan-Werner Müller, "Populism and Constitutionalism," in Cristóbal Rovira Kaltwasser, Paul Taggart, Paulina Ochoa Espejo and Pierre Ostiguy (eds.), *Oxford Handbook of Populism* (Oxford: Oxford University Press, 2017), pp. 590–606 at 593 (emphasis in original).
[13] Ibid., p. 601.
[14] Jan-Werner Müller, *What Is Populism?* (Philadelphia: University of Pennsylvania Press, 2016).
[15] Cristóbal Rovira Kaltwasser, "Populism and the Question of How to Respond to It," in Cristóbal Rovira Kaltwasser, Paul Taggart, Paulina Ochoa Espejo and Pierre Ostiguy (eds.), *Oxford Handbook of Populism* (Oxford: Oxford University Press, 2017), 489–507 at 490 (emphasis added).
[16] Bart Bonikowski, "Ethno-Nationalist Populism and the Mobilization of Collective Resentment," *British Journal of Sociology*, 68/Suppl. 1 (2017), S181–S213 at S186.
[17] Jane Mansbridge and Stephen Macedo, "Populism and Democratic Theory," *Annual Review of Law and Social Science*, 15 (2019), 59–77 at 60.

> We must also analyse the ways in which populism in power *mutates* existing institutions and procedures.[18]

This is not to deny the importance for populist politics of a specific discourse. Discourse matters a great deal, and as we shall see in this book, populist discourse carries distinctive characteristics, with its own style of demagoguery, easy simplifications, occasional paranoia, targeting of enemies, unattainable promises, aggression, wild exaggerations, and the like (Chapter 5, below). But to fully hinge the characterization of pluralism on rhetoric, narratives or discourse is risky: Politicians often use their speech in strategic or deceptive ways. Their language serves *their* purposes, and analysts of populism do not have to take it at face value.

As a result, the discursive account, if meant as a defining trait of populism, captures too much and too little at the same time. In other words, it risks being both over-inclusive and under-inclusive. It may be *over*-inclusive (i.e., capture too much): The discursive criterion is unlikely to provide a sharp distinction between populists and perfectly unimpeachable democrats who, in a pluralist democracy, often (though not always) claim that they have a better grasp of the *true* common interests of their community than their opponents. Such claims are a common staple of democratic politics, and making them does not immediately taint a politician or a party as "populist." (Self-doubt and skepticism about the value of one's own diagnosis of social ills, and about the usefulness of proposed remedies, are unlikely qualifications for a successful democratic politician.) Especially in democracies where ideologically determinate political parties have declined in importance, as is the case today, politicians increasingly appeal to a broadly understood public good rather than to the sectoral interests of this or that constituency. This does not necessarily render them "populist"; rather, it may show them to be nonsectarian and non-self-interested (at least, in their rhetoric), for which they should be congratulated rather than reprimanded. As Mark Tushnet and Bojan Bugarič in their recent book correctly observe, "Casting yourself as the candidate of the people against the elites isn't distinctively populist."[19]

On the other hand, the discursive definition may also be *under*-inclusive (capture too little). Populists such as Kaczyński, Orbán, or Duterte do not necessarily say "we and only we are the people,"[20] and that those who disagree with them are beyond the pale of the nation. Rather, they may characterize and try to delegitimize their opponents by

---

[18] Urbinati, *Me The People*, p. 16 (emphasis in original).
[19] Mark Tushnet and Bojan Bugarič, *Power to the People: Constitutionalism after Populism* (Oxford: Oxford University Press, 2021), p. 42, footnote omitted.
[20] Müller, "Populism and Constitutionalism," p. 601.

presenting them as corrupt, mistaken, treacherous, in the service of foreign powers, and the like. (And, as Tushnet and Bugarič remind us, for all we know they may be right: "Sometimes the opposition is indeed disloyal.")[21] Such grandiose declarations that "We are *the* people" are rare in a literal form, and more often than not are interpretations placed on populists' statements by analysts unfavorable to them. Hence, to hinge our understanding of populism on making anti-pluralist claims is to hook it on to the shifting sands of public rhetoric.

So, an alternative understanding of populism identifies it with *actions*, which usually speak louder than words. This sense of populism is different from the discursive approach because it views populism not as an ideology but rather as a form of political organization reflected in institutional structures. Of course, it overlaps with the discursive understanding in that it is, among other things, connected with anti-pluralism, or more specifically, hostility to *institutional* pluralism. As shown in this book, populists typically try to build bridges to the "real" people, above the heads of intermediary institutions that mediate between the people and the exercise of power in a well-ordered constitutional democracy (Chapter 2, below). They dislike and disparage these institutions even if they pay lip service to them, but in the process, denude them of the reasons that underlie the creation of these institutions in the first place. They hollow them out through various devices such as capture, erosion, duplication and so forth. Electoral political conduct is usually of a plebiscitary character (either yes or no to the incumbents), aimed at translating the will of a mythical, pre-political people into political action. Once elected, populists try to bypass all forms of intermediation.

Perhaps the most eloquent student of *institutional* populism is a professor of New York University Law School, Samuel Issacharoff. who has long argued that populism marks a departure from the central tenets of democratic governance, in particular "by using the power of incumbency to thwart institutional divisions of authority and by forcing increased domains of state decisionmaking into the hands of unilateral executive authority."[22] In his yet-to-be-published book (at the time of writing these words), Issacharoff will provide a detailed institutional analysis of populism (and anti-populist remedies) aimed at showing the deep *anti*-institutional animus of populists aimed at (inter alia) privileging "elections over mandates," the use of unconstrained executive power, and repudiation of

---

[21] Tushnet and Bugarič, *Power to the People*, p. 68.
[22] Samuel Issacharoff, "The Corruption of Popular Sovereignty," *International Journal of Constitutional Law*, 18 (2020), 1109–1135 at 1114.

institutional accommodation of societal divisions.[23] As one can see, the main institutional aspect of populism under this account is a frontal assault upon the separation of powers. This populist resistance to any dispersal or limitation on power is joined with radical majoritarianism, under which all institutions must reflect and express the will of the current majority, which in a *pars pro toto* way is taken to be the will of the entire polity. Hence the crucial significance of both the ritual of elections that generate or entrench the political majority and the principled antipathy to any counter-majoritarian institutions and procedures.

It is no coincidence that the institutional approach is favored by constitutional scholars rather than political theorists; disciplinary foci (if not *déformations professionnelles*) inform, to a large degree, the approach taken. This is often highlighted by the use of adjectives like "institutional" or "constitutional" in conjunction with "populism." But it is not only disciplinary specialization that inclines some scholars to adopt an institutional rather than discursive perspective. It is also largely driven by the subject matter of their analysis. Observers of populist movements that merely *attempt* to win power, so far unsuccessfully, will necessarily be inclined to focus on discourse or rhetoric because, to put it crudely, this is all there is. In contrast, scholars who describe and analyze "actually existing populism" (a formula here deliberately parroting what used to be known as "actually existing socialism," a.k.a. the Soviet bloc) have lots of material related to institutional reform (or deformation, depending on your perspective) to describe populism in terms of unconstrained majoritarianism and assaults upon the separation of powers.

But the discursive/institutional divide is too crude a device to adequately reflect the landscape of contemporary approaches to populism. Many commentators attempt to find a synthesis and merge discursive accounts with institutional versions. One of the leading students of constitutional authoritarianism and populism, Kim Lane Scheppele, in one of her numerous contributions on the subject, analyzed populism as a form of political strategy for autocrats, by drawing on Hungary as an example.[24] In her view, the Orbán regime's ethno-nationalist majoritarian philosophy is a *rhetorical* gambit, one that is parasitic on a legitimate academic and popular discourse about liberal constitutionalism, that exploits its tensions in order to blunt opposition to institutional changes that centralize power and erode constitutional constraints. Her view of

---

[23] Samuel Issacharoff, *Democracy Unmoored* (in press). I am very grateful to Professor Issacharoff for letting me read and refer to his manuscript.
[24] Scheppele, "The Opportunism of Populists," p. 314.

populism therefore has a discursive tinge, but it is still primarily strategic and focused on *institutional* control. It is just that the most sophisticated populists, "in places that value intellectualism," engage in a skillful distortion of liberal constitutional values by actively intervening in elite and popular discourses: They "mirror and mimic the language of constitutional liberalism in order to undermine it in practice."[25]

*

"Mirror, mimic, undermine." This is not a pretty picture. Populists feed on, and further contribute to, a highly moralized and negative polarization; a division of the polity into Us and Them. It is *moralized* because "They" are evil, not just mistaken, and it is *negative*, because "We" hate "Them" more than we love "Ours." We are on the side of angels, and They are the mortal enemy of Us, of the real people, working hard for a living. This Manichean story – which I will describe in some detail in Chapter 5 – is transposed onto the institutions: They all should, uniformly, serve Us (remember, the real, decent people, with children and stuff); hence any checks and balances, separation of powers and independent institutions such as courts (Chapter 4) only upset the achievement of justice. When populist leaders can, they will write this institutional homogeneity into their constitutions (Chapter 3); when they cannot, they will flout formal constitutional separation of powers (Chapter 2).

The pandemic – like a war or any natural calamity – is a powerful reality check brought to this picture (Chapter 6). In the pandemic, as in a war, the unified people stand by their leaders, mustering all the self-discipline they can afford, postponing their disagreements to better days. But the pandemic – like a war – also tests the leadership. And in the face of the disaster that Covid-19 brought to the world, the test was not passed well by populist leaders. Not with high distinction, at least. This is a generous statement. They have by and large failed miserably – this would be a more realistic assessment. What could have been a God-given opportunity to show the superiority of a system of an omni-powerful and wildly popular Leader over slow and wavering liberal democracies turned into a picture of incompetence, trivialization of the danger, disdain for scientific evidence, and chaotic indecisiveness of populist elites.

The microscopic foe, 600 times smaller than a grain of salt, has revealed and exploited the flaws of populist governance: its reliance on generalized societal mistrust, its low-quality personnel, its sub-optimal

---

[25] Ibid., p. 315.

epistemic base, largely due to selection of mid- and high-level management founded on political loyalties rather than skills. And although the jury is still out, one thing is sure: The pandemic has *not* reinforced the global attractiveness of populist rule. Even if the cliché "The world will not be the same again" is correct, it is not the case that the masses of precariat and commentariat in democratic states will cry in unison: "We all want to be like the Hungarians (the Poles, the Brazilians – add your favorite populists here)!" The price to be paid for this lesson is exceedingly high, but then no one chose the test in the first place.

*

This book was completed *before* Putin's horrific invasion of Ukraine. The conflict has provoked not only immediate military questions, but also broader reflections on the nature of the political regimes involved, and the growing contest between liberal democracy and alternative models of governance.

Neither the invader nor its victim belongs to the category of states discussed in this book, which deals with novel political systems in-between the full blown autocracy of Putin's Russia and the democratizing project of pre-war Ukraine. The case studies discussed here are less oppressive than Russia but on a converse trajectory from that of Ukraine.

It is impossible to know what Russia's aggression will mean for populism, both on the continent and around the world. Two of the case studies discussed in this book have already been affected by the invasion's shockwaves. Poland has overnight become one of the world's largest host countries for refugees and the venue for US presidential speeches about hope and liberal democracy. Suddenly, the Polish government has switched from attacking refugees to housing them, while simultaneously using the war as an opportunity to wrap itself with the flag, step up attacks on pro-rule-of-law forces within, and seek to distract the world, particularly Europe, from its multiple forms of democratic backsliding. Hungary's government meanwhile has been exposed as a Putin-sympathising pariah and has earned the admonishment of Ukraine's President Zelenski. In the midst of this, it has decisively won elections for the fourth time, partly by doubling down on the tactics described in this book, and partly with the promise that pandering to Putin will keep gas and petrol prices down. Doubtless, some of these trends will persist, others will fade, and still others are yet to emerge. Whether they will strengthen populism or weaken it, and unite liberal democracies or divide them, are key questions yet to be answered. What is at stake is more clear, and the subject of this book.

1

Why Populisms?

One of the most quoted opening lines is from Leo Tolstoy's *Anna Karenina*: "Happy families are all alike; every unhappy family is unhappy in its own way." One may paraphrase it: "Good democracies are all alike; every defective democracy is defective in its own way."

Political scientists and constitutional lawyers will immediately protest: Surely, the first half of the sentence is incorrect. Well-ordered democracies vary enormously from country to country. Some are republics, others constitutional monarchies; some are federal, other unitary; some are strongly secular, others have an established religion; some have strong constitutional courts that may undo problematic laws, others espouse the supremacy of the parliament, which has the last word on what constitutes binding law. Some good democracies have parliamentary systems with governments formed by a parliamentary majority; others are presidential, with the chief executive not accountable to parliament, but only to the electorate. Indeed, the wealth of different democratic solutions is mind-bending.

And yet, beneath all this diversity, democracies converge on certain points, on certain irreducible minima for any democracy worth its name. First, the top executive and legislature are formed as a result of regular, free, and fair elections. This means that policies and laws they adopt are, at least indirectly but very meaningfully, authored by the people to whom they apply. This is the self-government aspect of democracy. Second, power is in many ways dispersed. Methods of dispersal differ: some along the elegant tripartite architecture of different branches of government going back to Montesquieu; others along the lines of the rather chaotic US-style checks and balances, where decision-making is split and fragmented so as to "preclude the exercise of arbitrary power."[1] But the point is the same, and it is best articulated in a negative rather than positive

---

[1] Famous dissent by Justice Louis D. Brandeis in *Myers v. United States*, 272 US 52, 293 (1926).

manner: All political power is *not* concentrated in one place. This is the separation-of-powers aspect of democracy. Third, individual rights are strongly protected, especially rights related, directly or indirectly, to political self-government. This not only includes the right to vote, but also rights that eventually facilitate a free and informed vote: freedom of association, of speech, of movement, of religion, of choice of employment, and so forth. This is the civil rights aspect of democracy. And fourth, rulers are subject to rules of the game that they cannot, at their whim, change whenever it suits them politically. Of course, no law is or should be set in stone, but these rules cannot be changed at any time during the game. A "higher" law (at the constitutional level in particular) binds rulers. Thresholds for changing it are quite high, meaning it is entrenched against day-to-day modifications. This is the rule-of-law aspect of democracy.

Free and fair elections, the separation of powers, civil and political rights, the rule of law – observance of these principles is the common denominator of properly working democracies. They are all parts of an absolute minimum, not a lofty aspirational ideal. While of course achievement of each of these standards may be matters of degree, rather than being a binary yes-or-no, there is in each of them a certain point below which they must not fall. In contrast, populist regimes, such as those discussed in this book, fail on at least one, but often more of these yardsticks. Even if they respect free and fair elections to a point, they usually breach the principles of the separation of powers, civil and political rights, and, in particular, the rule of law.

Populists' Answer – But What Was the Question?

But the populist regimes that breach these principles do so for different reasons and in different ways. Here, the maxim from *Anna Karenina* kicks in. There is no one populism, but diverse populisms – plural. The language of "populism advancing in the world" conveys the sloppy idea that there is a single movement or trend or tendency crisscrossing the world, overtaking ever more nations and regions. Something like "a spectre is haunting the world – the spectre of populism" (to paraphrase yet another great first line of a well-known text, this time by Karl Marx and Friedrich Engels, *The Communist Manifesto*).

But we should resist the temptation of thinking along these lines. There is no Populist Manifesto available on the marketplace of published ideas (even if someone has written one, of which I do not know, it would not be worth much), for the simple reason that there is no singular populism. Populisms respond to real problems. And real problems are local, differing from one polity to another. Hence, populist answers are different.

To be a little more precise: populists usually give wrong, dangerous, simplistic, and disingenuous answers, but the questions to which they respond are real. They are not phantasmagorical, but correspond to actual concerns, worries, and fears of real people. These concerns and fears must be recognized and respected; we dismiss and trivialize them at our peril. The peril's name is "populism." But the peril's shape is different, as a function of different local concerns expressed by people who do not find liberal democracy provides them with satisfactory solutions to their problems. The easy solutions to complex problems offered by populists begin to look different once we realize that the problems themselves are different.

But, from the diversity of problems and solutions offered, it does not follow that the list of grounds for these populisms' successes is infinite. Far from it; the list is not long, and there are many commonalities between the various social contexts that give rise to populist successes. Factors from this list appear in different countries in different configurations: All factors are almost never present, at least with the same intensity. Rather, a convincing typology of populisms may take the form of specific combinations of two, three, even four factors that help to explain the popularity of populist politicians and ideas in a given country. A successful populist leader – that is, a leader who attains power through elections based on their populist program – owes their success to skillfully combining *several* of these concerns and presenting them, in a convincing way, as a simple, easy-to-understand package.

Consider this American journalist's colorful description of the grounds for Donald Trump's success in the 2016 presidential elections: "Donald Trump's campaign was massively fuelled by racism and xenophobia. But racism and hatred and fear of foreigners were not irreconcilable with hatred of the arrogant establishment that controlled major-party politics. Many voters out there hated both, and some hated those latter folks with the heat of a thousand suns."[2] My interest in this description is not so much in whether Matt Taibbi has properly described the sources of Trump's victory – a combination of racism, xenophobia, and anti-

---

[2] Matt Taibbi, *Insane Clown President: Dispatching from the 2016 Circus* (New York: Spiegel and Grau, 2017), p. xx.

establishment sentiment – although probably he has. Finding a common enemy in an unlikely blend of the most privileged (the incumbent political elite) and the most disadvantaged (would-be migrants escaping hunger, debilitating poverty, and wars) is a good depiction of two easily targetable groups against whom to mobilize social hatred. But what I wish to retrieve from this passage is the idea that populists are successful when they manage to combine policy responses to *several* societal concerns that are not necessarily consistent with each other. Of course, no algorithm for such a combination is available. But the idea of combining several elements into one easy solution is certainly convincing.

Before I catalog the "factors of populism," however, a digression on perplexity.

Perplexity of Political Pundits

February 2020, New York, a few weeks before the lockdown that would make the meeting impossible: In a nice Italian restaurant in Greenwich Village, just a stone's throw from the main New York University buildings, I am meeting Professor Adam Przeworski. Without any unnecessary preliminary pleasantries, I ask him: "Why? Why all that is happening in our home country, Poland?" For we are now in the fourth year of the populist bulldozer that was destroying the institutions of Polish democracy.

Adam Przeworski is a legend in the branch of political science that studies democracy: both democratization and *de*-democratization. Born and educated in Poland (just as I was), he has been a professor of political science at NYU for many years, and (here similarities between us end, I'm afraid) has achieved a worldwide reputation as a leading student of democracy. He has collected plenty of prestigious awards for his numerous books, including the Johan Skitte Prize – the Nobel of the political sciences. And at the end of his recent book, he quotes an old Polish adage – "A pessimist is but an informed optimist" – and to be sure, Przeworski *is* certainly informed.[3]

So again, I ask Przeworski – "Why?" – and I hear a straight "I don't know. Theoretically speaking, it should not have happened." And my immediate thought is, if Adam Przeworski does not know, no one does.

---

[3] Adam Przeworski, *Crises of Democracy* (Cambridge: Cambridge University Press, 2019), p. 206.

Of course, the conversation did not end there, and I am pleased to inform that it continued exactly a year later, in the same Tre Giovani restaurant after New York's lockdown was lifted, step-by-step. The conclusion I drew from these two conversations was that the populist counterrevolution took political scientists by surprise, and the most candid of these scholars – including Przeworski – had the courage to admit to perplexity in explaining its roots. In an interview given to a leading Polish weekly, *Polityka*, in January 2018, he said that "consolidated democracies," defined as those that had seen at least two cycles of consecutive democratic (electoral) transitions in power, are fundamentally durable. Of the eighty-eight cases of "consolidated democracies" (so defined) after 1918, only fourteen had collapsed. And, in 2015, Poland had acquired the status of a consolidated democracy.

It should have stayed that way. But it did not.

The fall of liberal democracies in countries such as Poland or Hungary was not well explained by the factors that usually accompany democratic collapse: poverty, slow economic growth, very high inequality, or low rates of professional employment in industry. In addition, presidential democracies are more likely to fail than parliamentary systems, because the latter have better mechanisms for responding to government crises: but neither Poland (a mixed system) nor Hungary (a pure parliamentary system) share this vulnerability.

Let me now broaden the sample of countries and explanations. Two leading political scientists, one from the United States and the other from Canada, published an important article in 2015 in which they summarized a large body of their own and others' empirical research on cases where democratization was unlikely to be successful: either because democratization is unlikely or short-lived or prone to relapse into the bad old ways. The account, which Steven Levitsky and Lucan Way provided, led them to the complex conclusion that "stable democratization is unlikely in":

- very poor countries with weak states (e.g., much of sub-Saharan Africa),
- dynastic monarchies with oil and Western support (e.g., the Persian Gulf states),
- single-party regimes with strong states and high growth rates (China, Vietnam, Malaysia, Singapore),
- countries with very low linkage to the West (e.g., Central Asia, much of Africa), and
- regimes born of violent revolutions (China, Ethiopia, Eritrea, Vietnam, Cuba, Iran, Laos, North Korea).

To all this, Levitsky and Way added philosophically: "While the recent stagnation on the overall number of democracies in the world may be normatively displeasing, it is entirely consistent with existing theory."[4]

But note that "existing theory" has huge difficulties in explaining the populist deformations of liberal democracy today. None of the paradigmatic populist states that form the list of usual suspects – today's Hungary, Poland, Philippines, Venezuela, India, or Brazil – match any of these five categories. Not one is a very poor country with a weak state (as in sub-Saharan Africa) or is a single-party strong state with impressive economic growth. Most have strong and traditional linkages to the United States (think of the Philippines or South America) and/or Western Europe. None was born of violent revolutions, at least of a reasonably recent vintage, and they are not dynastic monarchies. With some exceptions (Venezuela, much less Brazil), none have much oil (and in Venezuela and Brazil, not in conjunction with a dynastic monarchy). And, of course, these factors apply even less to successful populist politicians who have not managed to undo liberal democratic institutions (such as Donald Trump) or politicians who are successful but are not (yet) in power (such as Madame Le Pen).

So it is clear that conventional political science (at its best, one must add, since we are talking about scholars of the highest academic caliber) has been spectacularly unsuccessful in providing "structural" explanations, as we may call them, for the growth of today's populism. We must search for answers elsewhere.

Agency and Structure; Supply and Demand

If "structural" explanations such as those suggested by political scientists like Levitsky and Way fail to provide explanations, and scholars such as Przeworski throw up their arms, perplexed, perhaps it's necessary to look at the other side of the political equation: not structures but people, not "demand" but "supply," not long-term processes but short-term actions. In a word, at individual *agency*. Some scholars call this line of thinking "agentic," as it places more weight on often contingent events controlled by shrewd leaders who "supply" electorates with attractive slogans. We need to observe the formation and preferences of individual leaders and determine whether they seek moderate policies and have a normative

---

[4] Steven Levitsky and Lucan Way, "The Myth of Democratic Recession," *Journal of Democracy*, 26/1 (2015), 45–58 at 54.

preference for democracy. As political scientists Ellen Lust and David Waldner say:

> In these theories, we lift the structural constraint so that political actors have a high degree of freedom of choice. We explain the outcome by reference to this relatively unconstrained choice or action; by calling an action or choice contingent, we assume that it could feasibly have been otherwise, given the sum total of external conditions.[5]

Looking at the supply side of politics means that we need to discover what is on offer in a given political bazaar. What kind of party programs, political manifestos, leaders' qualities are available in the market of political strategies open to citizen-shoppers? Societal grievances, fears, and claims based on economic anxieties or identity concerns rarely express themselves in packages with specific policies and programs. They need to be enveloped in stories, narratives, and policy proposals that confer a clear meaning and significance on those inchoate claims.

In the end, both "supply" and "demand" matter. Structural factors (falling usually on the "demand" side) create the framework within which populism is likely to succeed. But the dominant programs, strategies, and leadership ("supply") determine the specific character of such success. Just as in economics, in any comprehensive account of politics there is room for supply-side and demand-side analyses – and for interactions between both. Even if the leader is able to skillfully supply certain ideas, they will not be effective without an audience that is strongly predisposed to accept them. And vice versa, even solid societal preferences for populist policies will not ripen into reality unless there is a leader or group of leaders determined to propagate and pursue them in a politically effective way.

Just as with commercial advertising, ads create needs for commodities, but only to a point – if you hate anchovies, no amount of attractive advertising will make you buy them. Supply and demand do not operate in realms totally divorced from each other. Political sociologist Bart Bonikowski describes this source of populist success as "resonance – that is, congruence between the content of the message and the predispositions of the audience," which explains "a social movement's ability to

---

[5] Ellen Lust and David Waldner, "Unwelcome Change: Understanding, Evaluating and Extending Theories of Democratic Backsliding," USAID 2015, www.pdf.usaid.gov/pdf_docs/PBAAD635.pdf, p. 9.

mobilize supporters around the movement's core message."[6] On the demand side, there is a process that aggregates various concerns and fears around the slogans and ideas the populist leader provides. The following description by Bonikowski is worth citing in full as it describes the demand side and the supply side of the populist phenomenon well, as

> a process whereby populist, ethno-nationalist and authoritarian discourse leads those in the target public to connect their experiences (e.g., fears associated with social, cultural, and economic changes) with their pre-existing beliefs (e.g., ethno-nationalism, distrust of elites, scepticism toward democratic institutions), and to support candidates that offer radical solutions to the resulting problems (i.e., minorities, immigrants and politicians being jointly responsible for undesirable social changes).[7]

Whether the supply side favors a particular entrant (for example, a populist party) depends to a large extent not only on that party's assets (including the charisma and skills of its leaders), but also on the preexisting condition of the political market. This is a matter of whether populist newcomers can find opportunities on the political stage including, for instance, how crowded it is with rivals trying to capture the same segment on the demand side.

For instance, the success of populism can be largely explained by the programmatic shift of left-wing parties (which had previously addressed themselves largely to the "working classes"), rendering them less attractive to their traditional electorate. When searching for alternatives, this electorate often finds them in new populist parties and candidates. The traditional Left has moved to the center and has become more occupied with concerns important to the urban higher-middle class, leaving the lower-middle class (especially white workers in developed economies) with the sense that there is no one to speak for them. Populists fill this gap. They do so, in particular, when they combine the economic concerns of the lower-middle classes with anti-immigrant and anti-globalization claims. This may explain the sociological finding that the share of votes enjoyed by right-wing populist parties has greatly increased in developed democracies especially at *lower* levels of income and wealth hierarchy.[8]

---

[6] Bart Bonikowski, "Ethno-Nationalist Populism and the Mobilization of Collective Resentment," *British Journal of Sociology*, 68/Suppl. 1 (2017), 181–213 at 192, reference omitted.

[7] Ibid., p. 193, footnote omitted

[8] For the finding about high support for right-wing populists among white working class, see Noam Gidron and Peter A Hall, "The Politics of Social Status: Economic and Cultural Roots of the Populist Right," *British Journal of Sociology*, 68/Suppl. 1 (2017), 57–84 at 60.

So back to the catalog of "factors of populism" and to the idea that effective populism – that is, populism that attains power – owes its success to the way it is able to combine at least two items, sometimes more, which correspond to local grievances, fears, and claims. The following is a rough list of factors determinative of today's populisms:

1. a sense of economic insecurity and status anxiety;
2. xenophobic attitudes toward "Others," in particular migrants and refugees;
3. disenchantment with incumbent political elites, combined with the perception that the establishment is arrogant, remote, and insensitive to the needs of "real people";
4. resentment against globalization, internationalism, and renewed support for nationalism (economic and other);
5. cultural and religious resentment, expressed in anti-modernism, anti-Enlightenment, and anti-secularism; and
6. impatience with liberal constraints upon government, with checks and balances viewed as an institutional obstacle to "getting things done" and to the expression of the will of the People.

There are more factors, no doubt, but these seem to me to be at the top of any convincing list. Varieties of contemporary populisms may be understood as resulting from different combinations of two or more of these sources of populist resentment, but the specific repertoire is country-dependent. Populists are successful when they aggregate various demands and grievances – rarely all of them, but at least more than one – into a coherent whole, and then offer a simple, easy response to the mix. The response places populists on the side of the pure People and at loggerheads with the corrupt elite.

There are of course important overlaps between factors that drive the demand for populism and await assembly into a single project supplied by populist politicians. Let us look at them one by one. We will have an opportunity to review some of these factors more closely later in this book. What follows is just a bird's eye view.

Status Anxiety

The most memorable image that readers take away from Arlie Russell Hochschild's bestselling book, *Strangers in Their Own Land*, is that of waiting in line. A long line leading up a hill.

A liberal, left-leaning Berkeley sociologist went to the bayou country in Louisiana to find out why people in this region, which is in almost every possible respect among the most disadvantaged in the United States – financially, environmentally, medically, educationally, and culturally – are at the same time politically arch-conservative. Why do people who have everything to gain and seemingly nothing to lose from a more expansive welfare state hate the state and perceive it as the problem, not the solution? And why do they vote for politicians whose programs, objectively speaking, disadvantage them even further?

There are many explanations offered by Hochschild to this apparent puzzle, but the "Waiting in Line" story is her most graphic and moving encapsulation. You are standing in the middle of the line leading up the hill, alongside others like you who are "white, older, Christian, and predominantly male,"[9] and just over a brow of the hill is the American Dream. It is a dream of material security and prosperity and progress – that your children will be better-off, just as you were better-off than your parents. And yet you do not seem to be *moving* in the line, you do not come closer to your goal. "[A]fter all your intense effort, all your sacrifice, you're beginning to feel stuck."[10] Now and again there are line-cutters: the beneficiaries of affirmative action, African-Americans, women, immigrants, refugees, public sector workers, and the like. And they seem to be aided by the government – the controller of the waiting line. Concluding her "deep story" about waiting in line, Hochschild says:

> In the undeclared class war, expressed through the weary, aggravating, and ultimately enraging wait for the American Dream, those I came to know developed a visceral hate for the ally of the "enemy" cutters in line – the federal government. They hated other people for needing it. They rejected their own need of it – even to help clean up pollution in their backyard.[11]

As it happens, my friend and colleague at Sydney Law School, Michael Sevel, a brilliant philosopher of law, was born a few miles ("if you went by boat, but by car it is thirty minutes' drive") from the territory explored by Hochschild – on the Mississippi side of the state border, in a small town, Gulfport. Environmentally and economically the Mississippi River delta is in the same world as Hochschild's Louisiana. His parents are still

---

[9] Arlie Russell Hochschild, *Strangers in Their Own Land* (New York: The New Press, 2016), p. 136.
[10] Ibid., p. 137.
[11] Ibid., p. 151.

fishers there, and they are working in the Gulf of Mexico, catching fish and shrimp. Even as we speak his Mum sends him a smartphone photo of the sunrise in the Gulf, a postcard view of great beauty: gentle waves of dark blue water crowned with white foam, sparkling in an early sun. Born in 1976, Michael has seen a steady deterioration in conditions of the fishing community in which he grew up and helped his parents at work. "They have a deep sense of decline," says Michael about his parents and their neighbors, "and in their case it is backed by facts." There was a world oil prices crisis in the 1970s, much later there was the economic downturn that followed 9/11, hurricane Katrina, the BP oil spill: steady decline, punctuated by traumatic events. After the oil spill, corporate lawyers advised the fishermen to work to remove the damage, for otherwise they would get no compensation. The great expansion of free trade in 1990s resulted in much cheaper imported shrimp to the United States, mostly from southeast Asia; this drove down the price for shrimp caught by US fishermen such as Michael's family and their neighbors. There was no state, no government, to be seen; the impression was rather that the government favored the economic interests of people on the other side of the world over those of Americans. The only time the State of Mississippi had any presence in their lives was when it decided to close the fishermen's harbor in Gulfport, which forced his parents to transfer their fishing boat to Pass Christian. So there were no special reasons to be fond of the government and its programs; people in Michael's community liked President Reagan's: "[T]he nine most terrifying words in the English language are: I'm from the government and I'm here to help." And yes, there were also episodes of xenophobia and racial tensions, especially after some Vietnamese immigrants brought into the United States by President Carter's orders settled in the fishing community where Michael's family lived. They did not speak English, they had their peculiar ways of fishing, the conflicts were frequent. And local white fishermen resented that the Vietnamese got government assistance – while traditional locals did not. "Many people in the community have the tendency to blame all those who take advantage of government assistance," says Michael, echoing the theme of Hochschild's depiction of the people stuck in the waiting line, with the American Dream ever receding.

The American Dream has its parallels everywhere: the Hungarian Dream, the Brazilian Dream, the Filipino Dream. The Dream is mainly economic, and its opposite – the failure of your dream to come true – has to do with a sense of economic loss or decline: real or imagined, absolute or relative. This is the fishing zone for populists. Sociologists note that relative decline in the social status of individuals whose economic situation has deteriorated the most generates concerns that lead them to reject the traditional political establishment in favor of populist right parties.[12] This is clearly the case in developed democratic countries, where there is significant support for populist parties and politicians, including in Britain, France, Italy, Spain, and the United States. In Britain, for instance, "supporters of Brexit tended to be much more pessimistic about their own economic prospects."[13] And it is at this point that *collective* identity enters: status insecurity is often more based on concerns for one's own group (for "others like me") rather than for one's individual predicament, which may be stable and secure.

There is abundant sociological evidence for the proposition that on both sides of the Atlantic popular support for radical populism comes from groups most threatened by rapid social and economic change. In Western Europe, this comes from the working and lower-middle classes, which have benefited the least from integration within the European Union. In the United States, support for populism was mainly triggered by "the economic insecurity and racial resentment of working-class white men."[14] There is a near consensus in the scholarly literature that economic insecurity is a powerful factor associated with voting for populist parties. For instance, Europe's poorer regions and regions with higher unemployment register a higher populist vote: the correlation between economic insecurity and populism is unmistakable.[15]

But concerns about loss of status may be more of a cultural than economic character. And the former category is tightly connected with the latter. Those who see themselves as economically underprivileged often at the same time feel culturally distant from the dominant groups in society. In particular, they disapprove of "liberal" causes such as multiculturalism, globalization, or the green movement.[16] Economic vulnerability (real or perceived) is part and parcel of a broader sense of

---

[12] See Gidron and Hall, "The Politics of Social Status."
[13] Ibid., p. 58.
[14] Bart Bonikowski, "Nationalism in Settled Times," *Annual Review of Sociology*, 42 (2016), 427–449 at 434.
[15] Luigi Guiso, Helias Herrera, Massimo Morelli, and Tomasso Sonno, "Demand and Supply of Populism," *ResearchGate* (October 28, 2018), www.researchgate.net/publication/325472986, pp. 7–8.
[16] See Gidron and Hall, "The Politics of Social Status," p. 57.

one's group being marginalized by political elites to the benefit of hitherto disadvantaged minorities and immigrants.

Sometimes the cultural distance is relatively autonomous from economic deprivation. This is, in my view, consistent with the examples of Poland and Hungary. PiS and Fidesz (the ruling parties in these countries) voters feel a sense of distance from the cultural values of the liberal elite. In particular, they feel anxiety related to immigration and multiculturalism, and this is not clearly correlated with their relative socio-economic deprivation. The anxieties and concerns of PiS and Fidesz voters are generated largely by their concerns about "Others," not because these *other* people (migrants) are likely to take their jobs and wealth, but rather because they may import unwanted cultural meanings to Polish and Hungarian collective lives. So it is not uncertainty about one's individual material well-being that matters, but rather a sense of affront to a group's cultural identity.

In addition, status anxiety is often specifically felt by *men* who feel that, as many more women move into traditionally masculinized occupations, their (male) status has relatively declined. Status, at least in a subjective sense, is partly a "positional good," such that "when many others acquire more status, the value of one's own status may decline."[17] If for some men their sense of superiority is based on their gender, and they lack other significant sources of status, they may suffer a loss of self-respect as a result of gender equality. It is no wonder that more men support populist parties than women.[18]

Xenophobia; Hatred of "Others"

The year is 2015, the year of the double (presidential and parliamentary) elections in Poland, following eight years of a liberal-centrist hegemony. The influx of migrants and refugees from Africa and the Middle East onto European shores during that time was a God-given gift for the populist Law and Justice party leader, Jarosław Kaczyński, who was able to stir up anti-migrant (often racist) attitudes in an ethnically and religiously homogenous Poland. In his most infamous, but not atypical, diatribe against admitting refugees, Kaczyński warned that refugees

---

[17] Ibid., p. 66.
[18] Niels Spierings and Andrej Zaslove, "Gender, Populist Attitudes and Voting: Explaining the Gender Gap in Voting for Populist Radical Right and Populist Radical Left Parties," *West European Politics*, 40 (2017), 821–847.

would import various "parasites" to which "these people" are immune, but which may be deadly to their Polish hosts.[19] Analogies between this rhetoric and the language of Nazi propaganda in occupied Poland that the Jews were bearers of typhoid and lice was not lost on PiS's Polish critics. (And, as I am writing these words, in October 2021, a similar story is being replayed on the Eastern border of Poland, with refugees from Afghanistan trying to enter Poland via Belarus.)

Anti-immigrant impulses in Poland and Hungary were inextricably related to racially tinged and anti-Muslim concerns. Opinion polls in late 2015 showed that two-thirds of Poles were against accepting refugees from the Middle East and Africa (a major shift from only a few years before), and that "[t]his reluctance is linked to the fact that the vast majority of refugees are Muslim and/or non-whites."[20] This group's sense of self-esteem and dignity became somewhat perversely founded on a sense of superiority to those over whom they could for once exercise power, even if only by saying "No" to their desperate pleas for admission to a safe place.[21] Drawing national, cultural and religious boundaries between "Us" and "Them" helped to exploit the fear of Otherness and sustained a sense of self-esteem. And in this resolute "No" to refugees, Kaczyński was strongly reinforced by Orbán's policies. By June 2015, Hungary had begun to build a border fence. Later these two countries, joined by the Czech Republic and Slovakia, rejected the European Union's proposed quota system for taking in refugees. All this in the name of resisting an alleged "Muslim invasion."

How the inhumane resistance to accepting even a limited number of children and women from war-stricken Syria could have been, in Poland, squared with Christian benevolence and love in a nation where over 90 percent identify themselves as Christians, is an intriguing question. But it worked, partly thanks to the connection successfully drawn by the government propaganda between being Muslim and being a terrorist. Opinion polls found that the overwhelming majority of Poles connected Muslims with terrorism. As sociologist Maciej Gdula (later to become a member of parliament as part of a left-wing party) said when reporting on his interviews with PiS supporters, "When it applies to strangers, the

---

[19] Quoted in Yascha Mounk, *The People vs. Democracy* (Cambridge: Harvard University Press, 2018), pp. 175–176.
[20] Andrzej Balcer, Piotr Buras, Grzegorz Gromadzki, and Eugeniusz Smolar, "Polish Views of the EU: The Illusion of Consensus," Warsaw: Stefan Batory Foundation, January 2017, p. 10.
[21] Sociological evidence is provided by Maciej Gdula, *Nowy Autorytaryzm* (Warszawa: Wydawnictwo Krytyki Politycznej, 2018).

impulses of empathy are suspended and the language used unpleasantly resembles a liberal laissez-faire philosophy."[22] He further explained that one of Kaczyński's sources of success is that he gave many people a sense of importance based on their superiority and strength by comparison with vulnerable Others, as well as a sense of community "the members of which are equal in their distinction from elites and from strangers."[23]

Self-respect *and* contempt for others, the less fortunate...This is not an unusual combination. As Noam Gidron and Peter Hall report, there is some sociological evidence that, for instance, "men in the French and American working classes sustain their sense of dignity or status, in part, by drawing sharp boundaries between themselves and North African migrants or African Americans."[24] Many Hungarians could have derived a guilty pleasure from watching masses of starving, frightened migrants on their way to Germany, in the Keleti railway station in central Budapest. A *Guardian* reporter quoted Syrian student Jamal al-Deenberra, aged 23, one of hundreds stranded at Keleti, as saying: "Hungarians look after animals more than people, they treat dogs and cats better."[25] Those upon whom fate had smiled could have derived satisfaction from watching, at a short distance, the most miserable in the world whose only guilt was to risk a life-threatening trip in order to escape war, hunger, and all-encompassing suffering.

The individual feeling of superiority toward the unfortunate Other is at the same time combined with a sense that one's *group* (and not only oneself individually) is threatened in its dignity and self-respect by allegedly excessive concern for traditionally despised groups or, what comes to the same in this constellation of concerns, immigrants. This attitude is well summarized (though not with respect to Poland or Hungary) by Bonikowski:

> The combined effects of economic, cultural, and social changes are perceived as impinging on the life chances, dignity and moral commitments of in-group members, who perceive themselves as increasingly sidelined by elites and mainstream culture and who view members of other groups as having been granted unfair advantages in society, often by those same vilified elites.[26]

---

[22] Ibid., p. 71.
[23] Ibid.
[24] Gidron and Hall, "The Politics of Social Status," p. 63.
[25] "At Keleti station in Budapest, the refugees could wait no longer." *The Guardian* (September 5, 2015), www.theguardian.com/world/2015/sep/06/keleti-station-budapest-refugees.
[26] Bonikowski, "Ethno-Nationalist Populism," pp. S201–S202.

By opposing concerns for the Others, populists restore (though in a perverse way) a sense of dignity and self-respect to those of their supporters who may acquire a sense of power and superiority from saying "No" to immigrants. Or "No" to other "Others," such as members of sexual minorities.

Anti-elitism

Anti-immigrant resentment is often combined with anti-elite sentiment. This may sound bizarre but in the hands of canny populists (the supply side!), the link is easily established. Incumbent elites are seen as not only arrogant and corrupt, but at the same time so cosmopolitan, deracinated, and anti-national that they are willing, for whatever reasons (to allay their own sense of guilt?) to let in masses of migrants and thus dilute the group's sense of nation-based unity and community. In the end, both groups are strangers to the common folk; they are "Them" rather than "Us."

In Stephen Holmes's description of elections bringing (or consolidating) populists to power, "Populist voters, feeling ignored and victimized go to the polls to avenge themselves symbolically against out-of-touch elites and under-the-radar immigrants."[27] Out-of-touch elites and under-the-radar immigrants...This is a good picture of right-wing populists' targets. Elsewhere in the same essay, Holmes adds:

> By clamoring against inner enemies,...[populist leaders] can channel voters' frustration and resentment away from themselves and toward two eminently targetable social groups: those who endorse liberal-humanitarian values as a matter of principle and those who benefit personally and concretely from a liberal *Wilkommenskultur*.[28]

"For too long, a small group in our nation's Capital has reaped the rewards of government while the people have borne the cost" – these words from Donald Trump's inauguration speech reflect a universal template for populist anti-elitism. At the same time, the speech strictly confines anti-elitist animus to *politicians* ("Politicians prospered – but the jobs left, and the factories closed" – continued Trump). It targets just

---

[27] Stephen Holmes, "How Democracies Perish," in Cass R. Sunstein (ed.), *Can It Happen Here? Authoritarianism in America* (New York: HarperCollins, 2018), pp. 387–427 at 412.
[28] Ibid., p. 418, footnote omitted.

one elite, not necessarily the only or even the most responsible for the disappearance of jobs and factory closures.

Distrust of *political* elites is probably the most constant force of populism these days. One has to emphasize "political" because many populist leaders, before they entered active politics, belonged to top echelons of business (Trump, Berlusconi), the arts (Beppe Grillo), the military (Chavez), or were administrative elites (Duterte) themselves. And, of course, different elites overlap to a great degree. Populism's targeting of political elites over others is largely self-serving but also rational having regard to the special visibility of politicians, compared with businesspeople or the military. And, as Nadia Urbinati observes, "the hostility of populism is directed at the *political* establishment, because it is this establishment that has the power to connect the various social elites and undermine political equality."[29] One may say that the political elite is at the same time the most central (capable of linking up various other elites) and the least independent, relying as it does on resources (money, force) held by other elites. That is what renders it an attractive target for populist anger and capture at the same time.

Populists insist on *their* anti-elitism, on their newness in politics, on their outsider status – even if it is an evident deception. (Prior to his double victory in 2015, Jarosław Kaczyński had been at the very center of the Warsaw political establishment for at least the past sixteen years or so, including stints off and on in government.) This is a frequent paradox: while in power, therefore elite by definition, populists cultivate the embattled image of being under constant threat from the "enemies of the people," who somehow maintain their "elite" or "mainstream" status despite losing political power. (There is an interesting empirical project to be conducted about the proclivity of populists in power to use vast protective forces, incommensurate with protection of other politicians in liberal democracies; this is partly triggered by their actual fears, but partly sends a message about how endangered these populist rulers are.) In the rhetoric of the Polish pro-government media, the word "mainstream" (in English, without its Polish equivalent) serves as an epithet used against media critical of the PiS government.

One of the favored concepts used often by Kaczyński and his followers before PiS returned to power in 2015 was that of "*układ*." The concept roughly corresponds to "establishment" or "arrangement" but carries an

---

[29] Nadia Urbinati, *We the People: How Populism Transforms Democracy* (Cambridge: Harvard University Press, 2019), p. 41, emphasis in original.

ominous meaning, much like the way "deep state" is used by Donald Trump. Beneath formal institutions, the story goes, there is a structure of interrelations and connections, invisible to ordinary citizens, but that ultimately controls all the important decisions. Members of the "*układ*" are of course completely egoistic and anti-social. In Kaczyński's optic, the "*układ*" was mainly composed of ex-Communists, ex–secret service personnel, and the nouveaux riches with strong connections with the former two groups. The specific contours and composition of such deep structures are unimportant for populists – what is important is that such stories are useful for directing the anger of "ordinary people" against the elites.

To be sure, much of the reaction against entrenched elites is perfectly justified: Oligarchies of money and power are a frequent pathology of today's democracies. Where there is infrequent alternation in office, political elites tend to ossify into arrogant plutocracies. Synergies between wealth and power contribute to build an unfair, polarized, and highly stratified society. Populist anti-elite slogans resonate with popular grievances against this type of injustice. But populist leaders convert these anti-oligarchy grievances into protest against the very institutions that render rulers slightly more accountable and constrained in their activities. The anti-elitism of modern populism becomes a movement against institutional constraints on power, thus further entrenching the distance between the People and the elite. Except that it is now a *different* elite. A healthy distrust of political power is then converted into the executive aggrandizement of a new oligarchy.

Perhaps a large polity without an elite is possible. But at the time of writing these words, no such phenomenon has yet been noticed in human societies.

Anti-globalism and Nationalism

Jobs exported to countries with low-cost labor; merchandise imported from low cost countries. Cheaper merchandise in supermarkets does not seem like an attractive trade-off to those shoppers who have become unemployed as a result of the chain of processes leading to their neighborhood shops being stocked with cheap goods. Globalization is blamed for massive job losses and the loss of a way of life contingent upon stable employment.

The liberalization of trade has important distributional consequences. The internationalization of the world economy – the opening up of markets for goods, services, and capital – does not affect all classes evenly, and the winners rarely compensate the losers. Even if there is a net utility from free trade, this is only a meaningless statistical fiction to those whose total losses are lower than others' total gains, unless these losses have been offset by social transfers from the better-off.

Globalization "drives a wedge between the cosmopolitan, professional, skilled groups that are able to take advantage of it and the rest of society" (Dani Rodrik), especially in developed societies.[30] On the one hand, high-paid managers of multinationals, exporting companies, investors, and international banks benefit from larger markets. And as a bonus, globalization liberates them from having to make difficult choices at home. It is easier to outsource than to deliberate with other stakeholders (including unions) about labor relations or environmental impact. On the other hand, it is the "rest of society" that creates a fertile soil for anti-globalization: unskilled or semiskilled workers, low- and middle-level managers, and the like, who cannot take their (meager) resources across international borders. Their services can be easily replaced by workers across national borders, in contrast to the expertise and assets of the first category. This, Rodrik had argued some time ago, is what led to the collapse of the postwar social bargain between workers and employers "under which the former would receive a steady increase in wages and benefits in return for labor peace."[31] The same bargain was described by Adam Przeworski as one in which "working-class parties and trade unions consented to capitalism, while bourgeois parties and organization of employers accepted some redistribution of income."[32] This compromise has now been largely broken, as evidenced by the declining power of unions and sharply rising inequality in developed economies.

Despite the immense net benefits of globalization, there is a significant army of losers from it. These losers have two natural remedies available to them: first, to demand that globalization winners compensate them for their losses (and still remain better-off than before) or, alternatively, to call for protectionism, that is, an end to globalization.[33] The former is a

---

[30] Dani Rodrik, "The Politics of Anger," *Project Syndicate* (March 9, 2016), www.project-syndicate.org/commentary/the-politics-of-anger-by-dani-rodrik-2016-03.

[31] Dani Rodrik, "Has Globalization Gone Too Far?" *California Management Review*, 39 (Spring 1997), 29–53 at 32.

[32] Przeworski, *Crises of Democracy*, pp. 18–19.

[33] Similarly, Italo Colantone and Piero Stanig, "The Trade Origins of Economic Nationalism: Import Competition and Voting Behavior in Western Europe," *American Journal of Political Science*, 62 (2018), 936–953 at 937.

left-wing strategy; the latter, a right-wing (populist) strategy. But to pursue the first strategy is increasingly difficult under conditions of globalization. The very conditions that had produced net benefits of free trade make it difficult to finance a generous, redistributive welfare state because of capital mobility across borders. Money simply migrates toward low-taxation environments. As such, protectionism presents itself as a feasible alternative that corresponds to economic nationalism, and in the political reality of today's developed world, to nationalism simpliciter. Globalization's losers in developed countries turn "naturally" to right-wing populism, just as those same groups in the past "naturally" turned to left-wing, pro–welfare state parties. Under globalization, welfare state solutions have lost their credibility, and hence attractiveness.

Grievances based on the perception of economic disadvantage produced by globalization merge seamlessly with anger based on identity claims built upon religion, ethnicity, and nationhood. Those who find themselves at the margins of the *global* flows of goods and capital are likely to find themselves on the margins of *their own* society. The status of exclusion produced by the cross-border mobility of capital is converted into a sense that the unique identities of national communities have been canceled. In this way economic nationalism resonates with nationalism per se. The presence of immigrants and refugees helps foster identity-based nationalism even if the root causes of Rodrik's "wedge" between the beneficiaries and victims of globalization belong in the domain of the economy.

The economic losers of globalization do not stop at calls for *economic* protectionism and criticism of various free-trade agreements, but often escalate their anger to the level of fully fledged belligerent nationalism. Anti–free trade tirades lend themselves well to such nationalistic excesses because usually it is relatively easy to nominate racially or ethnically defined targets as guilty of the domestic negative externalities of globalization: in particular the Chinese, other Asians, or Mexicans. This is all the easier for populists since globalization embraces some of the practices in developing countries that would be excluded – on the grounds of fairness or humanitarianism – and legally banned at home in developed countries. Think of the use of slave or quasi slave labor, child labor, hazardous working conditions for miserable pay, and the like. In this way, anti-globalism may connect with some perfectly plausible moral arguments. When child labor in Bangladesh displaces workers in Louisiana or lax safety in sweatshops in Indonesia leads to the closure of factories in Austria, more is at stake than just frustration with the negative side effects of bringing down restrictions on international trade. In an ironic manner, the moral underpinnings of anti-globalization animus go hand-in-hand with the visceral racism of the demonization of the Chinese, the Mexicans, or the Muslims, who are depicted as being responsible for the fate of the lower-middle class of the majority race in the United States or Europe. But come to think of it, the irony may not even *be there* because different standards and practices between developed and developing countries in terms of labor rights, environmental protection, or corruption lend themselves easily to interpretations that are contemptuous and even racist in nature ("They just do it that way there.").

And so exposure to globalization is a pathway to populism. There is a clear correlation in developed countries, for instance, between the degree of import penetration from China and support for right-wing, nationalist-populist politicians. Two Italian economists from the Bocconi University in Milan have convincingly shown this correlation in fifteen Western European countries. Their study showed that the "China trade shock" played a statistically significant role in the shift toward radical, nationalist, right-wing parties. The backlash aspect of globalization may help solve the puzzle of "Why do members of the 'natural' constituencies of left or social-democratic parties (low-skilled manufacturing workers, the unemployed, etc.) vote for radical-right parties?"[34]

But there is no necessary connection between a typically populist hostility to immigrants and a strong national identity: The latter does not *have* to lead to the former. "[L]ove for the country and even perceived superiority of the country do not necessarily have to result in perceptions of migrant threat and Euroscepticism...Associations between nationalistic attitudes and anti-immigration attitudes are far from perfect."[35] National identification and national pride may *but need not* lead to intolerance toward strangers, including refugees and immigrants. (After all, theoretically at least, one may derive national pride from the sense that one's nation is particularly generous and sympathetic toward others in need.) In addition, nationalism may be connected with a nostalgic construction of the nation as it (allegedly) *was*, rather than with its current state of affairs. Nationalism need not lead to "national hubris," understood as a set of beliefs about one's own nation entailing invidious

---

[34] Ibid., p. 937.
[35] Marcel Lubbers and Marcel Coenders, "Nationalistic Attitudes and Voting for the Radical Right in Europe," *European Union Politics*, 18 (2017), 98–118 at 101.

comparisons with other nations – another word for this is "chauvinism."[36]

Usually, a necessary condition for intolerance is the sense that one's national identity is *under threat*.[37] And of course the most obvious menace as perceived by public opinion in states with strong populism is a migrant threat, for example, a Muslim or Latin American influx. Envisioning their nation under siege by immigrants and refugees of an unfamiliar background and religion helps convert nationalism into a vehicle of anger and intolerance. Within this vision, the love of one's own nation translates into hatred toward undesirable Others. Populist political elites supply such a vision, which is likely to become toxic.

This may happen when political institutions embrace an exclusionary or supremacist notion of nationalism but also, to the contrary, when institutions *fail* to recognize the importance of national identity for many people. There was an interesting sociological study in Germany about the relationships between vocational schoolteachers and their students at the end of the first decade of the 2000s. In contrast to earlier generations of Germans who had largely rejected nationalism as evoking the horrors of the Nazi past, for school students in the study the nation was an important symbol giving them a frame for identification, orientation, and solidarity. But since national identification was officially disfavored and delegitimized by the public educational system, many students were attracted to radical right-wing politics.[38]

Anti-modernism

Witold Waszczykowski is not a household name. Currently holding office as a member of the European Parliament from the Law and Justice Party (PiS), he was until early 2018 the Polish minister for foreign affairs. His name briefly appeared in European newspapers in early 2016 when, in a press interview, he denounced "a Marxist pattern" according to which the world is supposed to move toward "a new mix of cultures and races, a world of bicyclists and vegetarians."[39] Somewhat less

---

[36] See Bart Bonikowski and Paul DiMaggio, "Varieties of American Popular Nationalism," *American Sociological Review*, 81 (2016), 949–980 at 951.
[37] Lubbers and Coenders, "Nationalistic Attitudes," p. 112.
[38] The study described by Bonikowski, "Nationalism in Settled Times," p. 433.
[39] See "Poland's New Government Dislikes Critical Media, Vegetarians and Cyclists," *The Economist* (January 4, 2016), online edition, www.economist.com/europe/2016/01/04/polands-new-government-dislikes-critical-media-vegetarians-and-cyclists.

comically, during a state visit in Hungary in March 2016, Andrzej Duda, the president of Poland, deplored the crisis "of the values on which European civilisation was built...that has Latin roots and is based on the stem of Christianity...All these ideals in today's Europe are being lost, are being forgotten and trampled on by other ideologies that in fact distort the essence of humankind and humanity."[40] Similarly, in one of his first TV interviews after elevation to high office, Prime Minister Mateusz Morawiecki asserted Poland's mission of "re-Christianising Europe."[41]

This anti-modernist and anti-progressivist program was not limited in Poland to *words* uttered, often in a preposterous manner, by politicians and the ruling party's propagandists. A number of existing offices and programs to combat discrimination were discontinued as soon as PiS came to power. For instance, in June 2016, just six months after its electoral victory, PiS extinguished the governmental Council for Counteracting Racial Discrimination, Xenophobia and Intolerance. Significantly, this happened at a time when acts of violence – verbal and physical – against non-whites were rising in Poland. Public schools ceased to accept visitors from NGOs running workshops against intolerance and xenophobia, while at the same time opening their doors to radical nationalistic groups such as the openly neo-Nazi ONR (The National-Radical Front).

The government stopped subsidies for civil society activities such as the so-called Blue Line, a phone-in for young persons in desperate psychological situations, often on the verge of committing suicide. It also announced its intention to withdraw from the Council of Europe's Convention on preventing and combating violence against women and domestic violence (known as the Istanbul Convention). In turn, governmental subsidies were generously conferred upon religious and right-wing groups, such as the network of organizations connected with the Catholic-fundamentalist Radio Maryja or a radical right-wing network of NGOs around the fundamentalist organization Ordo Iuris. All these manifestations of cultural counterrevolution have been enthusiastically

---

[40] "Poles and Hungarians Have Preserved Good Values," speech by Andrzej Duda, March 19, 2016, www.president.pl/en/news/art,126,poles-and-hungarians-have-preserved-good-values.html.

[41] As reported in "Poland's New Prime Minister: Return to Christian Roots Only Way to Stop Europe's Decline," *LifeSiteNews* (December 14, 2017), www.jtcontracelsum.blogspot.com/2017/12/polands-new-prime-minister.html.

promoted in public education, the public media, and the pro-PiS commercial media. Just before his nomination as minister of education in 2020, Mr. Przemysław Czarnek characterized the "LGBT ideology" as having the same roots as "Hitler's German national socialism."[42] As minister in charge of schools, Mr. Czarnek later announced that schoolchildren should learn about the fundamentals of business and entrepreneurship from the encyclical letters of Pope John Paul II.[43]

Even though Hungary is much more secular than Poland (just over half of the population profess themselves to be Christians, compared to around 90 percent in Poland), Viktor Orbán has also frequently used religious language and appeals to Christian values. In one of his speech-manifestos in 2018, he declared the primacy of Christian democracy over liberal democracy (or an "open society"). Orbán's vision of Christian democracy gives priority to Christianity over multiculturalism, is openly anti-immigration, and rests on the traditional Christian family.[44] This is not a version of "Christian democracy" as espoused by the great Christian Democratic parties in Western Europe after the Second World War, like the Italian DC or German CDU/CSU, but a narrow, mean, fundamentalist, thoroughly (and expressly) illiberal vision.

The new Hungarian Fundamental Law of 2011 is so replete with religious references, including a solemn preamble with its "God bless the Hungarians," that one Hungarian historian was able to speak of the "sacralization" of new Hungarian politics.[45] The preamble, significantly called "Avowal of National Faith," further recognizes "the role Christianity has played in preserving our nation" and emphasizes that Hungary is "a part of Christian Europe." Also mentioned in the preamble, the Holy Crown has become part of an important narrative under Orbán. The Fundamental Law proclaims that the Crown "embodies the constitutional continuity of Hungary's statehood," even though one striking fact about Hungary's constitutional history is its spectacular *lack* of constitutional continuity. The Fundamental Law itself constitutes an express and radical repudiation of the earlier two decades of post-

---

[42] Quoted in www.oko.press/czarnek-ministrem-edukacji-i-nauki-otwarta-furtka-dla-homo fobii-nacjonalizmu-i-antysemityzmu/, September 29, 2020.

[43] See www.money.pl/gospodarka/czarnek-zdecydowal-dzieci-nauki-o-biznesie-beda-czer pac-z-tekstow-jana-pawla-ii-6644859249121888a.html, May 29, 2021.

[44] Quoted in Kim Lane Scheppele, "The Opportunism of Populists and the Defense of Constitutional Liberalism," *German Law Journal*, 20 (2019), 314–331 at 323.

[45] See Bogdan Góralczyk, "Axiological Disintegration of the EU? The Case of Hungary," *Yearbook of Polish European Studies*, 18 (2015), 81–109 at 87 n. 17.

communist constitutionalism. The holy relic of St. Stephen, Hungary's first Christian king, has been elevated into an apex of national imagery, thus amalgamating religious with nationalist themes. "The holy crown doctrine," says Sándor Radnóti, professor of philosophy of art at Eotvos Lorand University in Budapest, has "placed the mystic 'membership' ahead of the idea of constitutional patriotism and citizenship."[46] Orbán has shrewdly used the exalted place the Crown occupies in Hungarians' collective memory. During his first period of rule, he made the Parliament adopt Act I of 2000 "On Commemoration of Saint Stephen's State Foundation and the Holy Crown," which determined that the National Museum was not a worthy enough site for the Crown. Instead, it was transferred to the Parliament building ("the idea of the Parliament [as a site for the Crown] rested on no tradition whatsoever," Radnóti observes caustically),[47] thus "re-sacralizing" it, or, again in the words of Radnóti, "resuscitat[ing]...the tradition of the crown as a symbol of the adoption of Christianity," for purely pragmatic political considerations.[48]

It is no wonder that some political psychologists connect populism (especially, right-wing populism) with the adulation of the spiritual over the cognitive, passion over reason, emotions over knowledge. "[A]s it offers as [sic] degraded view of people's cognitive abilities, [right-wing populism] celebrates their emotionality. With its focus on realizing the national will and the action it requires, the individuals' feelings and their vigorous expression are valued over their thoughts and useless contemplation. The former is strong, alive and vigorous, the latter weak, decadent and diminishing."[49] These words of Shawn Rosenberg, professor of political science and psychology and social behavior at University of California, Irvine, may sound too harsh. After all, political appeals to democracy, human rights, and liberalism are also often emotional. But it seems plausible that of all the ideologies (in a broad sense of the word) on the table today, populism is at the forefront in dismissing rationality,

---

[46] Sándor Radnóti, "A Sacred Symbol in a Secular Country: The Holy Crown," in Gábor Attila Tóth (ed.), *Constitution for a Disunited Nation: On Hungary's 2011 Fundamental Law* (Budapest: CEU Press, 2012), pp. 85–109 at 95, footnote omitted.
[47] Ibid., p. 105.
[48] Ibid., p. 107.
[49] Shawn W. Rosenberg, "Democracy Devouring Itself: The Rise of the Incompetent Citizen and the Appeal of Right Wing Populism," UC Irvine Previously Published Works (2019), www.escholarship.org/uc/item/8806z01m.

verifiable truths, and empirically falsifiable knowledge. (We shall see many examples of this in Chapter 5.)

And just as there is strong *supply* of irrationality and sheer falsehoods in politics (cyberspace is full of them), there is also a lot of *demand* for it, and populist politicians build their strategies on the people as they are rather than as they should be. Populist anti-modernist supply responds to the demand for a return to a world of known certainties, established hierarchies of authority (as much in the state as in a family), and traditional faiths. Populist voters are much more negative about social causes related to modernism that they view as contrary to the traditional outlook they endorse. Around the time of the Brexit referendum, "Remain" voters en masse supported, multiculturalism (70 percent), feminism (71 percent) and the green movement (73 percent), while support for these three causes among the "Leave" voters was, respectively, 26 percent, 44 percent, and 42 percent.[50] Anti-modernism is often aligned with nationalism and the assertion of national identity against colonialism, foreign domination, or the dreaded elitist cosmopolitanism. For instance, regarding Modi's India, one student of anti-Western populism explained in a recent article that: "India's anti-colonial struggle has shaped its anti-Westernism, but populism here is also a post-colonial 'local' assertion against a modernizing and cosmopolitan elite that is responsible for secularism and 'liberalism' in the American sense."[51]

The democratization of public space created by social media has prompted an unprecedented dissemination of silliness and nonsense that would have previously been screened off, censored, relegated to the fringes, or swept under the carpet. Cultural and media elites no longer control the mainstream production of information and commentary, at least not to the same degree as before. In Rosenberg's stern words, "[n]ow an alienated, uneducated, working-class ranch hand living in east Texas has access not only to the information disseminated by the major television channels or the national newspapers controlled by elites, but also to a myriad of smaller, more varied and less culturally sanctioned sources."[52]

Political phenomena are complex and difficult to comprehend without specialized knowledge. "Explaining" them by resort to irrational tales of

---

[50] Gidron and Hall, "The Politics of Social Status," p. 59
[51] Ralph Schroeder, "The Populist Revolt against the West," *Comparative Sociology*, 20 (2021), 419–440 at 426.
[52] Rosenberg, "Democracy Devouring Itself," p. 27.

conspiracy or divine intervention makes politics more accessible to many. It provides sense, value, and security to many people in a world fraught with dangers and challenges.

Illiberal Impatience with Institutions

Illiberal impatience leading to the delegitimizing of institutions is best reflected in the notion of legal or constitutional "impossibilism," a term used by PiS leader Jarosław Kaczyński, and is meant to signify the obstacles and barriers that law erects, in order to render it impossible to carry out necessary and desirable reforms. Dutch legal sociologist Paul Blokker describes this trait of populism as "legal skepticism," which means that "populists are wary of the institutions of and limits of liberal constitutionalism."[53] Law is perceived by populists as an impediment to the achievement of justice, and not just that, it is also perceived as an obstacle to democracy and effectiveness. Consider the case of presidential term limits, such as those introduced in Venezuela in 1999 by Chávez himself just as his constitutionally limited term was coming to an end in 2009. The question raised by his apologists was simple: if the best man for the job was still available, why would the People be denied the right to reelect him?

For many people, the centrality and autonomy of the law is not easy to comprehend or to value. If all that matters is the efficiency of authorities in achieving easily recognizable goals, legal institutions and procedures may be viewed as irrational obstacles to the achievement of those goals. Why would law be anything else than a means to a goal? If it is suitable, all is fine, but if it is unsuitable, it should be changed or disregarded. The sense that the law binds not only all citizens (a truth codified in a popular even if thoughtless maxim *"Dura lex sed lex"*) but also authorities is not something that comes naturally but is an acquired taste. So too is the idea of judges independent of the current majority's will. Or of procedures and protocols to be followed "no matter what," even if the urgency of a perceived problem dictates abandoning them.

The very idea of rights encompassing a right to do wrong seems to many absurd and confusing: If something is wrong, it should be legally prohibited, and if something is right, legally compelled. Liberals who deny those implications are seen as incoherent or perverse: Why should

---

[53] Paul Blokker, "Populist Constitutionalism," *ResearchGate* (September 20, 2017), www.researchgate.net/publication/319938853_Populist_Constitutionalism, p. 2.

they permit what they abhor? Why should people value claims they believe to be wrong, and respect individuals whom they loathe? Why should an exercise of a claimed right be immune to a moral veto by a majority? Why should someone be protected in conduct that offends the others' sensibilities?

This point was very well expressed by János Kis, Hungarian political philosopher and brave dissident under Communism, who later became a leader of a liberal-democratic movement in his country. Describing what he called "a basic rights shock," which many in his country have experienced with the advent of democracy, Kis says:

> for many, it was extremely hard to come to terms with the discovery that freedom of speech does not mean just freedom to criticize the government but also freedom to mock on others' sacred beliefs or to vent hate on vulnerable groups; that equal protection of the law involves the coming out of gays and lesbians and their demand for access to the institution of marriage; that the due process of law protects not just the innocent but also the criminal, and so on.[54]

"And so on," alas, stands for an awful lot. The elimination of the death penalty to many is unpalatable: It offends their sense of justice captured best in a version of lex talionis. And if the Council of Europe forbids its member states to have it on the books, so much the worse for those European organizations, in the eyes of populists.

But authoritarian sentiments and impatience with law are not present in all movements dubbed populist. The pro-Brexit movement, for example, is often depicted as one of the main pieces of evidence for advances of populism today, and certainly it displays some unmistakably populist traits: anti-immigration animus, economic nationalism, status anxiety. But many British were uncomfortable with the "ever closer Union" on the Continent for reasons that do not resonate with authoritarianism or illiberal impatience at all. A clever title "Never closer Union" in the *Economist* magazine almost on the eve of the fateful referendum (October 24, 2015) was an emphatic response to a federalist vision, a response *not* motivated by some dark aspirations for pursuing authoritarian ways at home without any supranational oversight. If anything, it was the opposite: It was a response to a perceived threat from Brussels to

---

[54] János Kis, "Introduction: From the 1989 Constitution to the 2011 Fundamental Law," in Gábor Attila Tóth (ed.), *Constitution for a Disunited Nation: On Hungary's 2011 Fundamental Law* (Budapest: CEU Press, 2012), pp. 1–21 at 12.

the established British model of the rule of law, with its own checks and balances, which many British citizens may have sincerely believed to be superior to those offered by EU legal supremacy.

Hence, as a legal scholar at New York University, Gráinne de Búrca, argued, "the vote to leave the EU, and the 'take back control' slogan, must...be understood as referring to the restoration of British parliamentary democracy, with its own distinctive set of domestic checks and balances."[55] And de Búrca recalls that even if there were some politicians in the United Kingdom (e.g., Theresa May) who flirted with the idea of British withdrawal from the European Convention of Human Rights, it was accompanied by the prospect of adopting a domestic bill of rights. For all we know (my comment, not de Búrca's), such a bill might have offered superior protections for individual rights than an old, largely anachronistic (despite some newer protocols) European Convention.

Different Lego Toys

The different configurations of different factors on both the supply and demand side help explain the various trajectories of populisms around the world. Why, for example, has Latin America seen strong advances of left-wing populism (with vote totals around the mid-20 percent level) but for a long time, low successes for right-wing populism (around 2 percent, up to 2015)? In Europe it is just the reverse (with left-wing populist parties under 5 percent in the aggregate electorate of European countries, while right-wing populism is up more than 20 percent)?[56] The salience of different anxieties and concerns (on the demand side), accompanied by politicians who emphasize anxieties that resonate with their programs (the supply side), is different. In Latin America, the most salient concern is economic inequality and the exploitation of the working classes, farmers, and the unemployed. Hence, populism generated by this supply-demand factor drives mainly left-wing populism. But in Europe, the more prominent concern is migrants and minorities, which resonates

---

[55] Gráinne de Búrca, "How British Was the Brexit Vote?" in Benjamin Martill and Uta Staiger (eds.), *Brexit and Beyond: Rethinking the Futures of Europe* (London: UCL Press, 2018), pp. 46–52 at 51.
[56] For these statistics and their sources, see Dani Rodrik, "Populism and the Economics of Globalization," *Journal of International Business Policy*, 1 (2018), 12–33 at 24–26.

with ethno-cultural divisions – thus triggering a right-wing brand of populism. It is not to say that economic class cleavages are insignificant in Europe, but rather that they have been amalgamated into a package of concerns and programs that respond to the influx of immigrants and to the grievances of internal minorities. Economic grievances are translated into anger against immigrants, who are presented as taking jobs and eroding domestic welfare systems.

This explanation of the comparative significance of different populisms in different parts of the world also applies, though with a lesser force, to the division between Southern Europe and the rest of the Continent. The unique phenomenon of the huge successes of left-wing populisms in Greece and Spain (respectively, Syriza and Podemos), and also (but less so) in Italy (Cinque Stelle), has similar roots to left-wing successes in Latin America, with the added factor of cultural interactions with Latin America in the case of Spain, of course. (And one has to add that in each of these three Mediterranean states, left-wing populist parties have powerful populist competitors on the *right*.) Just like Latin America, Greece and Spain have experienced similar socio-economic effects of financial globalization: in Latin America, through International Monetary Fund programs, in Southern Europe, through the euro. Pressures from the common currency and from austerity measures decided by the European Union amplified the consequences of the global financial crisis in a similar way to pressures from foreign corporations and the World Bank in Latin America.[57] An additional factor weakening anti-immigration hatred and therefore the ethno-cultural cleavage in the case of Spain was that the bulk of migrants came from Latin America (mainly Spanish-speaking Ecuador, Colombia, Peru, Bolivia, and Venezuela; fewer from Portuguese-speaking Brazil) and from other European countries (in particular, from Eastern Europe), which were by and large similar to Spain from the point of view of culture and religion. This contrasts with France or Germany, for example, where the most noticeable migrants came from Muslim countries of Northern Africa and Turkey, as well as from sub-Saharan Africa.

I will not end this overview by offering a taxonomy of contemporary populisms in power. Money can buy many such classifications today: left-wing and right-wing populisms, nationalistic, ethnocentric and authoritarian populisms, and so forth. More important than any

---

[57] See ibid., pp. 25–27.

taxonomies, which are inevitably arbitrary and overlapping, is the recognition of the different building blocks that create the demand for populism and trigger its supply. The catalog of these building blocks is not infinite, just as we do not have innumerable Lego pieces. But their different shapes, sizes, and colors *matter* for whatever comes at the end. And variants of contemporary populisms are just as diverse (and just as alike) as are Lego toys.

2

The War on Institutions

> Pure democracy is populism...The *innovation* is institutions that slow democracy down and filter it through legislature, courts, and agencies. The media, too, is meant to have a countervailing effect – people with domain expertise who can say, Let's interrogate the issue before banning immigrants from certain countries, removing grizzlies off endangered species lists, adding a citizenship question to the census, or restricting access to birth control because people in power at the moment decide it's a good idea.[1]

This passage from Scott Galloway, professor of business at New York University, nicely captures the two main characteristics of institutions in a democracy: first, their counterbalancing function and, second, their slowing-down role. The first is to have a set of devices that may oppose what at any given time "people in power" find to be a good idea; the latter is to hinder the immediacy of translating a "good idea" into binding law or official policy. These two checking functions are particularly disliked by populists. "Counterbalancing" means upsetting the purity of the will of the people, as discerned by populist leaders: It unnecessarily confuses, distorts, and clouds the simplicity of the issues at hand. "Slowing-down" reduces the effectiveness of governing, creates delays, and raises the real risk that the populists' programs will never become a reality.

And of course, if pushed to the extreme, both functions of institutions create real dangers, not just to populism, but to any democratic governance. "Vetocracy"[2] leads to a state of permanent stalemate, in which institutional checks and balances do the "checking" but with no visible outcome reflecting a satisfactory "balance" leading to an optimal decision. As Mark Tushnet and Bojan Bugarič observe in a recent book:

---

[1] Scott Galloway, *Post Corona: From Crisis to Opportunity* (London: Bantam Press, 2020), p. 199, emphasis in original.

[2] Ezra Klein, "Francis Fukuyama: America Is in 'one of the most severe political crises I have experienced'" (October 26, 2016), www.vox.com/2016/10/26/13352946/francis-fukuyama-ezra-klein.

"Policymaking at the national level in the United States has been stymied by 'gridlock' resulting from having too many veto gates."[3] So populists' impatience with the institutions may have a rational core: Institutions are there to get things done rather than to deliberate and mutually check each other ad infinitum. Hence the choice must be neither "ad infinitum" nor "immediacy," but a point on a continuum between both.

Where to draw the line in a principled way is not an easy thing to do in abstract terms, but it is not an impossible task. The opening passage from Galloway suggests that it must be controlled to some extent by a certain calculus of respective harms: the comparative risks of the harm of too much immediacy versus the risk of continuous institutional stalemate. And it is important to keep in mind that politicians in charge, especially those with plausible electoral mandates, will have strong incentives to push institutions in the direction of offering *no* counterbalance to the politicians' will.

Populists do not abolish or suppress institutions. Generally, populists are no Leninists in the sense of outright rejecting the institutional structures they inherit from the preceding regime.[4] While there are occasional examples of populists sidelining various institutions – for example, Hugo Chávez invented a fully malleable Constituent Assembly to sideline the existing parliament and the institutional configuration around it – when this occurs, it occurs in a piecemeal way, and usually not to all the central institutions at the same time. But when populists take these steps, they cross the line that separates authoritarian populism from authoritarianism tout court and open up space for their openly non-democratic followers, as was the case for Maduro, who had inherited ruins of democratic design from Chávez in Venezuela.

Typically, however, populists work within the inherited institutional architecture and subvert it for their purposes. The subversion is often hardly visible to outside observers. It may be as "subtle" as packing the institutions with their own loyalists or as brutal as redesigning the procedural rules and powers of the institutions. But the institutions persist with all the veneer of legality and the rule of law – they just change their function. Rather than "counterbalancing," institutions serve

---

[3] Mark Tushnet and Bojan Bugarič, *Power to the People: Constitutionalism after Populism* (Oxford: Oxford University Press, 2021), p. 24.
[4] Actually, once in power, Lenin tried desperately to hold on to tsarist state structures. But he wanted *effective instruments*, which he lamented Russians never knew, not *restraining* ones. I owe this observation to Martin Krygier.

the political purposes of the all-powerful rulers. Rather than slowing down, institutions accelerate decision-making. We shall see how populists have captured courts, and in particular constitutional courts, in Chapter 4. These fundamentally counter-majoritarian institutions were turned into enthusiastic helpers of the executive. But not every institution is of course "counter-majoritarian" in the way constitutional courts are supposed to be. As such, the process of subverting the role of institutions is better expressed by the metaphor of "hollowing out" than the more dramatic metaphor of "capture." This is less emotionally infused than some of the other categories used by the critics of populists' attitudes toward institutions, for instance "colonization,"[5] "occupation,"[6] or even "cannibalistic encroachment."[7]

Writing about the attitude of the Trump Administration to institutions during the Covid-19 crisis, Galloway observes: "Ironically, our national disregard for politicians has empowered [elected officials], because we've allowed them *to hollow out* the institutions meant to provide a long-term counterbalance."[8] The concept of "hollowing out" needs to be unpacked. This requires both a reflection on the theory of institutionalization, and also an account of the war on institutions conducted in many of the countries that may serve as exemplars of populists in power.

One important caveat: Despite the fact that some institutional deformations have taken place in all of the case studies considered in this book, it does not necessarily follow that this always happens whenever populists come to power. As Tushnet and Bugarič observe, neither the populist coalition of the League and the Five Star Movement in Italy nor the Austrian coalition government, which included FPÖ, a strongly right-leaning populist party, have done anything to undo liberal constitutionalism in those countries.[9] However, the survival of Austrian and Italian constitutionalism can be explained by two important factors relevant to those two cases: first, the relative brevity of the populist government's

---

[5] Jan-Werner Müller, "Populism and Constitutionalism," in Cristóbal Rovira Kaltwasser, Paul Taggart, Paulina Ochoa Espejo, and Pierre Ostiguy (eds.), *Oxford Handbook of Populism* (Oxford: Oxford University Press, 2017), pp. 590–606 at 596.
[6] Ibid., p. 596.
[7] Martin Krygier, "The Challenge of Institutionalisation: Post-Communist 'Transitions,' Populism, and the Rule of Law," *European Constitutional Law Review*, 15 (2019), 544–573 at 548.
[8] Galloway, *Post Corona*, p. 198, emphasis added.
[9] Tushnet and Bugarič, *Power to the People*, pp. 51–52.

tenure (in Italy, fourteen months over 2018 and 2019; in Austria, seventeen months from 2017 to 2019) and, second, the fact that in both these coalitions, radical right populists had to co-govern either with left populists (in Italy) or with center-right Christian Democrats (ÖVP in Austria). I am not claiming that it is inevitable that when populists of whatever color form government, they will always dismantle checks and balances. But populist governments do so in sufficient numbers to cause concern.

Hollow Institutions, Stuffed Institutions[10]

Martin Krygier says: Populists are de-institutionalizers.[11] But a page earlier in the same remarkable essay, Krygier asserts: Populists are institutionalizers.[12] Is he schizophrenic? (The answer is that he is not; I know him well.) So how can he reconcile these two assertions?

It all boils down to Krygier's understanding of "institutions" and "institutionalization." Following his intellectual guru, the late Philip Selznick, Krygier adopts a distinction between "organization" and "institution." Institutions, he says, are organizations "infused with value beyond the technical requirement of the task at hand."[13] So while they maintain their technical dimension, they also entail (in Krygier's words paraphrasing Selznick) "attachments, commitments and connections, typically not formalized," which become their "second natures."[14] They are social organisms. They embody certain desired aims and standards. And of course, these "attachments, commitments and connections" may be positive or negative, depending on one's perspective. The latter includes "engrained antipathies" or "hostility to strangers" or "differentiated patterns of behaviour and interaction among social strata and classes."[15]

Under this understanding, populists can be said to be "institutionalists," even "deliberate institutionalizers." They make use of institutions, and selectively value them in their strategies, whenever it suits them.

---

[10] With apologies to T. S. Eliott, "The Hollow Men" ("We are the hollow men / We are the stuffed men").
[11] Krygier, "The Challenge of Institutionalisation," p. 563.
[12] Ibid., p. 562.
[13] Ibid., p. 550, quoting Philip Selznick, *Leadership in Administration*, new ed. (Berkeley: University of California Press, 1984), p. 17, emphasis removed.
[14] Krygier, "The Challenge of Institutionalisation," p. 550.
[15] Ibid., p. 552.

Sometimes it *does* suit them. Krygier's description is well worth citing in full because, while originally describing post-Communist populists (especially in Poland and Hungary), it makes an important general observation on contemporary populists in power:

> They draw on institutionalised sources of attachment, resentment, and attitudes to public institutions and reforms of them, but they also seek to revive, develop, shape, distort, and exploit them...The values, loyalties, attachments, and their parallel anti-values and enemies are cultivated in order to strengthen the institutionalisation of new movements by linking them to old, uniquely authentically "our" values, or what are represented as such, that have been, or are alleged to have been, sloughed aside by alien elites.[16]

Occasionally, populists achieve their aims of hollowing out institutions inherited from the liberal-democratic past by creating their own, parallel institutions, which then overshadow the original institutions in importance, competences, and budgets. This is the strategy of duplication. Populists "engage in a strategy of duplication by creating parallel bodies tasked with carrying out the same functions as the 'original' institutions they aim to control...By shifting power to a parallel institution, they are able to quietly concentrate power without dissolving other branches of government, preserving the appearance that independent institutions continue to exist."[17] The Council of National Media in Poland under PiS is one such example. PiS inherited from the past a constitutionally entrenched National Council of Radio and TV. This was a large bureaucratic body with cumbersome procedures that the leaders of the party feared (without good grounds, as events have shown) would not be easily controllable. So, PiS established, by a statute enacted by the parliament they controlled, a five-person easily malleable council. With a guaranteed 3:2 majority on the council and streamlined procedures, PiS was able to better oversee all the main decisions concerning the appointments of top executives in all state-run broadcasters. This "institutional experiment" was of course completely disingenuous, and its sole aim has been to sidestep constitutional institutions that may have turned out to be unwieldy.

Another example concerns local government in Hungary. In 2010–2011, the Fidesz government established country and district

---

[16] Ibid., pp. 562–563.
[17] Will Freeman, "Sidestepping the Constitution: Executive Aggrandizement in Latin America and East Central Europe," *Constitutional Studies*, 6 (2020), 35–58 at 43.

government offices that paralleled existing local governments, but whose leadership was directly appointed by the prime minister. According to an OECD report, Fidesz then "drastically reduced subnational government responsibilities," transferring authority over social services and local administration to the government offices while slashing local governments' funding.[18] Similar events occurred in Venezuela in 2008, when opposition politician Antonio Ledezma was elected mayor of Caracas; Chávez's allies in the National Assembly passed a law creating a "parallel authority for the capital": a new administrative region with leadership appointed by the executive and its own budget. This was then replicated at the national level: The pro-Chávez bloc in Venezuela's National Assembly created a nationwide network of "local parallel institutions," executive-funded neighborhood organizations called Communal Councils, while at the same time reducing the powers and funds of the municipal governments.[19]

But at the same time, populists are *anti*-institutionalists. They are uninterested in institutions as opposed to extra-institutional mobilization, and are actually hostile to *independent* institutions: independent, that is, from populists themselves. This is "[b]ecause institutions would constrain the leader's latitude and impede their quest for unchallenged predominance, populism stands in unavoidable tension with institutionalization as such," says Kurt Weyland.[20] They interrupt the link that connects the leader and the people, and drive a wedge between the state and raw social interests. The populist state must be a direct, immediate expression of societal interests (those favored by populist leaders, of course) rather than something that stands "in between" and filters those interests by subjecting them to various institutional tests. Any institutional intermediation is abhorred as a possible distortion of the people's will, or even worse, an illegitimate competitor to the populist claim to exclusive legitimacy.[21] And so for leaders to *disregard* institutional rules and routines is seen by their followers not as an aberration or source of embarrassment, but to the contrary, a sign of authenticity. More than

---

[18] Ibid., p. 44.
[19] Ibid.
[20] Kurt Weyland, "Populism's Threat to Democracy: Comparative Lessons for the United States," *Perspectives on Politics* (2020). DOI: 10.1017/S1537592719003955, p. 3.
[21] See similarly Nadia Urbinati, *Democracy Disfigured: Opinion, Truth, and the People* (Cambridge: Harvard University Press, 2014), p. 132. See also Gianfranco Pasquino, "Populism and Democracy," in Daniele Albertazzi and Duncan McDonnell (eds.), *Twenty-First Century Populism* (Hampshire: Palgrave Macmillan, 2008), pp. 15–29 at 28.

democratic politicians, populists like to go "off script," literally and metaphorically, because the message to their followers is that they prefer to engage directly with their audiences rather than play by the rules, which are often seen as obscure and unnecessarily complicated. And, ironically perhaps, this anti-institutional stance often *intensifies* as populists gain power because they need to reconfirm to their base that they have not been co-opted by the institutional system and have not become a new establishment.[22]

Populists' grievances, often their anger, are addressed against *persons* inhabiting those institutions, just as their hopes are vested in *new* persons, rather than new institutions. In this, populists echo Stalin's maxim: "Cadres decide everything." The first step in the "hollowing out" of the inherited institutions is usually to staff them with loyal agents of the populists; it is only at the next stage that obedient institutions may see their competences enhanced and the tenure of its officials extended.[23] For instance, it is well known that for Jarosław Kaczyński, the main challenge in the political transformation of Poland was to replace the old elites with new ones; to substitute old personnel with people he could fully trust. (A popular slogan of Kaczyński's is there is a need for a "redistribution of prestige" – and this awkward concept is not meant in a sarcastic way!) To purge, rather than to redesign institutions, is his favorite strategy. Institutions can stay because they may one day be helpful for populists; but it is the people that have to go. Krygier again: "[T]he new populists are distinctive for their determination, having hollowed-out the independence (from them) of such institutions, to use and manipulate them for their purposes alien to the intentions that lay behind the generation of those institutions."[24] Similarly, Kaczyński's political friend and role model, Viktor Orbán, publicly rejected the view that "institution and principles are more important than personal power relations," and dismissively quipped: "Decisions are never made by principles and institutions."[25]

This is an important trope. Institutions are deflated rather than demolished by populist authoritarians. They may stay, but they must not be too

---

[22] See Nadia Urbinati, *Me the People: How Populism Transforms Democracy* (Cambridge: Harvard University Press, 2019), p. 6.
[23] Freeman, "Sidestepping the Constitution," p. 40.
[24] Krygier, "The Challenge of Institutionalisation," pp. 564–565.
[25] Orbán's speech of July 28, 2012, quoted by András Körösenyi, Gábor Illés, and Attila Gyulai, *The Orbán Regime: Plebiscitary Leader Democracy in the Making* (London: Routledge, 2020), pp. 79 and 91 n. 10.

strong (unless these are institutions such as the army and police) in the sense of effectiveness in enforcing compliance, and in the sense of stickiness and endurance. They should be capable of being changed at will because "the institutional settings are perceived and presented as resources to defeat political opponents, as strongholds to be occupied in a continuous and endless political struggle."[26] They are not something static, which may have some inherent value. They are not to be stabilized and preserved. Nor are they to be changed exceptionally, only when strong normative goals warrant change. Rather, they are assets if they are helpful at any given point to the movement, and obstacles when they are useless. And since any institution may show its detrimental face to the leader – even if only by constraining his need for immediacy – they are viewed with irritation. They don't "make decisions" – leaders do.

So, we may draw a tentative catalog of various forms of "hollowing out" of institutions, but this list is far from being exhaustive. *First*, institutions are rendered hollow by being staffed with new individuals who lack value commitment to the original rationales for having the institution in the first place ("capture"). From the point of view of an external observer, they perform the same acts and follow the same routines, but the considerations they inject into their decisions and so the substance of the decisions themselves are opposed to the raison d'être for the institution (the Polish and Hungarian constitutional courts are the best, or rather the worst, examples; central banks in India, Poland, and Hungary are other examples). *Second*, institutions may be paralleled by new ones, with ostensibly the same competences, which overshadow and sideline the original institutions, as exemplified by the new Media Council in Poland or the Budget Council in Hungary, which can veto any budget adopted by the parliament that even minimally increases the national debt ("duplication"). *Third*, the competences and powers (including budgets) of the institution may change, through formal legal changes or de facto changes, to the point at which they become purely perfunctory ("erosion"). It would be funny if it was not so tragic that in 2017, Duterte slashed the Commission on Human Rights' budget from $17 million to $25 (twenty-five dollars).[27] *Fourth*, institutions may obtain

---

[26] Ibid., p. 79.
[27] Barney Porter, "Philippines: Commission on Human Rights Budget Cut to Almost Nothing amid Duterte's Drug Crackdown," *ABC* (September 13, 2017), www.abc.net.au/news/2017-09-13/duterte-slashes-commission-on-human-rights-annual-budget-to-$25/8941088.

gally unlimited powers (think of the Venezuelan constituent assembly), which means that whatever input provided by a de facto leader is transformed into a binding decision ("expansion"). They are no longer meaningfully separated from the rest of the institutional setup. *Fifth*, the institutions may be transferred to another institutional context in which their independence and/or purpose are eroded, as was the case of the Hungarian data protection ombudsman whose office has been absorbed directly into the government ("migration"). *Sixth*, the oversight links between various institutions may be severed or even broken. In a well-designed institutional setup, institutions are interconnected with complex chains of accountability. But if those chains of accountability are broken, the institution's prerogatives are rendered indeterminate, and the institution becomes completely malleable in the hands of populists ("evasion"). As Will Freeman noted, "[t]he result is a series of gaps in the law, or oversight voids, which executives can then exploit to exercise unchecked power."[28] Such breaks in the chains of accountability prevent functioning institutions from providing checks on power.

Capture, duplication, erosion, expansion, migration, and evasion: These are some of the faces of the processes that largely keep inherited institutions in place – but also hollow them out.

Dispersion and Distrust

Leaders, not institutions, make decisions. And they make them fast. Many democratic theorists – including Samuel Issacharoff, Adam Przeworski, and Ming-Sung Kuo[29] – emphasize the "temporal aspect" of democracy. Democracy requires an extended time perspective. What is fundamental to democratic stability is a sense that democracy is a repeat play: Decisions must be taken in full awareness of the fact that soon someone else – currently in opposition – may be in power. Hence there is a need for compromises, trade-offs, consultation, and "negotiated accommodation"[30] – all of which take time and trigger a degree of moderation. Both (time delays and moderation, that is) are viewed by populists with distaste. Both are seen as signs of hesitation and of a shedding of

---

[28] Freeman, "Sidestepping the Constitution," p. 46.
[29] Samuel Issacharoff, *Democracy Unmoored* (in press); Adam Przeworski, *Crises of Democracy* (Cambridge: Cambridge University Press, 2019), Ming-Sung Kuo, "Against Instantaneous Democracy," *International Journal of Constitutional Law*, 17 (2019), 554–575.
[30] Issacharoff, *Democracy Unmoored*, chap. 2.

responsibility assumed at the point of election. The patient collaboration on legislation, with a canonical sequence of steps each separated from the other by required temporal spaces, is replaced by unilateral and impetuous measures. Populists behave as if they did not have to take out "insurance" for the future, in the form of supporting institutions that check their power today – and will also stay to check the power of today's opponents in the future.[31] Is it because they do not envisage the possibility of defeat? It's hard to tell – whenever populists establish strategically important positions with very long terms of office (as in Hungary where many constitutional positions are filled for nine years, including the head of the Electoral Commission), populists seem to plant their people in the apparatus of the state for years after their rule. Similarly, populists set in stone some substantive policies by entrenching them constitutionally.

The lack of any "intertemporal trade-offs"[32] may be a sign not only of impatience and impetuousness ("we have a mandate – let us act on it immediately, so that the Sovereign is not disappointed with us") but also of the absence of the separation and dispersal of powers. Such trade-offs are usually given effect by strong checks and balances, which is a pattern of the exercise of power that populists de facto reject, even if they occasionally pay lip service to it in official proclamations. The latter sometimes acknowledges the independence of the judiciary or the supremacy of parliament, but these narratives are laughable if one looks at how power is exercised in fact. The hostility to social and moral pluralism, so characteristic and indeed constitutive of populism in power, is translated into hostility toward the plural loci of political power.

Dispersed institutional schemes of power reduce, populists fear, the authenticity of the rulers' voice and actions. It waters down the (proclaimed) authorship of political decisions by a monolithic People. At the end of the day, all power is exercised by one person, and if some other officials have the last word on this or that, it is because they have been granted by the leader such authority, which may be revoked unilaterally at any time. Neither independent courts, nor the legislature with a recognized and respected parliamentary opposition, nor decentralized local units, nor single-issue agencies such as press boards or electoral commissions, nor inter-party factionalism or emerging alternative leadership, nor the soft power of media and civil society, are in the long term

---

[31] Tom Ginsburg, *Judicial Review in New Democracies* (Cambridge: Cambridge University Press, 2003), pp. 22–30.
[32] Issacharoff, *Democracy Unmoored*.

tolerated (and the "long term" is usually short). When they are, it is because the leader has so determined.

This is anathema to democracy. Dispersed powers – either along Montesquieu's tripartite elegant architecture or the messier US-style checks and balances, or any other scheme in between – is essential. And it is not only because the concentration of all powers in one person's hands poses mortal danger to individual liberty – though this is the main concern triggering separation of powers. But monolithic power is also likely to be inefficient. All institutions are vulnerable to temptations and perverse incentives that will lead to errors. "Preventing error is the most common reason for allowing friction within a constitutional order," N. W. Barber correctly states in a recent book.[33] And, as he continues, it is not only a prudential concern about preventing error that triggers separation of powers: it is also a rational division of labor, under which different institutions focus on different aspects of common good, for which they are the best suited, knowing that other institutions will weigh the considerations they have failed to take into account. In a well-designed constitutional system, this produces, Barber says, an invisible hand mechanism, where each institution pursues a limited good while the overall outcome is an aggregate public good. "Each [institution] fights for their own bit of a common good and, out of this conflict, the totality of the common good is achieved." And Barber adds: "Invisible hand mechanisms of this type are attractive where there are good reasons *to limit the range of considerations* that apply to an actor or institution."[34]

No such limits are contemplated in the ideal model of authoritarian populism. Institutions have the powers as delegated to them by the central executive. The public good pursued (or claimed to be pursued) by the leader is holistic and monolithic rather than partial and plural. Situations in which one institution "goes against the wishes of another," because it is an outcome of the limitation of concerns each institution is mandated to exercise, is seen as pathology and cacophony rather than a normal condition of separated powers. Friction, needed under Barber's scheme, both to guard against errors and to restrict the types of considerations different institutions include in their decisions, is seen as aberration, detracting from the unity of policy- and law-making. There is no division of labor, and there is no "invisible hand." Rather, the hand is all too visible.

---

[33] N. W. Barber, *The Principles of Constitutionalism* (Oxford: Oxford University Press, 2018), p. 72.
[34] Ibid., p. 73, emphasis added.

"Who Counts the Votes?"

An overview of the ways in which populists in power capture and deform previously established institutions (in addition to courts – to be discussed in Chapter 4) must begin with elections and electoral institutions. They are central to populists, in at least two ways. First, in the populist regimes discussed here, the rulers may genuinely worry about losing power, and everything that goes with it, which is much more than merely the perks of office. The probability is not very high – but nevertheless real. A purely (or predominantly) electoral mandate, by its very nature, renders the winners vulnerable. While populists do their best to tilt the playing field in their favor and to entrench themselves in power into the second (and third, and fourth...) terms of office, nevertheless their victory in the next elections cannot be taken for granted. Sometimes, as in Hungary, the field is so heavily skewed that their opponents must win the raw electoral votes by a very high margin in order to win the elections. But still, the democrats' victory is something that is *possible* – and not just theoretically, as it is in Russia or Belarus or Turkey, where elections are held too but for a host of other reasons than selecting a ruling team for the next term of office.[35] That is why these countries are not on my list of populisms in power but rather belong to the category of straight authoritarian rule. The countries discussed in this book can be located on a scale: from those where the entrenchment of populists in power is rather marginal and the victory of their opponents is quite likely (Poland and Brazil belong to that category) and, on the other extreme, those where either due to the actual popularity of ruling populists (as in India) or a heavy institutional, electoral, economic, and propaganda-based framework renders the defeat of populists highly unlikely (Hungary). But not impossible. Elections are not a sham even if they are unfair. And recent history carries examples of ruling populists voted out of power (e.g., in Ecuador in 2017 or in Sri Lanka in 2015).

The second reason for the centrality of elections is that winning elections is the main source of the political legitimacy of populists in power. It is also an important reassurance about avoiding political responsibility and legal liability in the future: "Leaders who come to

---

[35] For good analyses of the functions of elections in authoritarian states see John Keane, *The New Despotism* (Cambridge: Harvard University Press, 2020), pp. 98–109; and Ivan Krastev and Stephen Holmes, *The Light That Failed* (London: Pegasus Books, 2019), pp. 101–106.

power by elections rather than coups are more likely to avoid ejection from office and less likely to face punishment."[36] Electoral origin is what gives populists a key argumentative asset in their political struggle against the opponents. As Hungarian scholars observe, the various changes, for example, regarding fast-tracked parliamentary legislative proceedings and sidelining of the opposition, were "legitimised by the 'revolution in the polling booth.'"[37] And while in their first term in power, populists add additional legitimating resources to their portfolio – appeals to religion (Modi, Kaczyński) and national identity (Orbán), revolutionary tradition (Chávez), military values (Bolsonaro), or public safety (Duterte) – nevertheless their electoral pedigree is the main basis for their claim to power and institutional (often, constitutional) changes. So, the open flouting of the principle of free and fair elections would create a fundamental dissonance in this rhetoric and confuse their audiences. Not to mention the fact that it would greatly undermine their standing internationally, about which they usually care, at least to some degree.

Part of that legitimating rhetoric is to complain about alleged electoral frauds in previous elections, when populists were not victorious. Bolsonaro, Orbán, and Kaczyński all claimed, falsely, that earlier elections had been rigged. In Poland, a pro-PiS NGO headed by an extreme right-wing journalist, Ewa Stankiewicz, was founded and gained a good deal of prominence and a good many resources on the basis of completely unwarranted claims that a series of elections in the period between 2007 and 2015 were rigged. None of their complaints brought to courts were validated. In Hungary, Orbán's party questioned the integrity of elections in 2002, which it had lost, even if it was the Fidesz-controlled governmental apparatus that managed them.[38] Strangely enough, populists' complaints about alleged electoral fraud apply occasionally also to those elections they had *won*, with the implication that their victory would have been even higher were it not for the fraud. Jair Bolsonaro complained about alleged electoral frauds in the 2018 elections as part of his campaign against electronic voting, which he wants to remove in the next elections scheduled for 2022. This is one of the grounds on which Bolsonaro, but also Duterte in the Philippines,

---

[36] Ruth Ben-Giat, *Strongmen* (New York: W. W. Norton, 2020), p. 49.
[37] Körösenyi, Illés, and Gyulai, *The Orbán Regime*, p. 85.
[38] See Bálint Magyar, *Post-Communist Mafia State: The Case of Hungary* (Budapest: CEU Press, 2016), p. 227.

skillfully promote speculation that future elections will not take place according to a constitutional schedule.

The simplest step that many populist leaders take is to capture, or – if they cannot – delegitimize, electoral institutions. Capturing is the most effective method: If elections go really "wrong," populists can always count on their men and women in the commissions to supply a good result. It is in accordance with a maxim often attributed to Stalin: It does not matter who votes; what matters is who counts the ballots. In Chávez's Venezuela, the 1999 constitution gave the executive branch direct control over the national electoral council.[39] In Poland, the ruling PiS party has completely restructured the electoral machinery, by removing the requirement that electoral commissioners must be judges. The top body, the National Electoral Commission (NEC), which was previously exclusively composed of judges nominated by top Polish courts, now consists of two members nominated by presidents of two courts and seven members elected by the lower chamber of parliament, hence by PiS. The local commissioners heading 100 districts are appointed by the NEC but from among candidates proposed by the minister of the interior. So, at every level, votes are counted by officials who ultimately owe their positions to the ruling party and the administration. The law has also assigned the function of deciding about electoral complaints and controversies to a newly established chamber of the Supreme Court, fully composed of judges appointed by a council elected by the parliamentary majority – hence, again, by PiS. In this way, the party has composed a chamber that decides about its own victory or otherwise. And after the recent presidential elections, won by PiS candidate Andrzej Duda in 2020, this chamber summarily rejected a complaint about an unashamedly pro-Duda campaign run by public TV and radio.

In Hungary, after Fidesz-initiated changes to the electoral law, the entire institutional system of elections is now Fidesz-controlled. To start with, right after the 2010 electoral victory, the members of the previous Election Commission (a mix of representatives of different parties) were dismissed, halfway through their terms of office, on the basis of a new law that requires the commission be reelected after each national election (a bizarre principle, the majority of parliamentarians elect those who will conduct the next elections). A new commission quickly returned the favor: It permitted the government-aligned private media to televise

---

[39] Javier Corrales and Michael Penfold-Becerra, "Venezuela: Crowding Out the Opposition," *Journal of Democracy*, 18/2 (2007), 99–113 at 101.

political ads during campaigns for the 2014 parliamentary elections.[40] Members of electoral commissions at all levels are either delegated by the parliament with a two-thirds majority (enjoyed by Fidesz) or by the municipalities, most of which have a clear pro-government majority. The president of the National Election Commission – a Fidesz politician, of course – is appointed for a nine-year term, which guarantees political control over the election results for a long time to come. All in all, as Kim Lane Scheppele observes, in Hungary "all of the key players who will make the decisions about the election framework were assigned to their jobs by the governing party, in a system where the governing party just rewrote all of the rules."[41]

But when populists in power cannot simply capture the electoral apparatus, they either weaken it or go to war with electoral institutions. The first strategy has been successfully used by Modi in India. After introducing an ingenious "electoral bonds" scheme, without any consultation with the Electoral Commission, the result of which it is to greatly facilitate private contributions to party finances without any transparency, the government completely ignored initial objections voiced by the commission. As we are told by a knowledgeable observer: "The [commission] argued its objections to the Government on multiple grounds: concerns about foreign influence, the further consolidation of a corrupt business–politics nexus, and legal loopholes that could allow for dodgy money to be routed through shell companies. These concerns fell on deaf ears."[42] When an individual electoral commissioner behaves in a way that displeases the ruling party, there is a way of sending them a message. For example, when election commissioner Ashok Lavasa raised objections about violations of the electoral code by BJP in the 2019 elections, coincidentally at the same time his family members faced urgent inquiries by central investigative agencies.[43] In Brazil, where the

---

[40] Freeman, "Sidestepping the Constitution," p. 42.
[41] Kim Lane Scheppele, "Hungary: An Election in Question, Part 2," *New York Times* (February 28, 2014), www.krugman.blogs.nytimes.com/2014/02/28/hungary-an-election-in-question-part-2/, p. 4.
[42] Milan Vaishnav, "Electoral Bonds: The Safeguards of Indian Democracy Are Crumbling," Carnegie Endowment for International Peace (November 25, 2019), www.carnegieendowment.org/2019/11/25/electoral-bonds-safeguards-of-indian-democracy-are-crumbling-pub-80428.
[43] "Times Face-Off: Has the Election Commission's Independence Been Diluted?" *Times of India* (April 24, 2021), www.timesofindia.indiatimes.com/india/times-face-off-has-the-election-commissions-independence-been-diluted/articleshow/82206995.cms.

Electoral Superior Court enjoys high judicial standing and prestige, and is currently headed by a formidable justice (and professor), Luis Roberto Barroso, President Bolsonaro frequently verbally assaulted the court and its head, claiming that Barroso is a Worker's Party activist (read: a partisan leftist) and that he wanted ex-president Lula to win elections. Bolsonaro went further, calling Barroso "an imbecile" and claiming that he wanted "dirty elections" for Brazil.[44] (Under a new election code designed by Bolsonaro government, Congress will be able to override any decision of the Electoral Court on the basis that it has overstepped its boundaries. At the time of writing, the law has not yet been approved by the Congress, but the draft shows the direction of Bolsonaro's thinking.)

But capturing or attacking electoral institutions is just one step in the populists' war on fair elections. They have far greater ambitions: to fundamentally change the whole set of electoral rules so that having a friendly commission is not even necessary. Raw votes will translate into a result favorable to populists. No rigging is then necessary because the deck is stacked in favor of the incumbents. Bolsonaro is planning a big change by pushing for a model known in Brazil as "Distritao" (literally: "large districts"), which would fundamentally change the way in which members of the lower chamber of the Congress are elected. Today's system (in which citizens can vote either on individual candidates or on parties, with the seats then allocated on the basis of proportions of combined votes for candidates and parties) would be replaced by a purely majoritarian model that would only consider individual tallies, thus benefiting "celebrity candidates" (such as Bolsonaro) and purported outsiders (such as...Bolsonaro) as it would diminish the importance of political parties.

However, no populist can match the holistic, monumental manner in which Viktor Orbán changed the election framework in Hungary, resulting in a situation in which, as in the last elections, just under 48 percent of votes translated into nearly 67 percent of seats (133 out of 199) for Fidesz. It was so complete and comprehensive that it warrants a closer look – as it may be the shape of things to come in other, less accomplished populisms. The ingenuous system was composed of a combined effect of (1) changing the size of the parliament; (2) replacing two rounds of elections by a single round; (3) gerrymandering by

---

[44] Emilio Peluso Neder Meyer and João Andrade Neto, "Courts Are Finally Standing Up to Bolsonaro," in *Verfassungsblog* (August 9, 2021), www.verfassungsblog.de/courts-are-finally-standing-up-to-bolsonaro/.

redrawing the borders of electoral districts; and (4) changing the constituency of the electorate. It all resulted in a system in which it is extremely difficult for the opposition to win. A combination of (1) and (2) greatly increased the disproportionality of election results, and the outcome was immediate. In 2010, under the old rules, a party needed 52.7 percent of votes to have an absolute majority in the chamber; in 2014, a mere 43.6 percent was enough to produce a hefty 66.8 percent of seats.

How was it done? The size of the unicameral parliament was slashed nearly in half (from 286 to 199 members), which favors the strongest party in relative terms, while replacing two rounds with a single round produced a situation that additionally fragmented the opposition, because opposition parties must not only fight with Fidesz but also among each other. Gerrymandering (item #3 on my list) was so shameless that it was shown that on the basis of new, post-2010 borders, Fidesz would have won every election since 1998, including in both 2002 and 2006, which it had lost.[45] Redistricting was done unilaterally by the central government, with no reasons given for new borders. The pattern was always the same: "Historically left-leaning districts were partitioned and blended into historically right-leaning districts, creating fewer districts where left-leaning candidates were relatively certain to win."[46] Regarding (4), the change of the constituency amounted to what Magyar Balint calls nicely "a partial virtual replacement of the population."[47] On the one hand, hundreds of thousands of ethnic Hungarians who have lived permanently for generations in neighboring countries courtesy of the Trianon Treaty of 1920 were given an opportunity for dual citizenship, and a right to vote in Hungarian elections. To make it easy for them, they could vote by mail, and the criteria for voter identification were extremely lax. On the other hand, Hungarians who had recently emigrated, temporarily or continuously, usually to Western Europe or the United States, were only allowed to vote in person in a few selected consulates in their new home country, so most of them had virtually no means to exercise their right to vote, unless they went to a significant expense and loss of time. It just happened that the majority of the first category (ethnic Hungarians in Romania, Ukraine, Slovakia, etc.) were strongly pro-Fidesz, while the majority in the second category,

---

[45] Magyar, *Post-Communist Mafia State*, p. 222.
[46] Scheppele, "Hungary: An Election in Question, Part 2," p. 4.
[47] Magyar, *Post-Communist Mafia State*, p. 222, emphasis removed.

mainly younger, well-educated professionals, were strongly anti-Fidesz. In such an ingenious way, Fidesz "replaced a few hundred thousand government-critical voters with a few hundred thousand government supporters."[48] To complete the picture of this "population replacement," it should be added that the voters' lists for the first category were never made public or subject to any scrutiny and control, on the basis that having dual citizenship may be sensitive information in the case of Hungarians in Romania, Slovakia, or Ukraine. So, any numbers provided by the Fidesz-controlled electoral commission have to be taken as a matter of faith. The end result of all this is, as Kim-Lane Scheppele put it with only a little exaggeration: "the outcome of the election is cooked into the rules even before a single ballot is cast."[49]

Not every populist in power can boast such a comfortable and comprehensive design. But what most of them do at a minimum is to try to change the party finance and campaign finance rules in a way that favors them. The already mentioned "electoral bonds" scheme in India basically allowed "for limitless, anonymous corporate donations to political parties."[50] Its proclaimed aim was to assure more transparency (creating a mechanism for private actors to donate to parties via banks rather than in cash) but *without any duty of disclosure*, either on the part of the donor or the party. A non-surprising outcome was that a huge majority of such bonds (around 95 percent, on one estimate) went to the ruling BJP party.[51] In Brazil, under a new proposed electoral code, political parties will be able to reduce their legal liability for campaign finance violations merely by hiring private accounting firms: The punishment will be the amount deemed irregular plus a paltry 5 percent. The present rule that a candidate elected after a campaign-related financial irregularity would have to forfeit their position, would be discarded.[52] As an extra bonus for

---

[48] Ibid., p. 223.
[49] Kim Lane Scheppele, "Hungary: An Election in Question, Part 1," *New York Times* (February 28, 2014), www.krugman.blogs.nytimes.com/2014/02/28/hungary-an-election-in-question-part-1, p. 3.
[50] Gautam Bhatia, "Mouse under the Throne: The Judicial Legacy of Sharad A. Bobde," *The Wire* (April 24, 2021), www.thewire.in/law/mouse-under-the-throne-the-judicial-legacy-of-sharad-a-bobde.
[51] Vaishnav, "Electoral Bonds."
[52] Andrew Fishman, "Bolsonaro Allies in Brazilian Congress Push Sweeping Electoral Changes to Keep Hold on Power," *The Intercept* (August 12, 2021), www.theintercept.com/2021/08/11/bolsonaro-brazil-congress-elections-2022/.

candidates, the requirement for disclosure of their personal assets has been eliminated.

As on so many matters related to redesigning election rules in its favor, Hungary's Fidesz is a winner also when it comes to campaign finance. A rule is that, in addition to public money given equally to every party running a national list (which, in itself, has created a pathological phenomenon of "business parties" that have no chance of electing any candidate but are set up only to pick up funding, which has the effect of "disorient[ing] voters" and "fragmenting the government-critical votes"),[53] the donation rule is simple: Only private money is allowed, not donations from "legal persons." Sounds like a nice contrast to the US Supreme Court's *Citizens United* rule,[54] under which a corporate subsidy is a form of protected speech? Think again. Fidesz is funded by mega-wealthy oligarchs who owe the party well-deserved gratitude for their wealth while opposition parties rely on foundations and trusts. In Scheppele's words: "The campaign finance regulations are, like Anatole France's aphorism, designed to equally prohibit what the rich don't need and the poor can't do without."[55]

The Indignity of Legislation[56]

After the victorious elections, authoritarian populists face new parliaments – which they treat as rubber stamps, regardless of whether they enjoy a very comfortable supermajority with weak and fragmented opposition, as is the case in Hungary, Philippines, or India, or just a marginal and precarious majority, relying on coalition partners which are not all *that* reliable, as is the case in Poland. The strength of their majority does not affect their domineering attitude toward legislative bodies, only the methods of transforming their domination into law. Since assuming office, president of Brazil, Jair Bolsonaro, and his circle continued fiercely attacking the Congress and expressing dissatisfaction with its independence – despite the fact that constitutionally, the president has a strong dominance over the legislative agenda anyway. When

---

[53] Magyar, *Post-Communist Mafia State*, p. 221.
[54] *Citizens United* v. *FEC*, 558 U.S. 310 (2010).
[55] Kim Lane Scheppele, "Hungary: An Election in Question, Part 5," *New York Times* (February 28, 2014), www.krugman.blogs.nytimes.com/2014/02/28/hungary-an-election-in-question-part-5/, p. 6.
[56] With apologies to Jeremy Waldron, *The Dignity of Legislation* (Cambridge: Cambridge University Press, 1999).

THE INDIGNITY OF LEGISLATION 67

Congress overrode the presidential veto of the 2020 budget, close Bolsonaro collaborator and minister of the Institutional Security Cabinet, General Augusto Heleno, called it "blackmail" and suggested that the president should ignore this step by the Congress and act following the "voice of the people." And when the president cannot effectively threaten the legislature, he buys the party leaders with amendments in the budget that help them in the next parliamentary elections.[57]

Populists in power favor fast-tracking bills and super-speedy legislative procedures. In Poland, PiS has worked out a pattern of proposing their main legislative projects as private member's bills (an obvious fiction as they more often than not are prepared by the government), which allows them to avoid various compulsory consultations and pre-enactment audits. As a result, some of the most important pieces of legislation (including a suite of arguably unconstitutional statutes concerning the judiciary in 2017) have been passed very quickly, almost without any discussion. Some acts have been submitted and adopted in the middle of the night. In 2016, the first full year of PiS in power, some 40 percent of legislative acts had been adopted through a fast-track procedure – and these were among the most important ones.[58] Similarly, in India, in order to avoid a parliamentary debate on crucial financial issues, the government passed the Finance Bill and the Appropriation Bill under an extraordinary parliamentary procedure known as the "guillotine," which allows the Speaker of the House to put a bill to a vote without any discussion.[59] The fast track was not justified, in any of these cases, by any particular urgency at the time. The speed of legislative production is often mind-blowing. In Hungary in 2011–2012, at the height of the "legislative tsunami," the parliament legislated on average of one new law every one and a half days.[60] To facilitate such speedy production, the parliamentary standing orders were changed to help the government

---

[57] Thomas Bustamante and Emilio Peluso Neder Meyer, "Legislative Resistance to Illiberalism in a System of Coalitional Presidentialism: Will It Work in Brazil?" *The Theory and Practice of Legislation* (2021). DOI: 10.1080/20508840.2021.1942370, pp. 14–16.
[58] Wojciech Sadurski, *Poland's Constitutional Breakdown* (Oxford: Oxford University Press, 2019), p. 133.
[59] Tarunabh Khaitan, "Killing a Constitution with a Thousand Cuts: Executive Aggrandizement and Party-State Fusion in India," *Law and Ethics of Human Rights*, 14 (2020), 49–95 at 67.
[60] Bulent Kenes, "Viktor Orbán: Past to Present," European Center for Populism Studies, Leader Profile No. 1 (August 2020), p. 9.

introduce its agenda with minimal intervention from the opposition.[61] In the Philippines, some of the main pieces of legislation were also fast-tracked, with both chambers of the parliament fully acquiescing to Duterte's wishes. For instance, quick passage was given to controversial acts such as allocating (as already mentioned) the Commission on Human Rights a paltry 1,000 pesos (US $25) annual budget after it began inquiring into extra-judicial killings as part of Duterte's drug war,[62] or in 2020 passing the Anti-Terrorism Act,[63] widely viewed as a "human rights disaster," after Duterte certified it as "urgent" in a letter to Congress.[64] In India, the record was reached on March 13, 2018, when the parliament passed two bills and 218 amendments on fundamental financial matters (including new legislation on foreign funding of political parties, or salary increases for members of the parliament, the president, and state governors) without debate in thirty minutes.[65]

Parliamentary opposition in states ruled by populists is not treated as a partner for discussion but as an irritant, a necessary evil, which can be disregarded or – even better – demonized and marginalized. This is contrary to the rules of democratic accommodation of the opposition. True, those who lose in elections surrender much of their power but "there is no necessary rule that *all* power be shifted or that a political opposition be utterly disempowered."[66] Yet that is exactly what happens after the victories of populists. In parliamentary discussions in Poland, both in commissions and in plenary sessions, there were many instances where opposition MPs were given one minute for their speeches, with microphones turned off after the time was up. They were also often gagged from asking questions to ministers.[67] It became habitual to call

---

[61] Körösenyi, Illés, and Gyulai, *The Orbán Regime*, pp. 84–85.
[62] See Marc Jayson Cayabyab, "House Gives Commission on Human Rights P1,000 Budget for 2018," *Inquirer.net* (September 12, 2017), www.newsinfo.inquirer.net/930106/house-budget-deliberations-chr-p1000-budget-speaker-alvarez.
[63] Republic Act No. 11479 (signed July 3, 2020), www.officialgazette.gov.ph/2020/07/03/republic-act-no-11479/.
[64] Human Rights Watch, "Philippines: New Anti-Terrorism Act Endangers Rights, Special Council Would Usurp Court Powers" (June 5, 2020), www.hrw.org/news/2020/06/05/philippines-new-anti-terrorism-act-endangers-rights.
[65] Angel Mohan and Tish Sanghera, "In 30 Minutes Lok Sabha Clears Finance Bill, 218 Amendments without Debate," *Business Standard* (June 26, 2019), www.business-standard.com/article/economy-policy/in-30-minutes-lok-sabha-clears-finance-bill-218-amendments-without-debate-118031500115_1.html.
[66] Aziz Z. Huq and Tom Ginsburg, "Democracy without Democrats," *Constitutional Studies*, 6 (2020), 165–187 at 169.
[67] Sadurski, *Poland's Constitutional Breakdown*, pp. 133–134.

the opposition a bunch of traitors, most often in the context of the opposition "taking sides" with the European Union against PiS authorities. In Hungary, even the Fundamental Law was prepared with exactly zero input from the opposition – they were simply not asked for their views. In India, the opposition Congress Party has been sidelined by the decision of the parliamentary majority to break with the tradition of appointing the leader of the main opposition party as a formal "Leader of Opposition" – on the basis of a legally doubtful doctrine that such a privilege (and privilege it is, since the office attracts a salary and secretarial staff) belongs to a party that has at least one-tenth of the House membership, which the Congress Party failed to garner.[68] The Modi government has also failed to fill the constitutionally mandated post of "Deputy Speaker" – recognized as the second-highest-ranking legislative officer of the lower chamber, which normally goes to the opposition.[69] In Brazil, President Bolsonaro regularly accuses the opposition Workers Party of planning a Communist coup. In the Philippines, Duterte published a list of "narcopoliticians," which was seen as an effort to intimidate congressional opposition.[70] When the Hungarian opposition opposed the so-called Enabling Act in the time of the pandemic, president of the parliament, László Kövér (Fidesz), said: "This opposition is not part of the Hungarian nation."[71] Weakened, ridiculed, ignored, and sidelined oppositions produce weak, helpless, parliaments, not treated seriously by the populace because that is not where the power resides. Both in their legislative role and in their role of parliamentary oversight of the government, oppositions fail miserably.

Reporters within Borders

Populists care a great deal about controlling the press. In fact, control over media is for them the key to their success. Jarosław Kaczyński has

---

[68] Khaitan, "Killing a Constitution with a Thousand Cuts," pp. 64–65.
[69] Gaurav Vivek Bhatnagar, "Modi Govt Ignores Repeated Demands to Fill Post of Deputy Speaker in Lok Sabha," *The Wire* (August 10, 2021), www.thewire.in/government/modi-govt-ignores-repeated-demands-to-fill-post-of-deputy-speaker-in-lok-sabha.
[70] Pia Ranada, "5 ways Duterte Has Become a Threat to Philippine Democracy," *Rappler* (February 24, 2021), www.rappler.com/newsbreak/iq/five-ways-duterte-has-become-threat-philippine-democracy.
[71] Giorgos Katsambekis, Yannis Stavrakakis, Paula Biglieri, and Kurt Adam Sengul, "Populism and the Pandemic," *Populismus* (June 2020), www.researchgate.net/publication/342205771_Populism_and_the_Pandemic_A_Collaborative_Report, p. 30.

long held the view that whoever controls broadcast media holds political power. Orbán had blamed his party's defeat in 2002 on the public media, which were not sufficiently favorable to him and his party. Considering that populist politics is based on continuous communication between the leader and the people, the media must be under as close supervision as possible. It may be perhaps even claimed that for populism, compared to other political styles and ideologies, the media are *more* important because the very idea of attractive, entertaining, or attention-grabbing communication is intrinsic to populist strategy (see more on populism's uses of media in Chapter 5). And vice versa, in the era of infotainment, populists are often more attractive to media than other politicians. So even if they will not find friendly journalists or favorable editors in the mainstream media, merely by setting the agenda (for instance, by prioritizing the issue of immigration), they exploit media attention and turn it into an invaluable asset. And when in power, populists need media support and abhor critical media scrutiny of their rule.

The main institutional role in this regard is played by various media regulatory bodies. In populist states, they constitute a convenient device of making sure that media are properly disciplined. The Media Council in Hungary is the most emblematic board of that type. It is composed of five members elected by supermajority in the parliament for a long, nine-year term – hence all five being Fidesz activists or loyalists. The Polish National Media Council (NMC) is similar, except that it is elected by simple majority, and has three PiS members and two opposition members; of course, decisions always go in the direction of PiS preferences. Another difference is that, since PiS has no constitutional majority, the council is a statutory body, invisible to the constitution. A constitutional National Council for Radio and Television, fully staffed by PiS, still exists, but the key decisions about personnel are taken by the smaller and more malleable NMC. Of course, one of these is superfluous, but this does not bother ruling politicians in Poland.

The Hungarian Council has broad powers regarding media content: It can refuse and withdraw licenses, as well as impose heavy fines for "improper content." How the Media Council actually works has been well illustrated by its decision in March 2021 to deny the last big independent broadcaster the right to return to the airwaves. Initially Klubrádió (which had been broadcasting since 1999) was forced off the air in September 2020, after a decade-long campaign by Fidesz to muzzle the news-talk station, known for its criticism of the government from a left-liberal perspective. The Media Council at that time refused to extend the broadcast license under the pretext that the station failed to produce information on its programming. The radio appealed to the courts, which upheld the Media Council's decision. The rationale produced by the council for its final closure of the radio is that there were errors in the programming document. In reality, the errors were trivial: for instance, a particular show was specified as being forty-five minutes long, rather than fifty minutes. Another ground was the precarious financial position of the company. As the European Centre for Press and Media Freedom observed:

> This last justification is especially outrageous given that the financial difficulties faced by Klubrádió are in part the result of a state campaign over the past decade to weaken the economic position of independent media. State-controlled companies and ad agencies controlled by Fidesz loyalists or allied to the ruling party have systematically withdrawn advertising from the station, slowly starving it of resources.[72]

But capturing the regulatory institution able to grant and refuse licenses based on the political preferences of its masters is only one of a vast array of measures that assured Viktor Orbán a near-monopoly on media messages. The suite of such measures consists of (1) tight control of state-owned media and the use of these media for one-sided governmental propaganda, with no critical views allowed; (2) commercial and state advertising that is heavily tilted toward pro-government media titles and rarely goes to independent media (the state being by far the largest advertiser); (3) consolidation of private, pro-government media in centralized structures (a structure called KESMA, an acronym for the Central European Press and Media Foundation, which in 2018 gained control over 476 media outlets in the country after they transferred the ownership rights to KESMA); (4) the purchase of most private media by pro-government business leaders; and (5) the refusal of access to information, comment, or documents by independent journalists. The combined outcome of all these phenomena is that now "most Hungarians receive news only from pro-government outlets."[73]

---

[72] See European Centre for Press and Media Freedom, "Hungary: Fidesz-Captured Media Regulator Blocks Latest Attempt by Klubrádió to Return to Airwaves" (March 15, 2021), www.ecpmf.eu/hungaryon-national-day-new-hope-that-Klubrádió-may-return-to-airwaves/.

[73] Roberta Knoll, "Hungarian Journalists Are to Be Treated as Enemies of the State," ECPMF (November 27, 2020), www.ecpmf.eu/country-factsheet-hungary.

Every populist in power would love to enjoy such a formidable package of media-control measures. At present, they can only approach it. In Poland, the main means of control is by a combination of the National Media Council and an expressed intention to change the ownership structure, under the guise of "Polonization" of media, that is, those that have foreign ownership. At the time of writing, PiS has been partly successful in expropriating media with foreign ownership and subjecting them to PiS control. In early 2021, it managed to make the biggest state-owned oil company purchase a package of over twenty local newspapers from a Swiss-German syndicate, but it has been unsuccessful in grabbing the main national commercial station critical of PiS, the US-owned broadcaster TVN. This remains, however, its constant stated goal, and one may expect regular moves to "Polonize" (i.e., subject to the political control of PiS) the station.

Poland has not yet achieved a state of the full erosion of critical and independent media so characteristic of the Hungarian mediascape. Neither has Brazil, but it is significant that journalists draw the comparisons between Orbán's and Bolsonaro's aspirations, suggesting that the latter follows the former's playbook.[74] However, even though he has made inroads in all of Orbán's areas of achievements, he is not there yet. One way in which the Brazilian administration has favored the pro-government press has been to provide millions of dollars in ads to the friendly media. It reduced access to information by suspending the deadlines that the administration has in response to press queries.[75] And Bolsonaro targeted critical journalists for angry verbal assaults – for instance against investigative reporter Patrícia Campos Mello, a recipient of 2019 International Press Freedom Award, whom he had falsely accused of offering to trade sex for information.[76]

In this atmosphere, Brazilian journalists have come under increased threats of violence, tolerated and often instigated by Bolsonaro and his allies, to the point that Campos Mello said that she had to employ a bodyguard – something she had not done on her assignments on Syria or

---

[74] Patrícia Campos Mello, "Bolsonaro e a receita húngara para acabar com a imprensa crítica," *El País* (August 1, 2020), www.brasil.elpais.com/brasil/2020-07-30/bolsonaro-e-a-receita-hungara-para-acabar-com-a-imprensa-critica.html.
[75] Mayara Paixão, "Attacks on Brazilian Press Increase under Bolsonaro," NACLA, The North American Congress on Latin America (April 1, 2020), www.nacla.org/news/2020/04/01/attacks-brazilian-press-increase-under-bolsonaro.
[76] Ibid.

Afghanistan.[77] Reporters without Borders (RSF) calculated 580 verbal and physical attacks against journalists in 2020 by the "Bolsonaro system" – consisting of the president's family and his closest allies. As the RSF report states, "constant harassment by the president and his immediate circle poisoned the environment for journalists."[78]

The position is similar in India for media critical of Modi and his government. There have been several incidents of angry mobs attacking, with impunity, independent journalists; some journalists were even killed in attacks where the involvement of politicians has been suspected.[79] Just like Jair Bolsonaro, Narendra Modi engages in offensive name-calling, using derogatory terms such as "presstitutes." It is also generally known that "political consultancies" compile and constantly update lists of pro-BJP and anti-BJP journalists, commissioned by the ruling party, to keep track of hundreds of journalists.[80] But sanctions go further than just invective and blacklists. In 2020 alone, sixty-seven journalists were arrested, usually under colonial-era sedition laws.[81]

In Venezuela, under the rule of Hugo Chávez, the media came under increasingly tight control. The regulatory body Conatel, whose members were appointed by the president, shut down and seized equipment at more than thirty radio stations, with reasons ranging from technicalities to broadcasts about illegal squatters in the context of housing shortages. In 2004, a media law was enacted, and then reinforced in 2010, banning content that could be seen as inciting "disobedience to the current legal order." The legislation was largely criticized as too vague, and reporters pointed out that it could apply to subjects ranging from Venezuela's escalating street crime to the issue of sexually transmitted disease. Under

---

[77] Ibid.
[78] RSF Reporters without Borders, "RSF Tallied 580 Attacks against Media in Brazil in 2020" (January 25, 2021), www.rsf.org/en/reports/rsf-tallied-580-attacks-against-media-brazil-2020.
[79] Furquan Ameen Siddiqui, "Threats to Journalists in India: Journalism in the Age of Intolerance and Rising Nationalism," Reuters Institute Fellowship (University of Oxford, 2017), pp. 13–15, www.reutersinstitute.politics.ox.ac.uk/sites/default/files/2018-08/Threats%20to%20Journalists%20in%20India%20Journalism%20in%20the%20Age%20of%20Intolerance%20and%20Rising%20Nationalism.pdf.
[80] Ishita Mishra, "Pro-BJP or Anti-BJP: Inside the Modi-Shah Media Tracking 'War Rooms,'" *The Wire* (August 11, 2018), www.thewire.in/politics/narendra-modi-amit-shah-bjp-india-media.
[81] Geeta Seshu, "Behind Bars: Arrest and Detention of Journalists in India, 2010–2020," Free Speech Collective (n.d.), www.freespeechcollectivedotin.files.wordpress.com/2020/12/behind-bars-arrests-of-journalists-in-india-2010-20.pdf.

President Maduro, the executive crackdown on the free press has been further strengthened.[82]

Building Counter-elites: Populists and NGOs

Authoritarian populists dislike NGOs. This is an understatement. Their attitude was best encapsulated by Viktor Orbán, who once said, while setting up a parliamentary committee in 2014 to monitor civil society: "We're not dealing with civil society members but paid political activists who are trying to help foreign interests here."[83] While all governments, even those with impeccably liberal-democratic credentials, are averse to independent organizations critical of those in power (in 1985, French intelligence services sank the Greenpeace boat *Rainbow Warrior* in the port of Auckland; in 1988, Margaret Thatcher angrily accused Amnesty International of alleged insensitivity to the victims of terrorism in Northern Ireland; and President Reagan said in 1984 that criticism by the American Civil Liberties Union was for him "a badge of honor"), authoritarian populists have special reasons for this dislike. As Jan-Werner Müller notes: "[F]or them opposition from within civil society creates a particular moral and symbolic problem: it potentially undermines their right to exclusive moral representation."[84] Hence it is not only the program of many NGOs that is a problem, but it is their very existence, unless they strongly support the government: Populists deny that these NGOs are a true, authentic voice within society but are usually at pains to demonstrate that they are instigated from outside. That they are "foreign agents," in brief.

Often NGOs that benefit from external aid (otherwise they would simply not survive) have to register as just that, "foreign agents" (or an equivalent terminology), with all the negative symbolism and stigma carried by that description. That is the case in Hungary, which in 2017 adopted a law modeled on the Russian "foreign agents law" – if they receive foreign grants, they have to describe themselves as "organizations receiving support from abroad" and have to disclose the identities of their donors, and in a general climate of government-inflamed anti-foreign paranoia, suffer the multiple negative consequences of such

---

[82] RSF Reporters without Borders, "Venezuela," https://rsf.org/en/venezuela.
[83] Douglas Rutzen "Authoritarianism Goes Global (II): Civil Society under Assault," *Journal of Democracy*, 26/4 (2015), 28–39 at 31.
[84] Müller, "Populism and Constitutionalism," p. 597.

stigma. According to activists, "the political pressure and hostile rhetoric from the government achieve effects similar to 'legal persecution.'"[85] In this way, activists say, the government has divided the sector into "bad" (foreign-funded) and "good" (mainly religious and conservative) organizations.[86] It has also deterred those few domestic donors who would be ready to support human-rights–oriented NGOs. But then virtually no domestic funding is available for organizations that oppose the government. The same applies to funds from the European Union. In 2019, Orbán declared that EU money should not support NGOs, "which are acting against the will of the majority," read: against the government.[87] They also face hostilities from the local administration, for instance, denying them accommodation for offices.[88] Against the background of an all-out campaign against George Soros, NGOs are presented as vehicles of his invidious plans for Islamization of Hungary. Often NGOs' bank accounts, with foreign funds, are blocked, as is the case in India. And these are not rare incidents. The Modi government canceled foreign contribution licenses of some *20,000* NGOs, under vaguely worded provisions that allow the government to take such actions when it is "necessary in the public interest." These are usually human rights organizations, including Amnesty and Greenpeace.[89] Amnesty International had been forced to close its Delhi office after repeated government attempts to disrupt its funding. Other types of harassment include raids on NGO offices, usually to search for proofs of financial offenses: This happened both to Amnesty and Greenpeace offices.[90] As a result of these crackdowns, Greenpeace also announced that it had to close its several offices in India.

---

[85] Anonymous "director of a leading Hungarian NGO" cited in Amnesty International, "Hungary: Living under the Sword of Damocles. The Impact of the LEXNGO on Civil Society in Hungary," London (2021), pp. 9–10.

[86] Ibid., p. 10.

[87] Nataliya Novakova, "Civil Society in Central Europe: Threats and Ways Forward," GMF Policy Paper No. 21 (October 2020), p. 5.

[88] Amnesty International, "Hungary: Living under the Sword of Damocles," p. 12.

[89] Khaitan, "Killing a Constitution with a Thousand Cuts," p. 90.

[90] Swaminathan S. Anklesaria Aiyar, "Despite Modi, India Has Not Yet Become a Hindu Authoritarian State," Policy Analysis No. 903, Washington, DC: The Cato Institute (November 24, 2020), www.jstor.org/stable/resrep28731, p. 19; "Enforcement Directorate Raids Amnesty Office," Reuters (October 26, 2018), www.reuters.com/article/india-amnesty-regulation/enforcement-directorate-raids-amnesty-office; Arvind Ojha, "Raid at Greenpeace Office, ED Claims Evidence of Corruption," *India Today* (October 11, 2018), www.indiatoday.in/india/story/raid-at-greenpeace-office-ed-claims-evidence-of-corruption-1360468-2018-10-11.

NGOs are frequently the subject of populists' verbal rage, which easily translates into real harassment and discrimination. In the Philippines, where the tradition of vibrant civil society ("People's Power") is strong, Duterte targets left-wing, human rights–oriented groups for his special anger through "red-tagging," a label that describes human rights groups or trade union activists as communist. Human rights groups observe this "red-tagging" has not distinguished between "armed rebels and mainstream rights defenders, left-wing groups and other critics of the Duterte administration."[91] It has had some tragic consequences: Duterte himself had ordered the military to shoot and kill "armed communist rebels" – later nine NGO activists were killed.[92] Occasionally, just adopting a threateningly worded law is a message with a clear deterrent effect. In 2019, Brazil's Bolsonaro issued a sudden decree for the government to "supervise, coordinate, monitor and accompany the activities and actions of international organizations and non-governmental organizations in the national territory" – without providing any reasons.[93]

Sometimes populists in power simply prohibit NGOs from working on certain topics or from undertaking certain actions. Hungary's law of 2018 criminalizes the provisions of legal aid to asylum seekers and migrants and restricts the work NGOs can do on migration.[94] In Poland in September 2021, during a crisis on the Poland-Belarus border where a few dozen Afghan refugees found themselves on a "no-man's land" between the two countries, the Polish government declared a local state of emergency that made it unlawful for NGOs to approach the asylum seekers and provide them with humanitarian and legal aid.

But while human-rights organizations are being defunded and discriminated against, pro-government organizations are being cherished, fed, and cultivated. Poland provides a good example of such a two-tiered

---

[91] "'Appalled': UN Urges Probe into Killing of Philippine Activists," March 10, 2021, Al Jazeera, www.aljazeera.com/news/2021/3/10/un-urges-probe-into-killings-of-philippine-activists; Preeti Jha, "How Filipino Activists Ended Up on a 'Wanted' Poster," BBC News (October 6, 2020), www.bbc.com/news/world-asia-54144623.
[92] Catherine S. Valente, "Duterte Orders Military to 'Shoot and Kill' Armed Communist Rebels," *The Manila Times* (March 6, 2021), www.manilatimes.net/2021/03/06/news/duterteorders-military-to-shoot-and-kill-armed-communist-rebels/847906.
[93] Gabriel Stargardter, "Bolsonaro Presidential Decree Grants Sweeping Powers over NGOs in Brazil," *Reuters* (January 3, 2019), www.reuters.com/article/us-brazil-politics-ngos-idUSKCN1OW1P8.
[94] Nóra Köves, "Hungary to Imprison NGO Workers Helping Asylum Seekers and Other Migrants," Heinrich Böll Stiftung (June 26, 2018), www.boell.de/en/2018/06/26/hungary-imprison-ngo-workers-helping-asylum-seekers-and-other-migrants.

policy. On the one hand, civil rights and pro-democratic organizations (for instance providing assistance to battered women or to refugees) have been defunded by the government after it came to power (even a group of volunteers running an anti-suicide advisory lost its governmental support). On the other hand, right wing, religious, pro-government groups have found themselves in a situation of growing luxury, with enormous amounts of public money thrown at them by the government. A special governmental structure has been set up, with the Orwellian name of the National Institute of Freedom–Centre for the Development of Civil Society. It is chaired by the deputy prime minister, and its main function is to syphon a large amount of money to pro-government, right-wing NGOs (some set up shortly before the foundation of the institute, specifically to benefit from public money). For instance, an extreme nationalist organization, viewed by many as close to neo-Nazi, called National Guard/March for Independence, received in September 2021 a subsidy of PLN 3 million (EUR 650,000) – a large sum by standards of Polish NGO budgets.[95] Even larger grants have been given to radical Catholic organizations associated with an emporium of the priest-entrepreneur Father Tadeusz Rydzyk: Various state subventions for his multiple initiatives totaled in 2019 over PLN 214 million (EUR 46 million). As Stanley Bill correctly observes, the dual-track policy by the PiS government – negative pressure against the largest, established organizations, and promotion of pro-government, conservative groups – is aimed at "elite replacement" in accordance "with a broader rhetoric of 'counter-elite' populism."[96] (Disclosure: I sit on the boards of two large NGOs with liberal-democratic orientation: The Institute of Public Affairs and the Helsinki Foundation for Human Rights, Polish Branch; none received any grants from the National Institute of Freedom).

Trajectories

In contrast to good old authoritarians, populist-authoritarian assaults on institutions are often opaque and invisible – almost clandestine – for three main reasons.

---

[95] "3 mln zł dotacji dla Straży Narodowej i Marszu Niepodległości," *Business Insider Poland* (September 1, 2021), www.businessinsider.com.pl/finanse/3-mln-zl-dotacji-dla-strazy-narodowej-i-marszu-niepodleglosci-pieniadze-z-funduszu/gbqygt4.

[96] Stanley Bill, "Counter-elite Populism and Civil Society in Poland: PiS Strategies of Elite Replacement," *East European Politics and Societies*, 20 (2020), 1–23 at 15.

The first reason is that in the cases of populist rule explored in this book, institutional changes have been often incremental, even if they occur quickly. For instance, in Poland, it took over a year for the authoritarian government to fully paralyze the constitutional court and turn it into an obedient follower of political will. Changes do not happen all at the same time, although they do overlap. There is a sequence that differs for each of the different institutions dismantled by populist authoritarians. As a result, we know only that a certain line has been crossed with the benefit (a risky word in this context) of hindsight. There is no clear, identifiable turning point, a caesura between democracy and authoritarianism. As Aziz Huq and Tom Ginsburg say, using an unappetizing metaphor, it is like boiling a frog by slowly turning up the heat under the pot: We do not know exactly when it happened, but in the end, the frog is dead.[97] And they add, "[t]he precise point...at which the volume of democratic and constitutional backsliding amounts to constitutional retrogression will be unclear – both ex ante and contemporaneously."[98] The absence of this all-important turning point makes change less visible than in the case of a coup d'etat. Thus, it is difficult to mobilize people to protest against something that, by itself, does not seem to be so devastating to the democratic system. Our language – the language of liberal democrats outraged by these piecemeal changes – may seem often to be disproportionate and inflated in its critique.

Second, the relative obscurity of democratic backsliding is magnified by the fact that the truly invidious effect is produced not by particular laws or actions, considered in isolation, but rather by how they *interact* with each other. We have noted, earlier in this chapter, the different faces of the hollowing out of institutions: capture, duplication, erosion, expansion, migration, and evasion, none of which takes place in isolation from the others. It is the relationship between the different kinds of changes that truly erodes democracy, and it is the cumulative effect of various, seemingly disparate, changes that matters. For instance, in Poland, the truly invidious effect of the assault upon the judiciary could have been discerned only if one considered the cumulative effect of changes to the structures of the Supreme Court, of the ordinary courts, of the National Council of the Judiciary, and of the public prosecution offices. No new law, taken in isolation from the institutional context, can reveal the

---

[97] Aziz Huq and Tom Ginsburg, "How to Lose a Constitutional Democracy," *UCLA Law Review*, 65 (2018), 78–169 at 119.
[98] Ibid., p. 118, footnote omitted.

enormity of change that has occurred. Thus, Sujit Choudry writes about "La Suite Polonaise" to emphasize that various measures taken by PiS in Poland "are a series of distinct initiatives that nonetheless are components of a coherent strategy with thematic unity."[99] Taken separately, each of the legislative changes may seem innocuous enough, and our protests may sound exaggerated or even paranoiac.

This is exploited by pro-authoritarian propaganda: to any of the changes, an equivalent may be found in unimpeachably democratic systems. But in those democratic systems, those features exist in a context that reduces their possibly negative effect. In contrast, under populist authoritarianism, context bolsters the anti-democratic effects of these changes. It is rather like a virus that will not produce a major disease in an overall healthy body (indeed, may have some positive immunological consequences), but to a sick organism it may be fatal. Or, to use less charged language, Mark Tushnet, when discussing Singapore's authoritarian constitutionalism, constructed the figure of "a fallacy of decomposition" where "the components *lack* a property but the aggregate might have it." Hence, this analysis prompts his rejection of (what he calls) "a 'slice and dice' or disaggregated approach," which, Tushnet prudently says, "is almost certainly inappropriate."[100]

The third factor in the relative invisibility of democratic erosion is that, as we have seen above in this chapter, elected authoritarians often proceed without dismantling formal institutions and procedures: they leave them in place, but completely change their functions and meanings. As Anna Lührmann and Staffan I. Lindberg observe, "During contemporary autocratization processes, democratic institutions often are curtailed but left in place."[101] While they are still there – and to the unreflective public, it is still "business as usual" – they have stopped playing the role for which they had been set up in the first place.

So, institutions remain but the unwritten norms that give a proper meaning and value to those meanings undergo erosion. And that erosion has different dimensions, and they rarely happen all at once. Two American

---

[99] Sujit Choudry, "Will Democracy Die in Darkness? Calling Autocracy by Its Name," in Mark A. Graber, Sanford Levinson, and Mark Tushnet (eds.), *Constitutional Democracy in Crisis?* (Oxford: Oxford University Press, 2018), pp. 571–584 at 574.
[100] Mark Tushnet, "Authoritarian Constitutionalism," *Cornell Law Review*, 100 (2015), pp. 391–462, at 409–410, 410 n. 101.
[101] Anna Lührmann and Staffan I. Lindberg, "A New Way of Measuring Shifts toward Autocracy," in *Post–Cold War Democratic Declines: The Third Wave of Autocratization*, Carnegie Europe (June 27, 2019), www.carnegieeurope.eu/2019/06/27/post-cold-war-democratic-declines-third-wave-of-autocratization-pub-79378, p. 2.

constitutional scholars, Josh Chafetz and David Pozen, distinguish three different axes of "norm instability": Unwritten constitutional norms may be "decomposed" from the point of view of (1) what *conduct* does a given norm prescribe or proscribe, (2) to *whom* the norm applies, and (3) *when* (under what circumstances) is the norm liable to be overridden.[102] To use this helpful framework for our analyses, some individual examples of each of these phenomena may be identified: (1) norms against executive interference with the judicial process have been deemed not to apply to a presidential pardon of non-finally convicted persons in Poland; (2) norms against public calls by public figures for killing people are deemed not to apply to the president of the Philippines; (3) norms against legislative unilateralism reflected in sidelining the opposition in law-making were deemed not to apply to constitution-making in Hungary. The point to retain from the Chafetz/Pozen analysis is that the axes of the type of conduct, entities bound, and circumstances when a norm applies are disconnected in populist authoritarianism and happen according to different dynamics.

Trajectory matters. The concept of "backsliding" is helpful because its dynamism and path dependence is essential. In Poland, Hungary, the Philippines, Brazil, India, or Venezuela, in contrast say to Russia or Belarus or Turkey, we deal with instances of significant deterioration in democratic qualities *already attained*. This fact is significant to understand the specificities of the situation, because the trajectory of backsliding has to be distinguished from the absence of democratic progress in countries that have not achieved a satisfactory level of democracy in the first place, or where the current status quo has emerged as a result of the relative democratization or liberalization of an oppressive regime. Path dependence matters a great deal, and we need a language to distinguish cases such as Poland and Hungary (with recent democratic achievement fresh in its collective memory and in institutional legacies) from states that are "stuck somewhere on the assumed democratization sequence, usually at the start of the consolidation phase."[103] The states that have institutionally "backslid" from a superior position are held to higher standards by their citizens and by the outside world, because these higher standards had once been achieved or approximated. There are institutional legacies, such as constitutional interpretations in the case law or

---

[102] Josh Chafetz and David E. Pozen, "How Constitutional Norms Break Down," *UCLA Law Review*, 65 (2018), 1430–1459 at 1438–1445.

[103] Thomas Carothers, "The End of the Transition Paradigm," *Journal of Democracy*, 13/1 (2002), 5–21 at 10.

practices of good conduct by authorities, which exert normative pressure upon the current authorities. The coexistence and interactions of authoritarian leaders with the democratic institutions that evoke fully democratic standards latent in the collective memory of the society yields distinctive patterns of political behavior and legal actions not found in authoritarian states without such a past.

The use of the notion of "backsliding" emphasizes a temporal dimension and highlights a retrogression that is not visible in a time-slice account. Renata Uitz observed acutely (with regard to Orbàn's Hungary) that "[r]eflecting on the changes introduced by the new constitutional rules (rather than simply taking a snapshot of these rules) and accounting for the practical consequences of these changes, have revealed a pattern of elimination of constitutional constraints on the exercise of political powers and the resulting instances of self-perpetuation through constitution-making."[104] This reference to a "snapshot" is important because a system, if not viewed in a diachronic way, may carry resemblances to some similar systems in perfectly democratic countries. What is missing in a snapshot account is that the removal (or hollowing out) of certain institutions in comparison to the previous status quo erodes the system of safeguards, while in a different system that may carry superficial resemblances to a country that slid back, the role of such safeguards is played by different mechanisms or by legal and political culture. This is, for instance, the case of constitutional review that, when emasculated as in Poland or Hungary, leaves a gap because the system had used such review to provide crucial protections that elsewhere (e.g., in legal systems lacking a constitutional court) has been provided by other institutions.

The word "backsliding" accurately describes the process of reversal, and the fact that there is no rapid, immediate rupture, as in a coup. It also emphasizes a *process* as opposed to a state of affairs. As Ellen Lust and David Waldner describe it: "Backsliding occurs through a series of discrete changes in the rules and informal procedures that shape elections, rights and accountability. These take place over time, separated by months or even years."[105] But at the same time, one should be warned

---

[104] Renáta Uitz, "Can You Tell When an Illiberal Democracy Is in the Making? An Appeal to Comparative Constitutional Scholarship from Hungary," *International Journal of Constitutional Law*, 13 (2015), 279–300 at 296.
[105] Ellen Lust and David Waldner, *Unwelcome Change: Understanding, Evaluating and Extending Theories of Democratic Backsliding*, USAID 2015, www.pdf.usaid.gov/pdf_docs/PBAAD635.pdf, p. 7.

that the use of the word "backsliding" in this context should not connote (as the word *may* suggest to some) something impersonal, spontaneous, purposeless, almost haphazard. There is energy, restlessness, zeal, and purposefulness in countries described in this book, after Orbán, Kaczyński, Duterte, Bolsonaro, Chávez, or Modi came to power. There is restless agency at work. No lethargy or lazy apathy, as in many countries where nothing happens for decades. And come to think of it, this is also a cause for special concern.

3

Constitutions

Breaches, Abuses, and Literal Democracy

Populists in power dream of changing their country's constitution and writing into it as many of their pet projects as possible. For populists, this is one of the prizes for winning elections. The alternative of simply *breaching* the constitution inherited from their predecessors is seen as second-best, and much less satisfying, even if it is often useful. This is because populists derive their legitimacy from electoral victory, a victory won on the basis of current constitutional rules in place. For ruling populists to deny the legitimacy of the preexisting constitution by breaching it openly and frequently would be to saw off the very branch they are sitting on. And it doesn't look good internationally. When you breach the (unavoidably vague) norms of democracy, you can always retort: *which* democracy? But you will not get away as easily if you violate *your own* constitution, rather than some externally imposed standards.

It is no wonder that not only do many populists set about replacing or amending their country's old constitution, but also that they do so in haste, as soon as they obtain the requisite majority. Typically, these populists are not bothered about gaining broad support for their constitutional proposals, including from the political opposition. Actions by President Hugo Chávez in Venezuela (as well as in the Andean region, similar actions by Rafael Correa in Ecuador and Evo Morales in Bolivia) are symptomatic of such quick and unilateral constitutional replacements. Once elected to office in 1998, against the backdrop of a popular rejection of his predecessors as corrupt and elitist, Chávez was able to exploit his victory by quickly delivering a new constitution, in 1999. As Rosalind Dixon and David Landau explain, "Chávez rejected the 'total reform' [of the Constitution based on existing constitutional procedures] option because it would have required negotiating with an opposition-led legislature that he despised."[1] Rather than relying on the existing

---

[1] Rosalind Dixon and David Landau, *Abusive Constitutional Borrowing* (Oxford: Oxford University Press, 2021), p. 125.

institutions and procedures, he called a newly fashioned Constituent Assembly dominated by his followers, which managed to replace an old constitution in the span of several months. This led to the wiping out of many existing state institutions.

The idea of an extraordinary constitutional assembly had a good track record in Latin America prior to Chávez's innovative use of it. In several countries in the region (Peru, Nicaragua, Brazil), similar assemblies were called shortly after the overthrow of authoritarian regimes, as an important step toward democracy. In contrast, Chávez abolished a constitution that *was* democratic and enshrined separation of powers, federalism, and social rights in a country that, since 1958, had been a rare case of democracy and stability in the region. It was also based on consensus-oriented processes. As the Statement of Motivations accompanying the old 1961 constitution declared:

> In every moment [the Constitutional Commission] maintained the purpose of drafting a fundamental text that did not represent partial point of views, but those basic guidelines of the national political life in which there is and may be convergence of thoughts and opinions of the vast majority, or maybe we could say of the whole Venezuelan people.[2]

No matter how accurate this self-congratulatory description was, the approach by Chávez was the reverse: The constitution-writing he launched was fast and unilateral. His victory was decisive (56 percent of the vote), but he controlled only about one-third of the parliament, and most of state governorships were in the hands of the opposition. So rather than negotiating with the opposition about constitutional replacement (an action probably doomed to failure) and using the path prescribed by the incumbent constitution, he held a referendum on whether to convene a constitutional assembly. The Supreme Court obediently acceded to the terms of referendum, under political pressure. Chávez won the referendum by a wide margin and achieved a spectacular majority of seats in the Assembly (93 percent) – partly due to many oppositional forces boycotting the vote. A result was that the constitution was drafted quickly and with virtually no input from the opposition. We shall return to its contents in a moment.

---

[2] Quoted in Miriam Kornblath, "The Politics of Constitution-Making: Constitutions and Democracy in Venezuela," *Journal of Latin American Studies*, 23 (1991), 61–89 at 81.

Frantic

Hungary is another example of populist constitution-making in haste – and not quite according to the rules. To be sure, Viktor Orbán had gained a two-thirds constitutional majority of the unicameral parliament as a result of April 2010 elections. But the earlier constitution of 1989 (which was, in fact, the very heavily amended old Communist constitution), required a special majority for the *drafting* of the constitution (as opposed to the actual adoption.) In order to compel all major parties to reach a consensus immediately after the fall of Communism, constitution-makers required the future constitution-making parliament to adopt "regulatory principles" in the form of a resolution by a *four-fifths majority* of the parliament. The idea was that, while four-fifths is a clearly unrealistic threshold for the constitution itself, a near-unanimity condition would force politicians to strive toward an earlier consensus not about specific provisions, but at least about the general principles of a new constitution. (The technique of proceeding in two steps was very successfully adopted in the course of making of a post-apartheid constitution of South Africa, eventually adopted in 1996.)

But when Orbán came to power again, this time 53 percent of votes translated into a hefty 68 percent of seats. The last thing he wanted was seeking consensus and compromise with the opposition: After all, his popularity flourished on polarization and divisive rhetoric. So first he removed the four-fifths requirement for a "pre-constitution" by a resolution of the parliament adopted by, you guessed it, a two-thirds majority. (Such a change of the constitutional rules of constitutional change may be seen to be inconsistent with even the "thinnest" constitutionalism, under which "the constitution can be amended only by adhering to the amendment rules as they happen to be.")[3] Eventually the constitution was not prepared by a broadly based body, but by a three-person committee appointed by the government, led by a member of the European Parliament (from the ruling party, of course). The constitution was drafted in secret, inside a close circle of Orbán's friends, and was fast-tracked as a private member's bill, thus eliminating the requirement to consult. As a team of Hungarian legal scholars assessed: "[T]he preparation of the new Fundamental Law has been carried out exclusively by the governing party coalition...and was not preceded by the necessary

---

[3] Mark Tushnet and Bojan Bugarič, *Power to the People: Constitutionalism after Populism* (Oxford: Oxford University Press, 2021), p. 21, footnote removed.

political, professional, scientific and social debates."[4] The partisan, unilateral nature of the process (the constitution had been adopted only by the votes of the ruling party coalition) was best symbolized in the rejection by the rulers of a widespread call for a national referendum. Only a majority decision by the parliament would have made the calling of such a referendum possible.

It was constitution-making by stealth: Orbán had not foreshadowed constitutional change in his election campaign, so voters were not aware that their vote for Orbán would be a vote for fundamental constitutional transformation. Nothing in the election campaign promised radical regime change, which then occurred with unusual speed. Consider the timeline. Viktor Orbán won his constitutional majority in April 2010 (in two rounds, on April 11 and 25). On March 7, 2011, the parliament adopted a resolution on the rules and procedures for adopting a new constitution. And on April 18, 2011, Hungarians had a brand-new Fundamental Law.

The speed of adoption affected its quality as measured even by the standards of the ruling party. In the year and a half after its adoption, the Fundamental Law had already been amended five times. János Kis, a legendary ex-dissident, could not have put it better: "It is (and it is meant by its authors to be) a constitution of one half of the nation imposed on the other half against their will."[5]

On January 2, 2012, in the beautiful Budapest opera house, the government held a special gala to celebrate the entry into force of the constitution it had adopted, sidelining the opposition parties and large segments of public opinion. While members of the new Hungarian elite engaged in self-congratulatory talk and enjoyed a glass or two of Tokaji Aszú (or was it Egri Bikavér?), tens of thousands of protesters gathered in front of the venerable building, to show their anger at this unashamedly partisan exercise. The guests at the gala had to leave by the back door.[6]

---

[4] Andrew Arato, Gabor Halmai, and Janos Kis, "Opinion on the Fundamental Law of Hungary (Amicus Brief)," in Gábor Attila Tóth (ed.), *Constitution for a Disunited Nation: On Hungary's 2011 Fundamental Law* (Budapest: CEU Press, 2012), pp. 455–489 at 459.

[5] János Kis, "Introduction: From the 1989 Constitution to the 2011 Fundamental Law," in Gábor Attila Tóth, (ed.), *Constitution for a Disunited Nation: On Hungary's 2011 Fundamental Law* (CEU Press: Budapest-New York, 2012), pp. 1–21 at 20–21.

[6] This is described by Kis, ibid., p. 1.

Constituting a New Beginning

Hastily prepared populist constitutions carry certain common characteristics: the symbolism of a fresh start, centralization of power, erosion of individual rights, appeals to traditional moral and religious standards of the majority, and often the tendency to set various policy preferences in stone, thus making them capable of surviving the demise of populist rule. In presidential systems, the trend is toward increased presidential powers, while in parliamentary or mixed systems, it is toward increased parliamentary or executive power. In both cases, limits upon the political branches are eroded. As the Venice Commission remarked, acerbically, after one of its peregrinations to Hungary to discuss a constitutional amendment with Orbán's regime, "[d]uring the visit in Budapest and in the documentation provided, the Hungarian Government referred to parliamentary sovereignty as if it were the ultimate instance of legitimacy and no further checks applied."[7] This may be a good summary of populist constitutionalism in general, only with "parliamentary sovereignty" replaced by "constituent power" or "presidential supremacy," as the case may be.

In the new Hungarian Fundamental Law, limits on state power have been greatly reduced, and the powers of central government, greatly enhanced. The government has competencies to do everything that is not specifically assigned to another body – which is *a lot*. The judiciary has been subjected to the executive through the huge powers of the president of the newly established National Judicial Office – a person elected by a two-thirds majority of the parliament, hence by the Fidesz ruling coalition. (I write more about the subjection of the Hungarian judiciary in Chapter 4.) The structure of the ombudsman's office has been weakened. In the place of the former three ombudspersons plus a general commissioner for human rights, the constitution established one "general" commissioner, with many functions of former "specific" commissioners (such as data protection) transferred to the government, thus eroding their protected status.

There are other aspects of hyper-centralization. A newly established three-person Budget Council now has the right to veto the annual budget adopted by the parliament at its discretion: Its members are appointed by

---

[7] European Commission for Democracy through Law, Opinion on the Fourth Amendment to the Fundamental Law of Hungary, adopted June 14–15, 2013, VC CDL-AD(2013) 012, para. 137.

the parliamentary majority (hence, by Fidesz loyalists) for six years (two members) and twelve years (one member). This is unusual: Normally it is parliaments that have the power to express their political preferences through budgets, but here a non-parliamentary Budget Council has been given a power of veto over the parliament's crucial decisions. (In addition, the quorum for the council's decision is set at two: two people can veto the adoption of the country's budget, which may lead to the dissolution of the parliament and early elections.) The powers of the president (elected by the parliament, hence a completely compliant politician) have grown in importance from a purely ritualistic office. The president now has the right to dissolve the parliament if the budget is not approved by March 31. The dissolution may even take place shortly after the elections. The powers of municipal governments have been drastically reduced, their property rights in particular. This "de facto ends municipal autonomy."[8] In addition, the parliament has been given competence to dissolve local elected authorities if it finds them in violation of the constitution. Giving the majority party constitutional control over elected bodies, a power that normally should rest with a constitutional court, is a flagrant symptom of hyper-centralization.

The primary method of straitjacketing a future majority is by introducing a category of "cardinal laws" that may be adopted or changed only by a two-thirds majority. In this way, Orbán has exploited his party's temporary supermajority to bind future (simple) majorities. Currently there are thirty-three such cardinal laws, and they cover issues ranging from local self-government and organization of courts to pensions and taxes. As Imre Vörös, a Hungarian law professor and ex-judge of the Constitutional Court, lucidly suggests: "The intention...is clear: to reduce the room for manoeuvre of future governments, and to secure at any given moment a tool for paralysing the government for the respective opposition."[9] The same is the case with entrenching the power of specific officials appointed at the time of the Fundamental Law. Positions in almost all independent institutions of checks and balances that were occupied by Orbán loyalists at the time of the entry into force of the Fundamental Law have been extended far beyond the current election cycle of four years. With terms of office of six, nine, or twelve

---

[8] Bálint Magyar, *Post-Communist Mafia State: The Case of Hungary* (Budapest: CEU Press, 2016), p. 115.
[9] Imre Vörös, "Hungary's Constitutional Evolution during the Last 25 Years," *Südeuropa*, 63 (2015), 173–200 at 184, footnote omitted.

years, the constitution assures that they will hold office well into future election cycles.

The constitution is permeated with nationalistic and religious tones, merged together in its invocation: "God Bless the Hungarians." Symbolic too was the change in the very name of the state: Hungary, rather than "the Republic of Hungary," as had been the case up to then. These symbols are meant to mark a fresh start, a new beginning, and to distance the new constitution from the old, referred to disparagingly as "the communist constitution," which was "the basis of a tyrannical rule" and therefore is "proclaimed to be invalid." It was as if the massive 1989 and post-1989 amendments had not existed, and clearly disregards the contradiction between the declared invalidity of the prior constitution and the fact that the new one was being adopted on the basis of the old constitutional framework. I have already mentioned in this book the quasi-religious and exclusionary language of the constitution (in Chapter 1), and in particular its preamble, which stresses the Christian tradition and contains grotesquely anachronistic references to the medieval doctrine of the Holy Crown. There is a distinct nationalistic air to the references to the unity of the Hungarian nation ("We, members of the Hungarian nation" – starts the preamble pompously called "National Avowal," not the "people" or "citizens,") understood in an ethnic manner, and to Hungary's "responsibility for the fate of Hungarians living beyond its borders." At the same time, "the [other] nationalities living with us" are symbolically othered, the formula chosen intimating, as the widely respected Venice Commission observed, that members of those nationalities "are not part of the people behind the enactment of the Constitution."[10] After all, if they live *with us*, then they are not *us*.

The constitution is also strong on citizens' *duties*, with a puzzling statement that every person has an obligation "to contribute to the performance of state and community tasks to the best of his or her abilities and potential." What on Earth can it mean? Likewise, what can the statement that "every person shall be responsible for him or herself" mean? Probably nothing, but the insertion of such meaningless provisions in a constitution is dangerous because they may always be (ab)used by an enthusiastic legislator or a constitutional judge to restrict citizens' rights by extending their duties. In contrast, the constitution is singularly meek on individual rights, basically relegating any duty to specify them to

---

[10] European Commission for Democracy through Law, Opinion on the New Constitution of Hungary, adopted June 17–18, 2011, VC CDL-AD (2011) 016, para. 40.

"special Acts." The Venice Commission perceptively sees a possibility that "the constitutional provisions on freedom and responsibility might be *eroded* by special Acts."[11]

There are also myriad other illiberal provisions. To entrench a traditional definition of family and marriage against possible future legislation of same-sex marriages, the constitution explicitly defines marriage as "the union of a man and a woman." The constitution admits life imprisonment without parole, in contravention of international standards. Freedom of the press is not formulated as an individual right but only as an obligation of the state – thus reducing the possibility of recourse to courts against breaches of that freedom. Again, how prescient the Venice Commission was in 2013 to suggest that under the Fundamental Law "this freedom appears to be dependent on the will of the state and its willingness to deal with its obligation in the spirit of freedom."[12] Indeed, Orbán controls nearly all media in Hungary. Independent media have been pushed far into the margin, and are now financially non-viable.[13] Further, the recognition of religious communities has now been granted to the parliament (by an amendment of March 11, 2013), thus making this a political decision, expressing the views of the political majority about which religion deserves the distinction of recognition and the privileges related to it. Soon after, the parliament adopted a "Bill of Recognition," containing thirty-two "recognized" churches. Of course, any change in the composition of parliament may result in the recognition of new churches or the de-recognition of previously recognized churches. As Vörös observed, "the recognition of churches depends upon the outcome of parliamentary elections, a result that is incompatible with the state's obligation to remain neutral in matters of belief."[14]

The Venezuelan approach to the substance of a new constitution went further than the Hungarian approach because the Constituent Assembly, as we have seen, did not limit itself to writing a new constitution (which it did in 1999) but also effectively wiped out the main existing institutions of checking and controlling executive power. (It is rather as if a subcommittee that was set up to rewrite the rules of your club established a new statute, and added: and by the way, all existing committees of the club are now suspended or extinguished.) The new constitutionalism in

---

[11] Ibid., para. 59, emphasis added.
[12] Ibid., para. 74.
[13] Fábián Tamás, "Orbán's Influence on the Media Is without Rival in Hungary," *Euractiv* (March 30, 2021).
[14] Vörös, "Hungary's Constitutional Evolution," p. 192.

Venezuela was therefore more radical than the Hungarian act, which in fact remained at least notionally within the framework of the old constitutional rules of changing the constitution. In Venezuela, the change proceeded outside the existing institutional framework.

There, too, was a special symbolism aimed at capturing the authentic emotions of the people, though not by referring to religion as in Hungary, but (in the first sentence of the preamble) by referring to Simon Bolivar, Venezuela's national hero, and even naming the state the "Bolivarian Republic of Venezuela." This was to symbolize a fresh start, after decades of the despised elite rule, a sign of the constitution restoring power to the People.

The constitution replaced the earlier presidential term limit (four-year term, non-renewable) by two terms of six years, thus effectively giving Chávez twelve years in power. It greatly increased the competences of the president. According to one calculation, presidential power was increased by 121 percent.[15] He then used his powers to push through constitutional amendments that even further enhanced his powers, for instance by removing term limits altogether in 2009. Venezuela's bicameral Congress was reduced to a unicameral body, thus reducing its role as a veto point. But most importantly, Chávez used the Constituent Assembly to suspend the Congress, to create a council charged with purging the judiciary, and to remove many state-level officials. With the "original constituent power," he gave himself a blank check to wipe out preexisting institutions limiting the executive. In one particularly theatrical event, he even resigned from his position to the new assembly (only to be immediately reappointed), thus highlighting the paramount, unitary power of the assembly reflecting the "true" will of the people directly.

Less spectacularly but more significantly, the new Constituent Assembly helped Chávez to sideline and politically eliminate many of his political opponents, including those in state assemblies that were closed, by eroding the Congress, closing down the Supreme Court, and replacing many local leaders and trade union heads. "The result was a radically changed political landscape."[16] All countervailing powers were basically extinguished. Similar strategies of bringing about a new constitution to remove limits on the presidential powers were later applied in the region by presidents Rafael Correa in Ecuador (a new constitution of 2008) and Evo Morales in Bolivia (2009).

---

[15] See David Landau, "Abusive Constitutionalism," *University of California, Davis Law Review*, 47 (2013), 189–260 at 206 n. 59

[16] Dixon and Landau, *Abusive Constitutional Borrowing*, p. 126.

Constitutionalism by Stealth

But not all populist rulers have the luxury of bringing about a brand new, populist constitution. Rodrigo Duterte has made a constitutional change a core plank since he assumed the presidency; it became known as "cha-cha" (for "charter change" – the Filipinos have a taste for fun abbreviations). Duterte, himself hailing from the southern island of Mindanao, and resentful of "Manila imperialism," has pushed for a shift from a central government to federalism, for relaxing constitutional provisions restricting foreign ownership in control in economy (which would pave the way for increased Chinese investment), and, not surprisingly, for changes to the term limits (presidents have a six-year non-renewable term of office). Despite his repeated attempts, he failed to amend the 1987 post-Marcos constitution. Perhaps the main reason was a strong skepticism on the part of the electorate about any constitutional changes: This distrust has its roots in the Marcos era, when the dictator used constitutional change to duck term limits.

So rather than changing the constitutional text, Duterte has relied on a friendly Supreme Court, which engaged in creative constitutional interpretation to the benefit of the president, for instance by removing its chief justice, Maria Lourdes Sereno, in 2018, thus sidestepping the constitutional procedure of impeachment.[17] (More about it in Chapter 4.) Further, the president engaged in various acts of executive aggrandizement by introducing policies and laws that have been scandalous from a constitutional point of view, such as imposing an indefinite in time and open-ended in substance martial law across Mindanao (the southernmost island in the Philippines, with a predominantly Muslim population) in 2017, and unilaterally withdrawing from the International Criminal Court in 2019, without seeking the senate's consent. The latter move he defended on the basis of the need to protect national sovereignty.[18]

In India, BJP nationalist populists inherited a strongly liberal-democratic, egalitarian, secular, even if almost impossibly lengthy

---

[17] See Edcel John A. Ibarra, "The Philippine Supreme Court under Duterte: Reshaped, Unwilling to Annul, and Unable to Restrain," Social Science Research Council Democracy Papers (November 10, 2020), www.items.ssrc.org/democracy-papers/democratic-erosion/the-philippine-supreme-court-under-duterte-reshaped-unwilling-to-annul-and-unable-to-restrain.

[18] See Richard Javad Heydarian, "Subaltern Populism: Dutertismo and the War on Constitutional Democracy," in Martin Krygier, Adam Czarnota, and Wojciech Sadurski (eds.), *Anti-constitutional Populism* (in press).

constitution. The constitution entrenched a catalog of judicially enforceable rights, a system of separation of powers with a strong and independent judiciary, and a quasi-federal structure for the territorial division of power, as well as various devices for accommodation for minorities. In many respects it was – and is – a formidable document. As constitutional scholar Gautam Bathia said, "the Constitution's underlying theme of liberal constitutionalism intended to limit state powers and alter the colonial culture of authority into a culture of justification."[19]

Prime Minister Narendra Modi has not felt at ease within this framework, and has done much to undo it, without making any formal constitutional amendment. As leading India scholar Tarunabh Khaitan says of Modi's actions which have been aimed at undermining executive branch accountability, "[m]any of these acts were not so much unconstitutional (although some clearly were), but constitutionally shameless."[20] "Constitutional shamelessness" is a nice, if disheartening, formula capturing approaches by populist authoritarians who lack power to formally replace a liberal-democratic constitution.

In the case of Modi, constitutional transgressions have had two main forms. The first has consisted of assaults upon the constitution's secularism and equal religious rights. A constant Hindu-Muslim tension had been contained, less or more effectively, by strong constitutional guarantees of religious tolerance and non-discrimination. This has been the traditional, post-independence constitutional model of Indian secularism: to inhibit religious conflict and violence, but also to reform and contain Hinduism as the dominant religion, in order to protect fundamental rights and advance equality.[21] The model has not prevented multiple riots (including those following the provocative destruction by Hindu nationalists of the Babri Masjid in Ayodhya in 1992) and a large number of victims (mainly Muslims), but nevertheless the quasi-constant attitude of all ruling parties prior to the BJP has been to calm communal tempers and fall back on secularism as a constitutionally mandated response, with no clear privileges for the Hindu majority (four-fifths of

---

[19] Sandeep Suresh, "Gautam Bhatia. The Transformative Constitution: A Radical Biography in Nine Acts," *International Journal of Constitutional Law*, 18/2 (2020), 668–672 at 668.

[20] Tarunabh Khaitan, "Killing a Constitution with a Thousand Cuts: Executive Aggrandizement and Party-State Fusion in India," *Law and Ethics of Human Rights*, 14 (2020), 49–95 at 93.

[21] See Manoj Mate, "Constitutional Erosion and the Challenge to Secular Democracy in India," in Mark Graber, Sanford Levinson, and Mark Tushnet (eds.), *Constitutional Democracy in Crisis?* (Oxford: Oxford University Press, 2018), pp. 377–394 at 381.

the population). This model of secularism has permeated different state institutions and procedures, including not only the Supreme Court, but also the electoral process that contained prohibitions on appeals to religion by candidates and parties in elections. But this has all radically changed under Modi's leadership, with his BJP government promoting an anti-secular Hindu nationalist agenda, Islam came to be identified with Pakistan and patriotism with Hinduism.[22] This nationalist approach was implemented through law, including the anti-Muslim citizenship act of December 2019, which offered amnesty to illegal migrants from neighboring countries. The law offered a pathway to Indian citizenship for members of six religious groups, including Hindus, Sikhs, Buddhists, and the like, but with the conspicuous absence of Islam. It was the first time in independent India that citizenship was granted or denied on religious grounds, and it constituted a case of express religious discrimination. It specifically violates article 5 of the constitution, which proclaims *ius soli* (citizenship establishes at birth) as the only criterion for conferring citizenship. As the sociologist Niraja Gopal Jaya said, the law holds the "potential of transforming India into a majoritarian polity with gradations of citizenship rights."[23] The Supreme Court failed to uphold a challenge to the law, which many constitutional lawyers and judges of lower courts regard as clearly unconstitutional.

The second departure from the constitution has been through aggrandizement of the executive powers and weakening of most devices that disperse powers. It is true that assaults on India's constitution have been facilitated by various flaws in the constitutional text itself.[24] The constitution imported a British-style Westminster system into India, but without certain customary restrictions on the power of the parliamentary majority, for instance, without adequately protecting opposition rights. Modi has exploited these flaws by moving in the direction of granting full supremacy to the executive branch, for instance by using the procedure for "money bills" (which do not require scrutiny by the upper chamber) to pass all sorts of legislation, contrary to the original purpose of such acts, which is only to clear government expenses. Matters such as the

---

[22] Swaminathan S. Anklesaria Aiyar, "Despite Modi, India Has Not Yet Become a Hindu Authoritarian State," Policy Analysis No. 903, (Washington, DC: The Cato Institute, November 24, 2020), www.jstor.org/stable/resrep28731, p. 8.
[23] "Citizenship Amendment Bill: India's New 'Anti-Muslim' Law Explained," BBC (December 11, 2019), www.bbc.com/news/world-asia-india-50670393.
[24] See Khaitan, "Killing a Constitution with a Thousand Cuts," p. 93.

reform of existing tribunals, and more specifically, a 2017 law that shifted the authority to appoint the heads of the tribunals to the central government, have been decided in a shortcut way as "money bills." In addition, the "vertical" separation of powers, which takes the form of a quasi-federal system of government, has been decisively deformed to the detriment of states. This has been achieved through tax law – by reducing tax powers of state governments – as well as by revoking the autonomy of Jammu and Kashmir (a matter further discussed in Chapter 4). This last step basically showed that the central government can make "an Indian state extinct without consulting the elected representatives of its people."[25]

This all vindicates Khaitan's assessment that the BJP government has been "constitutionally shameless." Partly by violating the constitution outright, partly by departing from its spirit and the established precedents, and by ruthlessly exploiting its flaws, Modi has moved Indian constitutionalism in a Hindu-oriented, centralized direction, eroding the efficacy of veto points at the central level as well as federalism. This is evidenced by the "Kashmir lex" and strong fiscal centralization.[26] In the process, it has undermined the many rights guarantees for which the Indian constitution was deservedly praised.

Similarly to India, Polish ruling populists have not had the luxury that Hungarian and Venezuelan rulers had, and have been unable to change the constitution. When they came to power in 2015 – with a bare legislative majority, insufficient for a constitutional change – the populists did not have any constitutional drafts in their drawers. An older one, from 2010, had been all but forgotten, but if one were to retrieve it, one would be shocked how centralizing, pro-religious, and reticent on individual rights it was.

During the post-2015 populist rule, President Andrzej Duda at a certain stage tried to initiate a debate about a constitutional referendum. It was his desperate attempt to find a role for himself, having otherwise been relegated to a hapless rubber-stamp of his party's (PiS) initiatives. But the presidential initiative was a spectacular nonstarter. Not only was it ignored by his own party (a deliberate snub by party leader Jarosław

---

[25] Madhav Khosla and Milan Vaishnav, "The Three Faces of the Indian State," *Journal of Democracy*, 32/1 (2021), 111–125 at 118.

[26] See Chanchal Kumar Sharma and Wilfried Swenden, "Modi-fying Indian Federalism? Centre-State Relations under Modi's Tenure as Prime Minister," *Indian Politics and Policy*, 1/1 (2018), 51–81 at 55.

Kaczyński), but more importantly, in a polarized Polish society it was obvious to everyone that no draft generated by PiS would be endorsed by PiS opponents and thus win the required constitutional support of a supermajority. Duda's proposals ranged from the symbolic-sycophantic (highlighting the role of Christianity), redundant (the protection of labor and of pregnant women), silly (the supremacy of Polish law over that of the European Union) to harmful (the constitutional entrenchment of current levels of welfare payments). Mercifully, public opinion forgot about this ill-considered initiative as soon as the ruling party confined it to the dustbin. So all in all, the populist regime in Poland has operated in a formally unchanged constitutional context. The 1997 constitution – by and large liberal, pro–human rights, consensus-based – has been in force throughout the populist rule.

Rather than governing under a new "abusive constitution," Polish rulers abused the existing one. The 1997 constitution has acquired its value based on an old joke from the Communist times: "Why is our constitution so valuable? Because it has not been used." While they could not change the (capital-C) Constitution, they have changed the (lower-case) constitution – understood as the rules that govern the political game.

As I have evidenced elsewhere at length, the Polish Constitution has been routinely violated in a number of ways since 2015.[27] The takeover of the Constitutional Tribunal through a complex process of court-packing is one arena in which breaches of the constitution have been committed, as I shall describe in some detail in Chapter 4. The parliamentary resolution undoing the formal election of judges, the president's refusal to take an oath of office from those judges, the government's refusal to publish tribunal judgments it did not like – these are just a few steps that led to the dismantling of the tribunal through utterly unconstitutional means, and that have importantly changed the constitutional structure. Further, the regime has "amended" the constitution through simple statutes adopted quickly by a simple majority: It has fundamentally altered the method of selection to the National Council of the Judiciary (KRS), established a new Media Board by statute that overshadows the constitutional body, the Council for Radio and TV, and has adopted a statute lowering the retirement age for the chief justice, despite her constitutional term of office.

---

[27] Wojciech Sadurski, *Poland's Constitutional Breakdown* (Oxford: Oxford University Press, 2019).

The process of "amending" the constitution by fiat and simple statutes rather than by constitutional amendments is the main difference between Kaczyński's Poland and Orbán's Hungary. What Kaczyński occasioned by statutes, Orbán brought about by a brand-new constitution followed by a number of constitutional amendments. One may wonder which of these two situations is worse – worse, that is, from the point of view of the standards of liberal constitutionalism. On the one hand, one may claim that the Hungarian style of illiberalism via constitutional changes is *more* damaging in the long term because illiberal changes are being entrenched well into the future; thus a future non-Fidesz government may lack a constitutional majority and be straitjacketed in its conduct by the illiberal Fundamental Law of Hungary. On the other hand, one may speculate that constitutional amendments via statutes and simple breaches of the constitution, Polish-style, are more destructive of the principles of constitutionalism and the rule of law. In Hungary, the disempowerment of the Constitutional Court was accomplished in accordance with the law; in Poland, it was more a demolition job than the restructuring of an institution, fully disregarding constitutional provisions.

Parchment Barriers

The Polish case is a good starting point for considering how resilient a constitution may be against politicians orchestrating backsliding toward authoritarianism. Suppose you have a reasonably good constitution, which provides for a fair balance between different institutions, good protection of individual rights, safeguards for judicial independence, and so forth. How can you make sure that the constitution will deter authoritarians from dismantling these achievements? Or, more realistically, that the constitution will *slow down* the backsliding? Poland has had a reasonably good, liberal constitution since 1997, and yet it was incapable of preventing populist backsliding. So has India.

The main reason why it is difficult to consider the impact of non-resilient constitutional design on the rise of populism in Poland or in India is that, as already shown, PiS and BJP continued to govern through multiple *breaches* of the constitution. When a constitution is violated with seeming impunity, it is difficult to blame the constitution itself for the capacity of rulers to overcome constitutional checks and balances. Speculation about alternative designs that may arguably be thought to be more capable of withstanding the populist rise is just that, speculation, simply because the constitution itself is breached. For how do we know that a smarter constitutional design would not have been as easily discarded by determined authoritarians? The simple answer is, we do not know. This sort of counterfactual is simply impossible to support with a good argument.

But what we do know is that no constitution is *absolutely* resilient. To what extent constitutional design can make a difference in protecting a system against an authoritarian threat, especially when that threat comes from elected populists who enjoy a sizable public support, is a matter that is fundamentally context dependent. Much depends on the course of action taken by the elected rulers themselves. If they feel free to break constitutional rules and customs whenever they find them inconvenient, not much can be done by designing checks on the political branches.

As Aziz Huq and Tom Ginsburg say in relation to the United States:

> The decisions of party leaders and activists on both sides to prioritize the continuance of democracy as an ongoing concern, and their willingness to allow transient policy triumphs to offset concerns about antidemocratic behavior, will be of dispositive importance...Constitutions are, after all, just pieces of paper that take their force from the intersubjective understandings of elites and citizens.[28]

But the human factor is all the more significant in new, transitional democracies, where there has simply been less time for people to have had the opportunity to become convinced about the advantages of democracy. Democracy is stable when its citizens believe that it is "the only game in town" and that non-democratic alternatives are illegitimate.[29] The *newness* of institutions works against the resilience of the constitution because there is simply an insufficient reservoir of customs, conventions, established patterns of conduct, and collective memory as to the proper way of acting within these institutions.

This is not to suggest that the shape and design of institutions do not matter: There are ways of promoting and ways of minimizing the need for interparty dialogue and compromise through institutional design. In the United States, various devices of checks and balances – federalism, bicameralism, presidential veto, robust judicial review, and the like – mean that the leaders in power have to compromise with politicians of

---

[28] Aziz Huq and Tom Ginsburg, "How to Lose a Constitutional Democracy," *UCLA Law Review*, 65 (2018), 78–169 at 167.
[29] Juan J. Linz and Alfred Stepan, "Toward Consolidated Democracies," *Journal of Democracy*, 7/2 (1996), 14–33.

persuasions other than their own. These and other factors of institutional design constitute jointly what Samuel Issacharoff calls "the structural dimensions of democratic stability."[30] Rosalind Dixon and David Landau offer important advice to constitutional designers aimed at making constitutions more robust against the possible future capture of constitutional institutions.[31] Three such techniques, the authors suggest, are (1) tiering (some constitutional provisions are less easily amendable, and hence more entrenched), (2) sequencing (amendments of core provisions take longer to carry out, hence "creating speed bumps that can slow authoritarian projects"),[32] and (3) splitting (i.e., the fragmentation of authority over appointments, including to courts).

There is no doubt that smart constitutional design may increase the costs of constitutional breaches by the authoritarian leaders, but it will not eliminate such breaches. For instance, a system of electing/appointing constitutional court judges may make it easier or more difficult to capture the court. The Polish and Hungarian system is bad, from this point of view, because the parliamentary majority can appoint judges to all vacancies that open up during the parliamentary term. In a "winner takes all" system, the compromise-oriented election of judges depends largely on the political culture and good will of the ruling party or parties rather than being compelled by an institution. Germany has a very similar model for the election of constitutional judges, but a degree of cultural consensus about the process has prevented an outright capture by the ruling party or coalition. In Poland or Hungary, a different system for the election of those judges (for instance, as in many countries, splitting appointments to the court between different top institutions) would have made it more difficult for local authoritarians to quickly pack the court with party loyalists. But it would not prevent it: Those other institutions charged with appointing judges (the president, the judiciary council, etc.) could have been captured first. And if they did *not* appoint the "right" judges, their decisions may be struck down, misrepresented, or wrongly reported by the executive. It is all a matter of political costs – not of the physical impossibility of a capture.

To quote Huq and Ginsburg again, "constitutional enforcement requires the kind of intersubjective agreement on violations that is

---

[30] Samuel Issacharoff, *Fragile Democracies* (Cambridge: Cambridge University Press, 2015), p. 22.
[31] Dixon and Landau, *Abusive Constitutional Borrowing*, p. 179.
[32] Ibid., p. 179.

difficult to obtain, especially under mutative and precarious political conditions."[33] The test for the resilience of constitutions is whether powerful officials back down when institutions in charge of enforcing a constitution issue decisions those officials dislike or even abhor, as was the case of President Richard Nixon having to hand over audiotapes in connection with the Watergate scandal as ordered by the Supreme Court. So ultimately it is a matter of culture and ethics. When these are missing or uncongenial, even the best-designed constitutional institutions are rendered hollow. By contrast, when they are strongly ingrained in the professionals staffing various institutions – in parliaments, the public service, and courts – they are likely to prevail over determined and resolute populists. Consider this hypothetical a US legal scholar posed about a possible attack by President Trump on freedom of speech and the press in order to silence his critics:

> A frontal assault on the [Supreme] Court's First Amendment jurisprudence would fail for the time being. Justices on the left and right are committed to strong protections for political speech; Trump would need to replace at least five of them, securing the Senate's consent in each case, and *it would be hard, perhaps impossible, for him to find even a single qualified, mainstream jurist* who would supply the vote he needs.[34]

The confidence with which Eric Posner makes this assessment seems justified, but a similarly confident judgment could not have been made with respect to Poland or Hungary or the Philippines when the ruling elites went after the top courts. They *did* find a sufficient number of jurists who were willing to occupy high judicial positions. On the positive side, there was a strong sense of opprobrium targeted against those individuals. On the negative side, it was not strong enough to prevent these lawyers from volunteering or accepting these positions and, in the process, actively participating in the dismantlement of the rule of law.

Reading the Constitution between the Lines

Authoritarian populists behave as if all there is to a constitution is the constitutional text. Theirs is literal democracy, not liberal democracy.

---

[33] Huq and Ginsburg, "How to Lose a Constitutional Democracy," p. 168.
[34] Eric A. Posner, "The Dictator's Handbook, US Edition," in Cass R. Sunstein (ed.), *Can It Happen Here? Authoritarianism in America* (New York: HarperCollins, 2018), pp. 1–18 at 3, emphasis added.

When Polish president Andrzej Duda granted in 2017 a pardon to PiS politicians who had been sentenced in a non-final judgment for abuse of office,[35] he may have used his text-based constitutional power of pardon correctly (the text does not expressly qualify this right in any way). However, he breached an unwritten norm that states that a pardon is a means of last resort that can be applied only to those sentenced in *final* judgments. To think otherwise – that is, to allow presidential pardon at *any* stage of the judicial trial – would bring the chief executive right into the center of judicial proceedings and make them a super-judge, thus fundamentally breaching the very essence of the separation of powers. And, come to think of it, it does not make sense: A person not yet sentenced in a final judgment must be considered innocent, and how can you pardon a legally innocent person?

When the Polish ruling party PiS brought about a law with respect to the body for appointing judges, the National Council of the Judiciary (KRS), which transferred the power to elect KRS judicial members from the judges to the parliament, it may have been legally correct – the constitution does not explicitly say that these members are elected *by* judges, only that they must *be* judges – but the law breached an unwritten norm taken for granted from the beginning of the post-Communist history of Poland up to 2015. It had been ordained in a founding constitutive document of post-Communist Poland, that is, in the agreements of the Round Table of 1989.[36] It is also a generally recognized European standard with which Poland, as a member of the Council of Europe and of the European Union, has an obligation to comply, whether it is textually stated in its constitution or not. It also has the advantage of making sense: These judges are meant to be representatives of all judges, and the KRS representatives should be elected by those whom they represent.

When the government of India brings about various non-budget-related statutory changes via "money bills," thus avoiding a cumbersome legislative path and eliminating scrutiny by a higher chamber, it strictly speaking may be seen to remain within the four corners of the constitutional text that does not provide a clear definition of what exactly "money bills" concern. But when the Modi government introduced the controversial "Aadhaar project" in 2016, which sought to create a national, centralized biometric identification system for the whole

---

[35] For an account, see Sadurski, *Poland's Constitutional Breakdown*, pp. 80–81 and 253–254.
[36] On the constitutional significance of 1989 Round Table compromise, see ibid., pp. 36–39.

country, its constitutionality was more than dubious.[37] How can a citizens' identification system be viewed as the proper subject-matter of a "money bill"? But its unconstitutionality was not a matter of text but of interpretation, which is based on the *purposes* of having a particular procedure – in this case, a money bill – in the first place. The purpose is unwritten – as they usually are.

This, incidentally, is a trick many authoritarian populists use. In Poland, some of the populist government's most important pet projects after 2015 have been introduced as private members' bills, even though they were very much prepared by the government. (In 2016, the first full year of the PiS majority, over 40 percent of all PiS legislative proposals were presented as private members' bills even though they had been mostly prepared by the relevant ministers; the proportion in the previous years sat around 15 percent. And substantively, those bills applied to some of the most important legal changes, such as the law on common courts and the Supreme Court.)[38] The reason is simple: Private member bills allow the lawmaker to sidestep various procedural requirements of compulsory audits, public hearings, expert opinions, and the like. So if the government wants to fast-track its legislative proposal and immunize it from pre-enactment control, it can always use the ruling party's MPs to sign on to it as their bill. Of course, it is disingenuous, dishonest, and contrary to the norm of proper legislation. But where is there a black-letter provision that prohibits such practices?

Each of these norms was unwritten but considered clear and peremptory – until populists took power and breached them, pretending they did not exist. This uses the law against itself: acting within the literal meaning of the rules but disregarding the norms that are necessary in order to accomplish the original purposes for specific legal provisions. And this is characteristic of today's authoritarians' uses of law. As Martin Krygier notes, "[m]any illiberal regimes have aspired to use law for their purposes, but without submitting themselves to it in any ways that matter to them, at any event at times that matter to them. Here a regime might promote law and even fidelity (of officials and citizens) to law, but there are strict limits."[39] Those limits arise out of the authoritarian focus on the *letter* and disregard for the *spirit* of constitutions.

---

[37] Khosla and Vaishnav, "The Three Faces of the Indian State," 115.
[38] See Sadurski, *Poland's Constitutional Breakdown*, p. 133.
[39] Martin Krygier "The Spirit of Constitutionalism," in Jakub Urbanik and Adam Bodnar (eds.), Περιμένοντας τους Βαρβάρους: *Law in the Days of Constitutional Crisis: Studies Offered to Mirosław Wyrzykowski* (Warsaw: C. H. Beck, 2021), pp. 343–358 at 351.

Populists manipulate public opinion into believing that if a norm is unwritten, then it is not binding, and not really a norm. This means that unwritten norms are usually the first victim of populist actions that often observe the written norms to the letter. But unwritten norms are equally, if not more, important. Consider the catalog of examples of unwritten norms necessary for a democracy, provided by Anna Grzymala-Busse: "conflict of interest laws, financial transparency, respect for the opposition access and accountability to the media, and preventing party loyalty from becoming the basis for the awarding of tenders, contracts, and government responsibilities."[40] Yascha Mounk adds norms such as: the government does not change electoral rules shortly before the election in order to maximize its chance of winning, the incumbents losing in the elections do not restrict the powers of offices gained by their adversaries in the last moment of their rule, or "[t]he opposition confirms a competent judge whose ideology it dislikes rather than leaving a seat on the highest court in the land vacant."[41] Regardless of whether it is written into a law or not, there is obviously a norm that the top executive does not intervene in individual criminal investigations, especially those that involve him or his family.

The problem is that some of these norms are ascertained only in consequence of their *breach*; they become evident because of specific conduct that strikes us intuitively as highly improper. For often the norms become salient only when broken; as with health or plumbing, we know their importance in their failure. That is why the argument that populists would have been prevented from breaching them by making those rules *explicit* in the text in the first place, is so hypocritical. You cannot put everything into a constitutional text; you must rely on common sense and honesty in the text's interpretation, and in filling the gaps. In different countries the proportions between the written and the unwritten will be different, but there must always be something that remains unwritten, just as in love something remains unsaid. Articulating these unwritten norms may be controversial at times, and some proposed meanings may be contested, but in a healthy democracy there is a degree of consensus on unwritten norms. What is required is not just knowledge of the norms, but also knowing that others know them, and that they will

---

[40] Anna Grzymala-Busse, "Global Populisms and Their Impact," *Slavic Review*, 76 (2017), Suppl. S1, 3–8 at 6.

[41] Yascha Mounk, *The People vs Democracy* (Cambridge: Harvard University Press, 2018), p. 113.

abide by them, and if they do not, they will know that they have violated them.

Often, unwritten norms have a suitably *moderating* effect upon written rules, and supplement them in ways that render written rules more constraining upon public officials than what a mere reading of the textual rule would suggest. Mark Tushnet gives an example of the Canadian system for choosing Supreme Court justices. The formal rule gives the prime minister complete discretion in making appointments, subject only to the proviso that three out of nine justices come from Quebec. However, Tushnet adds: "That formal system...is supplemented by extremely strong norms of deference to professional judgments about potential appointees' ability. The prime minister would act inappropriately, and suffer politically, by departing from these norms."[42] The same textual rule, adopted in another country but without the accompanying unwritten norm, would be disastrous because there is little reason to think that elsewhere such informal norms would effectively constrain the top executive's choices.

In his important book *America's Unwritten Constitution* (note the title!), Yale law professor Akhil Reed Amar urges: "[W]e must read the Constitution as a whole – between the lines, so to speak."[43] This is a nice formula: reading the Constitution "as a whole" and "between the lines" demands that we must not read disparate passages and clauses in isolation from the document as a whole. This is a good passage (redacted, for brevity) in Amar's book, bringing together several conclusions from his case studies (including the composition of impeachment courts, the scope of congressional lawmaking power, the sweep of free-speech rights, etc.): "On each topic, clause-bound literalism fails. Sometimes the key clause in isolation is simply indeterminate...Other times, the most salient clause, in isolation, sends a rather misleading message...On occasion the Constitution's true meaning is very nearly the opposite of what the applicable clause seems to say quite expressly."[44]

This means that we must inquire into the *reasons* for having a particular constitutional provision in the first place. To go back to the example

---

[42] Mark Tushnet, "Comparing Right-Wing and Left-Wing Populism," in Mark Graber, Sanford Levinson, and Mark Tushnet (eds.), *Constitutional Democracy in Crisis?* (Oxford: Oxford University Press, 2018) pp. 639–650 at 642.
[43] Akhil Reed Amar, *America's Unwritten Constitution* (New York: Basic Books, 2012), p. 47.
[44] Ibid., p. 47.

of Poland's National Council of the Judiciary: The reason for providing a certain number of judges on the council is to make sure that they *represent* judges. Hence, there is some discretion for a legislator to regulate the mode of appointment but only in a way that renders the representation meaningful. There may be other ways of filling these positions than by having all judges elect them (although I am not sure of better ways) but, by contrast, allowing members of parliament (hence, the majority party) to elect them is not one such way. The constitution, if read "between the lines," precludes such a legislative choice.

Democratic unwritten norms are often *pre*-constitutional, not discernible even from a "holistic" reading of the Constitution "between the lines," but from the democratic culture underlying the system. Of course, there may be a legitimate disagreement about the exact meaning of such norms, but this is a different disagreement from the one that disputes whether such norms exist and are peremptory. For instance, there is a norm that democratic rulers do not push their legal competences to their limits, that is, by testing their outer boundaries, or by constantly being on the verge of overreaching. Steven Levitsky and Daniel Ziblatt define this as a norm of "forbearance," which is "the idea that politicians should exercise restraint in deploying their institutional prerogatives."[45] There is also a norm that, no matter how harsh the words said during the electoral campaign, there is a sort of reconciliation after the election, which allows the governing majority and the opposition to work in the parliament toward a public good. But in the countries where populists win, usually the opposite happens. The chasm between the winners and the losers grows larger, and accusations against the opposition become harsher. Public insults devastate the public sphere and contribute to a growing public cynicism about politics – a toxic element in a democracy, as Chapter 5 will show.

---

[45] Steven Levitsky and Daniel Ziblatt, *How Democracies Die* (New York: Crown Publishing, 2018), pp. 8–9.

4

Courts

The Least Resilient Branch

One of the classic books in constitutional law has the title: *The Least Dangerous Branch*.[1] Written by Alexander Bickel, a professor at Yale Law School, the book argued that the authority of the courts relies upon values-based, principled decisions that can gain acceptance. At the end of his book, Bickel wrote: "Broad and sustained application of the [US Supreme] Court's law, when challenged, is a function of its rightness, not merely of its pronouncements."[2] But rightness is in the eye of the beholder, and populist leaders know one or two things about how to quickly mobilize a large number of supportive beholders. As a result, the title of Bickel's book acquires a less benign meaning from that which was intended. As courts have no means for enforcement and no budget (other than for their own administration) – hence no sword or purse – rulers may regard them as sufficiently impotent to be tolerated. However, the same factors that render judges and courts the least dangerous branch at the same time make them the most defenseless in the face of executive assault.

And yet, populists in power often behave as if courts are the *most* dangerous branch. If being the target of assaults is a criterion for identifying apparent threats to populist rulers, the judiciary must take the number one spot in the demonology of populist rulers. After being elected, populist rulers almost invariably take on the courts, often with fervor and unusual animus. Judges are presented as "enemies of the People," as an (in)famous headline in the British *Daily Mail* proclaimed on November 4, 2016, depicting three British judges who had ruled that despite the referendum, the government was required to obtain the consent of Parliament legally to authorize Brexit. Also starting in 2016 in Poland, PiS's legislative proposals to dismantle judicial

---

[1] Alexander Bickel, *The Least Dangerous Branch: The Supreme Court and the Idea of Progress* (New Haven: Yale University Press, 1962).
[2] Ibid., p. 258.

independence were preceded by a well-orchestrated propaganda campaign against judges. All of a sudden, the pro-PiS media and public TV in particular began to publicize individual cases of judges' alleged corruption or petty offenses. In one instance, a judge was shown to have stolen a sausage from a grocery store. Subsequently it turned out that the judge in question had long been removed from the profession and was suffering from a nervous disability at the time she committed the theft. This was soon followed by a government-funded smear campaign against judges (huge billboards were displayed in public spaces), accompanied by top politicians attacking the judiciary. Prime Minister Beata Szydło referred to the judiciary as a "judicial guild" (or "caste") and said that "everyone knows someone who was hurt by the judiciary system."[3] These events were the artillery prelude to a full-blown legislative package to capture the courts.

In Hungary in April 2018, after the Supreme Court (now called the Kúria) handed down an unfavorable decision on absentee voting affecting his government, Viktor Orbán accused the Supreme Court of being "not intellectually up to its task" and alleged that it "interferes in the elections" and "takes a mandate away from our electors." The prime minister liked to complain about "the judicial state" and irresponsible judges.[4] In Israel in 2015, Ayelet Shaked, an outspoken minister of justice in the populist Netanyahu government, declared that "due to judicial supremacy," the elected branches "fail to achieve their goals and fulfil the will of the people."[5] Minister Miri Regev, Shaked's colleague in the same government, declared, after a Supreme Court judgment unfavorable to the government, that the court was "disconnected from the people."[6] And in India in 2015, Prime Minister Narendra Modi chided judges for not being impartial and fearless but, instead, in fear of social activists.[7]

---

[3] See Council of Europe, Bureau of the Consultative Council of European Judges (CCJE), Report on Judicial Independence and Impartiality in the Council of Europe Member States in 2017, Strasbourg, February 7, 2018, para. 320, www.rm.coe.int/2017-report-situation-ofjudges-in-member-states/1680786ae1.
[4] Zoltán Fleck, "Judges under Attack in Hungary," *Verfassungsblog* (May 14, 2018), www.verfassungsblog.de/judges-under-attack-in-hungary/.
[5] Quoted in Alon Harel and Noam Kolt, "Populist Rhetoric, False Mirroring, and the Courts," *International Journal of Constitutional Law*, 18 (2020), 746–766 at 755–756.
[6] Ibid., p. 756.
[7] "Congress Attacks Narendra Modi for Attack on the Judiciary," *The Economic Times* (April 7, 2015), www.economictimes.indiatimes.com/news/politics-and-nation/congress-attacks-narendra-modi-for-attack-on-the-judiciary/articleshow/46830797.cms?from=mdr.

Alternative Legitimacy

The most obvious reason for populist rage at the judiciary is that the courts are the most important bastion of *alternative* legitimacy. To many individual citizens and civil society, the courts may offer the most feasible channel for airing their grievances when the political branches are effectively shut to them. Broad social movements in Poland in defense of free courts, beginning in 2017 and continuing, though with a lesser force, to the present day, are a practical manifestation of this instinct. One summer evening in 2017, after a day of loud protests, the candle-lit crowd outside the Supreme Court building "stood peacefully listening to Chopin's piano compositions and sang the Polish anthem at the end" – as one *Euractiv* correspondent reported.[8] As a participant, I can confirm that it was an impressive and uplifting experience.

In contrast to the legislature and the executive who derive their legitimacy from popular support – mainly derived from free, fair, and regular elections – judges claim a different type of legitimacy. As American political scientist and constitutional scholar Martin Shapiro explained in a now-classic book, judges are legitimate by virtue of being impartial arbiters between conflicting parties. It is not so much that modern courts, as we know them, behave as go-betweens or mediators or arbiters; when we come as a defendant in a criminal trial, we would *not* have agreed to appointment of *this* judge; indeed, our presence has nothing to do with our consent. Nevertheless, judges' sources of legitimacy resemble that of a "triadic" structure because even if a defendant "did not consent to the judge, he must be convinced that judicial office itself ensures that the judge is not an ally of his opponent."[9]

Courts are not legitimate by virtue of electoral support but rather by virtue of a combination of professionalism and independence. Or so proclaims a democratic theory that needs to explain the existence of a branch that is not accountable to electors. As such, judges are direct competitors to state actors whose legitimacy *is* derived from such electoral support. If those state actors – legislators and governments – accept the principle of separation of powers, with different branches that draw on diverse sources of legitimacy, all well and good. But if they believe that the only legitimate power comes directly from the People, and so their

---

[8] Karolina Zbytniewska, "Thousands Protest Coup against Constitution' in Poland," *Euractiv* (July 17, 2017).

[9] Martin Shapiro, *Courts* (Chicago: The University of Chicago Press, 1981), p. 8.

own legitimacy is superior and cannot be shared with others, the existence of a branch of government that has a completely different source of legitimacy becomes intolerable.

There cannot be rightful competition, the populist story goes, between leaders generated by the will of the People and independent actors who do not need to submit to the scrutiny of the People. For if the true will of the People speaks through the elected Leader's mouth, anything external to it – anything that is not an expression of popular sovereignty as incarnated by the Leader – is extrinsic to "true" democracy. And as such, it is not only redundant but even dangerous. It may be even "linked to the secret work of an oligarchical enemy, the deep state, or an external power."[10] In this way, populist ideology legitimates anti-judiciary attacks.

When courts are already captured by the executive, they lose their capacity to solve conflicts that otherwise would have found their peaceful resolution in the courtroom. This is because a captured court is also *seen* as having been captured and is hence not impartial. Going to such a court to seek justice is pointless. This extends to constitutional courts, which in some cases can help the political class by taking some controversial issues off the political agenda and placing them on the court's docket – as has happened in different countries with abortion, doctor-assisted suicide, hate speech, or the ritual slaughter of animals. But parliamentary oppositions, lower courts, independent institutions (such as the ombudsman), or citizens will go to constitutional courts only if they feel they have some chance of winning, or at least if they believe that if they lose, they will have lost after a fair, reasonable consideration of their case. Their incentive to go to such a court is underwritten by their trust in it, and the hope that even if they lose today, they may well win tomorrow. As Adam Przeworski says, "[w]hen courts are blatantly partisan, this belief [in the likelihood of winning one day] is eroded, and addressing conflicting issues to constitutional tribunals becomes futile."[11] This is exactly what has happened in populist countries where constitutional courts have been captured by the state. In Poland, statistics show a dramatic reduction in the number of cases heard by the Constitutional Tribunal (CT). In 2015, the last year before it was captured, the CT received 623 motions of

---

[10] Andrew Arato, "Populism, Constitutional Courts, and Civil Society," in Christine Landfried (ed.), *Judicial Power: How Constitutional Courts Affect Political Transformations* (Cambridge: Cambridge University Press, 2019), pp. 318–341 at 331.
[11] Adam Przeworski, *Crises of Democracy* (Cambridge: Cambridge University Press, 2019), p. 166.

unconstitutionality and handed down 63 judgments. Two years later, it received only 284 motions and handed down 36 judgments. The trend has continued downward ever since. The main "supplier" of challenges is now the state itself: either the president, the prime minister, or the parliamentary majority, and their function is to support rather than scrutinize the government. This further strengthens the social perception that a court is part of a unified governmental bloc and cannot claim independence or professionalism.

When a court loses its independent legitimacy that is based on a widespread belief in its impartiality and professionalism, it loses its capacity to lower the intensity of social conflicts – a capacity that is helpful for democracy itself. It may be seen to be redundant. But it is not. It is helpful – but this time, for politicians.

Judges as Populists

While courts are universally viewed by populists as enemies of their institutional projects, and populists resent and resist the constraints on their powers emanating from courts, it does not follow that the judiciary is an unqualified impediment to populist rule. Occasionally courts themselves may be an engine of populism, often in a neophyte attempt to shed the odium of elitism and remoteness from "real people." "Judicial populism" is not an oxymoron: The concept is used by legal scholars to describe the use of severe penalties by criminal courts to please the public. But the concept is not limited to the criminal law. When an Israeli court considered the grant of a license to broadcast the Playboy channel, Justice Cheshin uttered the memorable phrases: "*Vox populi, vox dei.* The voice of the people is the voice of God...I am referring to the voice of the people, in the simple sense of the phrase...It is incumbent upon us, the judges, to go out into the street, to literature, to poetry, to the press, to the radio and television, to everyday conversation."[12] This sounds like a good opening to a manifesto for Judicial Populism. Rather than deliberating on the legal meaning of the freedom of speech and its limits, Justice Cheshin referred directly to raw public convictions.

The idea that a court should be sensitive to public morality is, in itself, unobjectionable. It has entered into the law of many countries under the garb of the "reasonable person" test, as an example of what standard of

---

[12] *SHIN Israeli Movement for Equal Representation of Women v. Council for Cable TV and Satellite Broadcasting*, HCJ 5432/03 [2004] IsrLR 20.

care a reasonable person would apply in negligence cases. It is one thing to use such standards to filter between public morality and judicial decisions. But it is another to suggest that a "raw" public view should directly shape a judicial decision. This is a task for legislators rather than for judges. The idea that judicial decisions should mirror the actual distribution of views on legally relevant matters is an example of "judicial populism" – inviting judges to act as enforcers of a majoritarian morality rather than of law, with all its moderating, filtering devices. In Bickel's words, "[t]heir insulation and the marvelous mystery of time gives courts the capacity to appeal to men's better natures, to call forth their aspirations, which may have been forgotten in the moment's hue and cry...Hence it is that the courts, although they may somewhat dampen the people's and the legislatures' efforts to educate themselves, are also a great and highly effective educational institution."[13] In contrast, if judges aspire to directly enforce a majority's view, they will adopt a quasi-representative function. In doing so, they will certainly do it worse than the parliaments do, and in the process, surrender their mission to act as a check on the representative and executive branches.

Courts who surrender their judicial mission become useful to populists. When problematic changes in law are rubber-stamped by a government-friendly constitutional court, these toxic changes acquire a patina of constitutionality. Further, any opposition can be depicted as anti-constitutional.

But the exploitation of courts for such purposes has, in a populist regime, clear limits: Populist rulers use courts only insofar as it serves their political goals. When they do not, populists abandon respect for courts and look the other way when courts issue judgments inconvenient to them. When the Supreme Court of India ordered that no compulsory use of the controversial Unique Identification Number (UIN) could be required while a case against the UIN was still pending, the Modi government simply flouted the court order – with impunity. And then, in its final judgment, the compliant majority of the court ignored the government's illegal conduct, and fully endorsed the controversial legislation on the basis that "the government was justified in restricting individual privacy for the collective good of providing welfare."[14] Or,

---

[13] Bickel, *The Least Dangerous Branch*, p. 26.
[14] Pawan Singh, "*Aadhaar* and Data Privacy: Biometric Identification and Anxieties of Recognition in India," *Information, Communication and Society*, 24 (2021), 978–993 at 978.

worse, populist rulers can simply declare the judgments illegal. When the Court of Competition and Consumer Protection in Poland in April 2021 suspended a transaction involving the purchase of a huge chunk of print media by the state-owned oil refining company Orlen (because it would eliminate competition in the media market), Orlen declared that the judgment was legally wrong, and the government of course stood by its own oil company turned-media empire.[15] Any court that interferes with the regime's plans enters a zone off-limits to it.

Willful Enablers and Cheerleaders

Populists are particularly keen to capture *constitutional* courts wherever they exist, or supreme courts whenever they perform (in addition to their regular role as a top appellate court) a function of constitutional review. The reason is obvious: These courts have the authority to strike down statutes as unconstitutional. This puts them directly on a collision course with the government.

In a democracy, the power to invalidate democratically adopted statutes is not seen as an aberration, but rather as a necessary corollary of the supremacy of the constitution over statutes. It is an additional check, exercised either before or after the adoption of a statute by the parliament. Democratic majorities accept constitutional courts, even if only grudgingly, as a "counter-majoritarian institution," not just out of an idealistic commitment to the constitution, but also based on their own, well-conceived self-interest. This self-interest tells democratic majorities that even if a constitutional court may upset some of their plans when in power, it will aid them when in opposition, and make sure that the majority of the day does not overstep constitutional limits or trample on rights.

But populists do not think this way. They often act as if there is no tomorrow. And any restriction on their authority – an authority that is after all conferred by a majority of the electorate – is viewed by them as unjustified, undemocratic, and thoroughly irritating. Hence, constitutional courts must be subordinated or captured. There is no room for "counter-majoritarian" institutions in a populist scheme.

---

[15] See Robert Jurszo, "Sąd wstrzymał zgodę na zakup Polska Press przez Orlen," Oko.press (April 12, 2021), www.oko.press/sad-wstrzymal-zgode-na-zakup-polska-press-przez-orlen-wniosek-zlozyl-rpo/.

The best that can happen, from a populist perspective, is when constitutional courts become helpful "enablers" of the executive. This became very clear in the case of Poland from 2017, when the captured Constitutional Tribunal began to play an important role in paving the way for the destruction of judicial independence and endorsed many unconstitutional actions of the government. These actions were perhaps not indispensable – the ruthless government would have undertaken them anyway. But they lowered the political costs of governmental misconduct. With a tribunal imprimatur, the government could tell the public – and European institutions – "Look, our hands are tied, the independent tribunal said so."

A good example of the CT playing its enabling role is the Polish CT judgment of June 20, 2017, on the National Council of the Judiciary (I will be using the Polish acronym KRS here), which is at the very center of the judicial system because it decides all judicial appointments and promotions. The system inherited by PiS consisted of a KRS mainly staffed by judges selected *by judges* in a complex system of voting at different levels. This was anathema to PiS because they could not control who gets onto to the KRS and thus control the appointment of personnel to the courts. So PiS used the CT to declare an existing law on the KRS unconstitutional – despite the fact that it had been in force for sixteen years and had not previously been objected to. The invalidation of the law by the CT was based on trumped-up, pretextual reasons that were really technicalities. But the actual reasons given for declaring invalidity did not matter. What mattered was to certify that the statute on the KRS was unconstitutional and to justify the enaction of a new statute. And it soon was enacted. Shortly after the judgment, the PiS-dominated parliament adopted a new law providing for the appointment of judges sitting on the KRS by...parliamentary majority. (It did not matter that the original law, struck down partly on the basis that it unfairly allocated seats on KRS to judges elected by judges of different levels of courts, was replaced by a law that simply extinguished all elections to the KRS by judges.) In this way, party control over judicial appointments was fully secured.[16]

Another case in which the CT obediently fulfilled the government's expectations and helped it to sort out an embarrassing situation was that of the grant of a presidential pardon to Mariusz Kamiński, one of the

---

[16] I provide a more detailed account of this episode in Wojciech Sadurski, *Poland Constitutional Breakdown* (Oxford: Oxford University Press, 2019), pp. 79–80.

closest and most powerful collaborators of Kaczyński, in 2017. Mr. Kamiński was found guilty of various improprieties in his office as head of secret services (a sort-of Polish FBI): He was fond of listening in on other people's phones without court warrant, and so forth. A criminal sentence would have been highly inconvenient to the government because if it was upheld on appeal, Kamiński would be prevented from continuing in public office and would possibly go to jail. The PiS-supported President Duda quickly granted Kamiński a pardon. But the thing was, the court judgment was non-final, and Duda by his pardon had effectively extinguished any further appellate proceedings. As well as constituting a blatant interference with the judicial process, granting a pardon for non-final punishments makes no sense (it is rather like granting a divorce when the marriage itself had not been properly formalized) – and this is exactly what the Supreme Court decided. PiS reacted with anger to the Supreme Court's decision – and appealed to the Constitutional Tribunal, which quickly announced that the presidential prerogative to pardon is absolute and unqualified, and that the Supreme Court had exceeded its competences in finding fault with a pardon for a non-final punishment. The CT characterized the problem as a "clash of competencies" between the Supreme Court and president, which was absurd. The Supreme Court had not usurped to itself the presidential power to pardon but had provided an interpretation of the law for the sake of a related, pending procedure. The CT's action saved Mr. Kamiński's head, politically speaking. In fact, as at the time of writing these words, Mr. Kamiński still occupies the position of security tsar, and is even more powerful than before.

Venezuela's top court also performs this "enabling" function in what legal scholar Sanchez Urribarri calls its "proactive" conduct (as opposed to "reactive," in the sense of frustrating the regime's opponents' plans, which it also does).[17] After various steps were taken to reinforce political control over the court, the Constitutional Chamber is now a fully fledged pro- and re-active enabler of the regime. The chamber has supported the government in several cases, insulated constitutional reforms from challenge, and permitted constitutional amendments to remove presidential term limits, leading to the subsequent removal of term limits in a referendum of February 2009.

---

[17] Raul A. Sánchez Urribarrí, "Populism, Constitutional Democracy, and High Courts: Lessons from the Venezuelan Case," in Martin Krygier, Adam Czarnota, and Wojciech Sadurski (eds.), *Anti-constitutional Populism* (in press).

The case of the RCTV (Radio Caracas Television) was telling in this regard. The station had been consistently critical of President Chávez's rule. In December 2006, Chávez announced that he would refuse to renew its license on the basis that the TV station supported "coup-plotting." At the same time, he sent a message to the Supreme Tribunal (TSJ) warning it against making any decisions favorable to the station. The TSJ refused to hear any petitions against the TV closure, except for one: that filed by a group of citizens against the Ministry of Telecommunications, asking the Constitutional Chamber of TSJ to allow the station to continue broadcasting beyond the license expiry date. The chamber agreed to hear the case and mandated the government to take over all the equipment of RCTV in order to secure continued broadcasting on the same frequency by any other TV station the government deemed appropriate. Which is of course exactly what the government did – and the government-owned station TVES picked up where RCTV left off when it stopped broadcasting.[18]

The court also provided critical support and "safeguarded the regime's stability" during Chávez's illness, for instance, by allowing Chávez to be sworn-in as president in absentia after his reelection in 2012. This type of proactive support has continued into the regime of his Chávez-anointed successor, Nicolas Maduro, with the court finally becoming "the main institutional arm" of populist attempts to "annul the opposition's use of the constitution to hold it accountable."[19] As the entire political system took a rapid authoritarian turn under Maduro, the court continued to offer reliable support to the executive. The ultimate act of endorsing autocratic rule was the TSJ's support, contrary to the constitution, for setting up a body called the "Constituent National Assembly," which asserts authority supreme over all other branches of government, including the parliament. In doing so, the court gave the green light to the final destruction of democracy.

Another example is the Supreme Court in India – for a long time praised as one of the most progressive and activist apex courts on the world – which has played both "proactive" and "reactive" roles when complying with the demands of the Modi regime. "Proactively," it triggered an unusual procedure ("public interest litigation" but activated by the court itself) to confirm the National Register of Citizens in the state of Assam – a signature action of the government that risked millions

---

[18] Account by Sánchez Urribarrí, ibid.
[19] Ibid.

becoming stateless because the law impossibly required individuals to produce documentary proof of citizenship going back to 1971. The Supreme Court's approach in helping the government in its quest to identify illegal migrants from neighboring Bangladesh was characterized as "harsh and cruel" by legal scholar Alok Prasanna Kumar.[20] As far as the Supreme Court's "reactive" role is concerned, it failed to consider many challenges against the Modi government. These included several controversial issues central to Modi's actions, such as a unilateral change made to the constitutional status of Kashmir by the central government, bringing an end to decades of semi-autonomous rule in the region.[21]

The court has also tolerated obvious lies told it with a straight face by the government. For instance, after a strict lockdown imposed by the government in March 2020 led to a massive crisis in which *millions* of Indians were forced to walk hundreds of miles to their homes during the height of the summer, with many dying as a result, the solicitor general declared before the court that not a single migrant was walking on the road at that point. But the court did nothing to reproach the government's counsel for telling such an outrageous lie. Instead, the court ordered the government to...form a committee to address citizen queries regarding the pandemic threat. Indian legal scholar Anuj Bhuwania concludes, with sadness, that "[d]uring the Modi period, not only has the [Supreme] Court failed to perform its constitutional role as a check on governmental excesses, it has acted as a cheerleader for the Modi government's agenda."[22]

Hostile Takeovers

The strategies employed by populist politicians against courts vary widely, ranging from a frontal assault and capture (Poland, Hungary, Venezuela) to doing next to nothing. The latter approach was taken by

---

[20] Alok Prasanna Kumar, "'More Executive-Minded Than the Executive': The Supreme Court's Role in the Implementation of the NRC," *National Law School of India Review*, 31 (2019), 203–210 at 203.

[21] For the background, see Hannah Ellis-Petersen, "India Strips Kashmir of Special Status and Divides It in Two," *Guardian* (November 1, 2019), www.theguardian.com/world/2019/oct/31/india-strips-kashmir-of-special-status-and-divides-it-in-two.

[22] See Anuj Bhuwana, "The Indian Supreme Court in the Modi Era," in Tom Gerald Daly and Wojciech Sadurski (eds.), *Democracy 2020: Assessing Constitutional Decay, Breakdown, and Renewal Worldwide*, IACL-AIDC Global Roundtable E-book (December 2020), 150–153 at 151.

Brazil's president, Jair Bolsonaro, who basically had avoided any structural interferences with the court system until the party recently announced that it had proposed a constitutional amendment to lower the retirement age for judges, which would possibly allow Bolsonaro to introduce at least two of his loyalists to the Supreme Court.[23] But by and large, he confined himself to verbal assaults upon critical judges[24] and the placement of loyalists in judicial positions. The institutional structure of the courts has also been left intact in India. Modi's proposed constitutional amendment changing the system of judicial selection by removing the system of "judges appointing judges" was invalidated by the Supreme Court in 2015 – and the regime stopped at that. But President Modi has not abstained from other attempts to influence courts, including, in particular, the nation's top court. He has refused to act on many nominations (so far, 140) to India's high courts, has sent back politically "undesirable" appointments to the Supreme Court, and allegedly blackmailed the chief justice to get him to assign politically sensitive cases to favorable benches.[25] However, so far he has given up on any radical institutional and structural changes. But judges in other countries ruled by populists have not been *that* lucky.

Admittedly, today's populists do not go as far as the arch-populist of yesteryear, Juan Peron, who had initiated the impeachment and trial of four out of five justices of the Supreme Court of Argentina. (An even better trick was used by a military government in Myanmar in 2012, which decided to impeach *all* nine judges of the Constitutional Court – but then no one would describe Myanmar as a populist state.) These days, the populist tool kit for dealing with recalcitrant judges is more subtle and includes a long list of measures, often applied simultaneously, including removing judges and court-packing, reducing the court's scope of jurisdiction, manipulating the rules of appointment, changing the

---

[23] See Katya Kozicki and Rick Pianaro, "From Hardball to Packing the Court: 'PEC do Pyjama' and the Attempt to Attack the Brazilian Supreme Court," in Tom Gerald Daly and Wojciech Sadurski (eds.), *Democracy 2020: Assessing Constitutional Decay, Breakdown, and Renewal Worldwide*, IACL-AIDC Global Roundtable E-book (December 2020), 59–62.

[24] See Emilio Peluso Neder Meyer and João Andrade Neto, "Courts Are Finally Standing Up to Bolsonaro," *Verfassungsblog* (August 9, 2021), www.verfassungsblog.de/courts-are-finally-standing-up-to-bolsonaro/.

[25] See Tarunabh Khaitan, "Introduction: The World's Most Powerful Court on the Brink?" IACL-AIDC Blog (May 15, 2018), www.blog-iacl-aidc.org/blog/2018/5/17/introduction-the-words-most-powerful-court-on-the-brink.

voting rules on the court, refusing to publish judgments, or changing salaries and other benefits or working conditions.

Whether a populist leader uses all of these strategies or just one (usually, court-packing) depends not only on his perception of how conducive current judges are to populist pressures, but also on his (here, a gendered pronoun is warranted) optimism about the future prospects of his own power. This, in turn, depends to some extent on the system of government. American political theorist Andrew Arato notes that presidents in strong presidential systems (where the president is largely immune to the changes in the composition of the parliament) usually restrict themselves to old-style court-packing: See, for example, in Argentina, Venezuela (initially, at least), or Peru.[26] But populist leaders who are less certain of their future, especially in parliamentary or mixed systems, as in Hungary or Poland, opt for the whole suite of measures. Such leaders also apply long-term measures, such as reducing the competences of the top court.

If court-packing proves to be sufficient, other measures taken may be redundant. This was so in the case of Poland. After a wide range of measures meant to disable the "hostile" CT were taken throughout 2016, the PiS-dominated parliament happily restored the status quo ante once the tribunal became fully "friendly" to PiS, as a result of a series of changes on the court's composition. In fact, the populists *needed* a strong, friendly court if it was to perform its "enabling" function.

The story about the capture and eventual enlisting of the Polish CT as an active helper of PiS is long and tedious. I have described it in great detail elsewhere.[27] Here, I provide only a bird's-eye view. (And the bird is instructed to ignore side stories.) First, it is important to realize why Poland's populist rulers considered the tribunal to be dangerous. This was because the CT had played a reasonably active role in fine-tuning the details of Polish democracy after the fall of Communism, and had derailed some legislative schemes as unconstitutional, such as the so-called lustration law, which would render a large group of people as second-class citizens for their, real or alleged, involvement in the ancient regime. Many of these schemes were concocted when PiS was in power for the first time in 2005–2007. Hence, when it returned to power in 2015, Kaczyński's party knew that they had a lot to fear from the tribunal. This was especially because PiS lacked the required supermajority (two-

---

[26] Arato, "Populism, Constitutional Courts, and Civil Society," p. 319.
[27] Sadurski, *Poland's Constitutional Breakdown*, pp. 58–95.

thirds) for constitutional change, and so all of the systemic changes had to be made in ordinary statutes, which were themselves vulnerable to the tribunal's scrutiny.

The Polish saga of how PiS disabled a hostile CT and then enlisted a friendly CT is a Play in Five Acts:

> Act 1: Already having its own president, as soon as PiS gains a parliamentary majority in late 2015, it adopts an unusual, irregular parliamentary "resolution" that the five new judges of the CT, elected shortly before the end of the previous legislative term by the former parliament, were elected improperly. This notwithstanding that the Polish parliament had no power to check the validity of judicial elections. Then the president refuses to take the oath of office from those judges (despite the president having a duty to take the oath of office of elected judges).
>
> Act 2: On the eve of a crucial session of the CT in December 2015 to deal with the situation, the Parliament elects five new judges, three of them illegally (hence now called "quasi judges;"); in the middle of the night the president takes the oath of office from them (hence they are also known as "midnight judges,") and the next morning, escorted by police they enter the building of the CT and take offices there.
>
> Act 3: PiS judges are still in a minority, so the parliament invents several new statutes, the main consequence of which would be to paralyze the CT's decision-making, with such ingenious devices as strictly requiring the consideration of cases in the order of their arrival at the court (which would basically immunize all new statutes passed by PiS for a long time, due to the existing backlog), the new and elevated requirement of a qualified majority in court votes (which would give the new pro-PiS judges the power of veto, etc.), the power of even a few judges to postpone the consideration of any case by several months, and so forth...
>
> Act 4: The CT, still without a PiS majority, invalidates all these statutes one-by-one, but the government refuses to publish these judgments in the official gazette (the government has no such authority, but the judgments enter into force only at the moment of publication); in addition, bombarded by consecutive legislative bills concerning *itself*, the CT has no time and resources to consider almost anything else – this can be considered "existential" jurisprudence[28] because it concerns the very existence of the CT itself.
>
> Act 5: In December 2016, almost exactly a year after the whole play began, after the terms of several "hostile" (non-PiS appointed) judges end and they have to step down, and new, "friendly" judges are appointed in

---

[28] See Tomasz Tadeusz Koncewicz, "'Existential Judicial Review' in Retrospect, 'Subversive Jurisprudence' in Prospect," *Verfassungsblog* (October 7, 2018), www.verfassungsblog.de/existential-judicial-review-in-retrospect-subversive-jurisprudence-in-prospect-the-polish-constitutional-court-then-now-and-tomorrow.

their place, the transformed CT elects Ms. Julia Przyłębska (in a questionable procedure, but never mind,) a favorite of PiS. A new CT is born, with a pro-PiS majority, and – surprise, surprise – all of the legislative proposals manufactured throughout 2016 are forgotten, and a new statute on the CT basically restores the status quo as it had been before 2015. No need for a disabled court anymore: The CT must be strong to perform the roles assigned to it by the PiS rulers.

This is the end of the play. And the end of the Constitutional Tribunal, as Poles had known it. Przyłębska's CT is part and parcel of the government – it criticizes the opposition, praises the government, invalidates those old laws inconvenient to the rulers, and happily endorses new laws, no matter their constitutional status.

And just as a one-page outline of a Shakespeare drama cannot give even an approximate picture of the thick storyline, so the above synopsis of five acts is incapable of taking in various meaningful details and turns of action. Though what is rich in the former is tawdry in the latter.

Such as the fact that, when various incapacitating laws reached the CT over the course of 2016, the government insisted that these new laws must be considered by the tribunal *under the procedures proposed by these very laws under scrutiny*; a truly Kafkaesque (or, to change a literary allusion, Catch-22) situation in which one and the same law would be the *subject matter* and the *standard* of scrutiny at the same time.

...Or that one of the proposed innovations was a proviso that the absence of the prosecutor general (under a new PiS law, the PiS minister of justice, and the most rabid anti-judiciary head-kicker in the government) in any case where he declares a legal interest would prevent the consideration of a challenge (hence, a government minister may disable the handing down of any judgment, without having to produce any reasons for his absence).

...Or that, as soon as Julia Przyłębska became chief justice, all references to the judgments (inconvenient to the government) that the government refused to publish disappeared from the list of judgments on the website of the tribunal, a truly Orwellian gesture of erasing the judgments as if they never existed.

...Or that, as soon as she took office, Chief Justice Przyłębska sent the vice-chairman of the court, Professor Stanisław Biernat, on compulsory retirement, on the basis that his accumulated entitlement for annual leave must be used, or it would become a financial burden to the tribunal. In this ingenious way, she had disabled her most vocal opponent until the end of his term of office in mid-2017.

...Or that two other "old" judges were excluded from participating in the tribunal until the end of their terms of office, as a result of an ingenious trick. The prosecutor general/minister of justice charged them with having been improperly elected many years before (a self-evidently baseless charge), and then objected to their presence in any case in which he or his representatives appeared, on the basis that these two judges may hold a grudge against him, and thus be biased. And since he can join any case before the CT, these two judges were effectively removed.

Or...but enough. The play is getting tedious. There is nothing particularly subtle about it. Just a vicious, unsubtle use of force against a once important pillar of Polish democracy.

The assault upon the Hungarian constitutional court was somewhat different than that wreaked upon its Polish counterpart. In some ways it was softer – there was no barrage of ever-changing legislation; no overt violation of express constitutional and legislative rules. In other ways, it was harsher because it was more comprehensive – it reduced the jurisdiction of the court, not simply attended to its personnel.

The government tool kit included the three Ps: altering the court's powers, procedures, and personnel. Regarding the first P: Fidesz stripped the Constitutional Court (CC) of its power to review budgetary matters and evaluate constitutional amendments on matters of substance. The removal of powers to scrutinize constitutional amendments was a reaction to a tit-for-tat that had been settled in the early days of Orbán's regime: The government would adopt a law, the CC would deem it unconstitutional, the government would overrule the CC's decision by codifying the problematic law as a constitutional amendment, the CC would then attempt to evaluate the amendment, and so on. So Orbán simply excluded this latter possibility. But perhaps even more shockingly, in an amendment to the Fundamental Law, Fidesz barred the CC from referring to *its own* rulings handed down prior to the new 2011 constitution. It therefore cut off the CC from its entire pre-Orbán case law legacy. I cannot think of any other court in the world that saw its entire doctrine elaborated prior to a new constitution thrown into a black hole by the eager constitution-maker. (I will come back to the issue below.)

Regarding procedures, from 1990 everyone could challenge a law to the court for its unconstitutionality, in what was called an *actio popularis*. Fidesz removed the *actio popularis* procedure, thus extinguishing citizen-initiated constitutional complaints. This has left only government-controlled channels for complaints. Moreover, the government has recently enhanced the role of the CC in *defending* the interests of the *government* itself. Under a new law on constitutional complaint procedure of December 2019, the authorities may challenge any judicial decision before the Hungarian CC, even if it has already become final, if it violates their rights and curtails their powers under the FL.[29] This firmly entrenches the CC in its status as the government's helper and enabler.

But it was the third "P" – personnel of the court – that Fidesz used to its greatest benefit. Court-packing was greatly facilitated by the way constitutional court judges were elected: Hungary is one of very few countries in the world (along with Poland and Germany) where judges are elected by a simple parliamentary majority. While in Germany this system has led to complex deals, bargains, and compromises between various parliamentary parties, Poland and Hungary settled on an unrefined version of majority election: Winner takes all. And having won a parliamentary majority, Orbán had no problem packing the court with his sycophants. Combined with the ingenious decision to increase the number of judges, the majority was soon pro-Fidesz.

The scenario in Hungary went more smoothly compared to court-packing in Poland. Almost immediately after his parliamentary victory in 2010, Orbán changed the composition of the parliamentary committee in charge of making recommendations for candidates, and quickly achieved an absolute majority in that committee. Soon after, a constitutional amendment increased the number of judges from eleven to fifteen, and these extra judges, plus two vacancies in 2011 and 2012, assured Fidesz's majority on the court. As a minor additional change, the method of selecting the president (chief justice) also changed. Originally, he or she was elected by the full court for a short period of just three years, to prevent too much power being concentrated in one office. Under the new rules, the *parliament* elects the president for the period of his or her mandate, which may be up to twelve years. This assures that a Fidesz-supported judge will preside over the court long after any possible transition of power in the parliament. In this way, the "insurance" functions of constitutional courts have been activated in Hungary – but to the benefit of Orbán only.

It is notable that the Constitutional Court's most vigorous response was mounted against the government's interference with its competencies. The explanation is simple: The alteration of competences strikes at the core of the court's nature and warrants more of a response than

---

[29] European Commission, 2020 Rule of Law Report, Country Chapter on the Rule of Law Situation in Hungary, Brussels 30.09.2020, SWD (2020) 316 final, p. 18.

changes to court procedures. As to the exclusion of the relevance of all case law prior to 2010, the Court gently tried to reintroduce this possibility in a 2012 decision in which it suggested (commonsensically) that if the new constitutional article under interpretation is substantively the same as the equivalent article in the old constitution, then judicial case law developed under the latter *may* be applied. But the court quickly appended a cautionary proviso: If the court wished to refer to old, pre-2010 case law, it must provide particularly strong reasons for doing so. A year later, in 2013, the court added that it may do so only if it finds it necessary. This was not a satisfactory solution, more like desperate face-saving than principled judicial doctrine. As Eszter Bodnár says: "[T]he risk is that the Court decides on a case-by-case basis whether or not to follow its previous case law, and it depends solely on the future composition of the Court."[30]

A different approach was applied in Chávez's Venezuela, focusing mainly on judicial appointments. It was through relentless court-packing that the TSJ (Venezuela's court of last resort, with a Constitutional Chamber) was captured, serving to reinforce populist control over the court at critical junctures in the populist regime's struggle against recalcitrant institutions and political opposition. Soon after coming to power, Chávez redesigned the apex court in a new constitution of 2000, which replaced the Supreme Court with the Supreme Tribunal, with an increased number of judges and different appointment rules. At the beginning, its justices were appointed for just one year, knowing full well that any renewal would depend on their behavior. After the second round of appointments, in which several justices were replaced, the court (and especially its Constitutional Chamber) found itself at the center of several conflicts, as civil strife and political polarization grew, punctuated by a failed coup in April 2002 and a planned recall referendum against Chávez. The year 2004 saw the further expansion of the TSJ to thirty-two judges, with only a handful of pro-opposition judges remaining on the bench. One of the leading anti-Chávez judges, Franklin Arreche Guttiérez, was removed by the legislature for his judgment refusing to prosecute the April 2002 military officers. By 2005, court-packing resulted in a complete takeover of the TSJ by the Chávez regime; the

---

[30] Eszter Bodnár, "Disarming the Guardians: The Transformation of the Hungarian Constitutional Court after 2010," in Martin Krygier, Adam Czarnota, and Wojciech Sadurski (eds.), *Anti-constitutional Populism* (in press).

tribunal was now the main tool of the presidency against a new parliamentary majority.

Court-packing is also a favored strategy used by the Philippines president Rodrigo Duterte since the beginning of his term in 2016, and his preferred measure is through impeachment procedures, which he has used against his own vice president, the head of the national election authority, and the ombudsman. But his top achievement was to oust the chief justice of the Supreme Court, Maria Lourdes Sereno. The enmity between the president and chief justice was obvious from the beginning of his tenure: She had criticized Duterte's heavy-handed approach to the "war on drugs," while he publicly stated to her not too subtly on April 9, 2018: "I am putting you on notice that I am your enemy."[31] (In fact, Duterte's antagonism toward Chief Justice Sereno was visible from literally day one of his presidency: He refused to take his oath before her.) The impeachment process developed quickly, with a two-pronged attack on the chief justice: the first was an impeachment complaint in the Congress (launched in August 2017 by a Duterte-aligned lawyer); the second was triggered by the solicitor general's "*quo warranto*" petition to the Supreme Court itself (a legal action to determine a person's right to hold office). The Supreme Court was faster than the Congress, and in an eight-to-six judgment, the court removed the chief justice from office on May 11, 2018. It did not escape the attention of one of the dissenting judges, Marvic Leonen, that the justices who voted to remove the chief justice also testified earlier in congressional impeachment hearings. In any event, after Sereno's removal, Duterte appointed four chief justices, each serving very brief terms, along with the majority of new justices to the fifteen-member court. As one observer notes, each of the Duterte appointees "ha[s] consistently and reliably voted in his favour."[32] As a result, under Duterte administration, the Supreme Court has not vetoed any legislation and action important to the government. And this includes matters as important as imposition of martial law upon the southern Philippines, the arrests of two opposition senators, and non-

---

[31] Nicole Lorena, "Timeline: The Many Times Duterte and Sereno Clashed," Rappler.com (May 20, 2018), www.amp.rappler.com/newsbreak/iq/202763-timeline-maria-lourdes-sereno-rodrigo-duterte-clashes.

[32] Edcel John Aibarra, "The Philippine Supreme Court under Duterte: Reshaped, Unwilling to Annul, and Unable to Restrain," Social Science Research Council Democracy Papers (November 10, 2020), www.items.ssrc.org/democracy-papers/democratic-erosion/the-philippine-supreme-court-under-duterte-reshaped-unwilling-to-annul-and-unable-to-restrain/.

release of Duterte's health records – all were challenged before the Supreme Court, unsuccessfully. The court's "co-operativeness" was assured by skillful court-packing.

But not all populist rulers have used such heavy-handed tactics. In Brazil, legal elites supported President Jair Bolsonaro and his family without any dramatic attempts by the government to attack or capture the courts. Brazilian legal scholar Alexandre Fleck notes that the Brazilian judiciary is in fact quite independent. Their salaries, tenure, and general immunity from punishment for their decisions have not been targeted by recent reforms. Nor has the nation's constitutional court, the Supreme Court, been captured. Nevertheless, Fleck argues, the Supreme Court helped in Bolsonaro's rise and also helped him attack his political opponents. Fleck's takeaway is that the Brazilian case shows how "members of the Judiciary can effectively turn into agents of illiberalism even if they are not apparently structurally vulnerable to attacks from the Executive."[33] This is, of course, quite different from the Venezuelan case. Bolsonaro has not presented any plans for any judicial reform. His attacks on the top court have been merely rhetorical, as evidenced in his verbal threats to "close the court."

Bolsonaro is the first Brazilian president since democratization to openly praise the former military regime and has appointed ten out of twenty-three cabinet members from the military. Over the course of his rule, he has learned to rely for support on not just the army, but also on Brazilian legal elites. As Fleck observes, these elites played an important role in making the rise of populists such as Bolsonaro possible, have assisted him to resist accountability, and have enabled his corruption. A significant factor clearing the way for Bolsonaro to assume power was the conviction of popular ex-President Lula in July 2017, just prior to the 2018 elections. In early 2018, Lula's defence team requested an order of habeas corpus from the Brazilian Supreme Court (STF), on the basis that Lula's appeals to superior courts from the initial conviction were still pending. There was some precedent for this dating back to a habeas corpus decision in 2009, which held that sentences should be served only after the exhaustion of all appeals. To put it most cautiously, there were legal arguments in favor and against arresting Lula immediately – but the political significance was unambiguous. As a result of the STF's judgment

---

[33] Alexandre Fleck Soares Brandao, "When Bolsonaro and the Judges Go Shopping: How Brazil's Legal Elites Opened the Door for Bolsonaro's Bad Populism," in Martin Krygier, Adam Czarnota, and Wojciech Sadurski (eds.), *Anti-constitutional Populism* (in press).

of April 5, 2018, Lula was arrested and was required to serve his jail sentence – just six months before the presidential election.

Capturing Common Courts

The Polish takeover, successfully executed against the Constitutional Tribunal, was subsequently repeated by Polish rulers vis-à-vis all courts, including Poland's Supreme Court. But here the task was much more difficult. It is one thing to take over an institution of fifteen members, fully elected by the chamber of parliament in which you have the required majority. It is another thing to establish full control over nearly 10,000 judges across the country – a broad structure headed by an apex court of more than seventy judges. All of these judges were professionals, non-politically appointed, and possessed security of tenure until retirement.

Hence, the capture of the "regular" judiciary has been a much more complex and time-consuming process, which began in 2016 and was only completed in early 2021.

The legislative package designed to handle this task was made up of three parts, involving the passage of new statutes on (1) the Supreme Court, (2) the "common courts," and (3) the National Council of Judiciary (KRS). The three statutes were of course easily bulldozed through the parliament in express time, in spite of theatrical hesitations by the president that caused slight delays.

The KRS, the body central to the entire judicial system and responsible for appointing and promoting judges (through recommendations to the president), was easiest to grab. The new statute extinguished the constitutionally guaranteed tenures of incumbent members. It also changed the mode of elections from the old system in which the KRS's judicial members were elected by judges, to a new system in which KRS members are appointed by the parliament, and hence by the parliamentary majority, and hence by Jarosław Kaczyński. As a result of the changes, twenty-three out of twenty-five members of KRS are now, directly or indirectly, PiS nominees. PiS has control over the central engine of the system controlling judicial personnel. But this was a comparatively easy task.

Much more difficult to achieve was the capture of the "common courts." To start with, the parliament adopted a whole package of rules that effectively subjected all judges to the minister of justice's whim. The vindictive, authoritarian minister, Zbigniew Ziobro (perhaps still reeling from his legal studies in which he graduated with very mediocre grades, and was later unsuccessful in various attempts at admission to the bar), restructured the courts in order to obtain full control over appointment of court presidents who play a central role in case assignment. Ziobro quickly replaced these main positions with his loyalists. In a few months following the adoption of the new law of 2017, he replaced ten out of eleven court of appeal presidents (who also exercise control over lower courts in their jurisdiction).

But it is the refurbished "disciplinary" system that has played the most significant and most invidious role in controlling what judges do. In contrast to rule-of-law states, where disciplining unjudicial behavior is natural, the Polish disciplinary system was built to punish judges for *judicial decisions* the authorities do not like. As a result, it has now become an alternative to a system of appellate judicial review, in which higher courts control the decisions of lower courts. But this alternative differs from regular appeals, in two respects. Appeals are not intended to *punish* judges, but rather to allow applicants to seek correction of legal mistakes. In the new system, the objections are political and the judges are truly *disciplined*, punished for conduct that displeases the regime. Indeed, in Poland under PiS, the system has been set up such that judges are disciplined – and removed from office – for exercising their official functions. In other words, for doing what they must do. For example, after an altercation between the PiS Speaker and an opposition member in the hall of the parliament (Sejm) on December 16, 2016, the Speaker (of course backed up by the majority) decided to transfer the proceedings to another room (the "Column Hall") with questionable facilities for vote counting, and with many opposition MPs absent, largely due to the overall chaos. The agenda was not insignificant: the budget for the next year was adopted in the "Column Hall." The case came before Judge Igor Tuleya of the Warsaw Court of Appeal, who was suspended for a judgment in which he held that it was illegal to hold a parliamentary session outside the main hall, in a way that precluded a proper vote count. At the time of writing these words, he is facing no fewer than seven disciplinary proceedings. Disciplinary action has also been taken against several judges for sending questions of preliminary reference to the Court of Justice of the European Union – which is not only the right of judges in a member state of the European Union, but also their duty, if they have doubts about the proper interpretation of EU law applicable to any case they consider.

The disciplinary system has been reconstructed at all levels of the judiciary to allow the minister to exercise direct control over court proceedings. At its apex, a Disciplinary Chamber has been attached to the Supreme Court. But it is a strange sort of chamber. For all practical purposes, it is a separate extraordinary court that has full independence of the Supreme Court. Its "judges" receive much better remuneration (40 percent loading) and are exclusively appointed by the newly established KRS (hence, by ruling politicians). Comparisons to a Star Chamber are not inappropriate when considering this body.

There are many independent and brave judges in Poland who decide in accordance with law and conscience. That is what I found when, in June 2020, I watched Judge Sylwia Urbańska in a Warsaw courtroom ruling in my favor in a trial in which PiS had charged me with defamation. And that is what I again felt in March 2021, when I watched (this time in an online hearing due to Covid-19) Judge Agnieszka Prokopowicz ruling for me in another trial in which the state-owned TVP had charged me with criminal defamation. It is of course easy to admire judges when they rule in your favor. But there was more to it than simply the result, I thought. Rather, both judgments were paragons of judicial interpretation of the highest quality, not just under the Polish codes (respectively, civil and criminal,) but also the Polish constitution and the European Court of Human Rights. "In this trial, the court determined that freedom of expression has primacy over the good name of the plaintiff," said Judge Urbańska – and the plaintiff was none other than the ruling party, PiS. And in the criminal defamation trial, Judge Prokopowicz said that "the right to criticize improprieties openly, even if it cannot be verified in terms of truth-falsity, promotes democracy and pluralism of opinion which has its basis in the Constitution of the Republic of Poland...Democratic society cannot survive without tolerance, openness and pluralism." While at the time of writing these words, both cases are still pending on appeal or cassation, I feel reasonably confident that I will encounter judges of similar integrity and wisdom in my legal clashes with Poland's rulers.

But brave judges in Poland have to pay a heavy price for their courage. They may be "disciplined" for their judgments, removed from office, suspended in office and forced to take huge pay cuts, demoted, or sent to a court far from their residence. They may be vilified in state-controlled media. The last thing actually happened to both "my" judges. For instance, a few hours after Judge Prokopowicz announced her judgment in my favor, the evening news bulletin of TVP featured a story in which she was denounced as member of the judicial association "Iustitia," which is critical of the government's deformation of the judicial system.

The TVP further informed its viewers that I am "friendly" toward "Iustitia" (true) and therefore Judge Prokopowicz may be biased in favor of me (not true.)[34]

While many judges are still independent in their minds and hearts, the institutional system is now fully politicized and subject to the will of politicians. And to one politician in particular – Zbigniew Ziobro – minister of justice and prosecutor general, who is also the leader of PiS's junior coalition partner, a party called "Solidary Poland." As a result of all the legislative changes of recent years, the minister of justice now directly or indirectly decides on (1) the composition of the body that nominates all judges (the KRS), (2) the appointment and discharge of court presidents, (3) the allocation of specific judges to particular courts, (4) whether to permit judges to continue working beyond retirement age, (5) the appointments of "lay judges" in the Supreme Court, (6) the composition of disciplinary panels against particular judges...and so forth. And among the many government apparatchiks who vilify independent judges, this guardian of the Polish legal order is vilifier-in-chief.

But the Supreme Court has raised a special obstacle against Poland's populist rulers.

The Masters and Margarita[35]

The Supreme Court in Warsaw is housed in a stunning modern building – all bright-green columns and glass. Situated at Krasiński Square, from which you see the elegant skyline of Warsaw's Old Town and across the square, the majestic, baroque building of the National Library, located in the old Krasiński Palace. Inscribed on each of the court building's seventy-six columns are huge Latin maxims ("*paremias*" is the scholarly word) along with their Polish translations: *Leges ab omnibus intellegi debent* (Statutes should be understandable to all), *Non omne quod licet honestum est* (Not everything that is permitted is honest), or *Lex retro non agit* (Law is not retroactive). A team of legal scholars compiled these maxims under the leadership of Professor Witold Wołodkiewicz, my old Roman Law professor at the University of Warsaw, when the building was completed in 1999.

---

[34] See account of the trial and of the TVP's attack on the judge in www.wirtualnemedia.pl/artykul/telewizja-polska-wyrok-proces-sad-wojciech-sadurski-wiadomosci-goebbelsowskie-media.

[35] With apologies to Mikhail Bulgakov, *The Master and Margarita*.

On a hot day in August 2018, a huge banner at the front of the Supreme Court building's main entrance dwarfed these classical statements. Held by several people wearing T-shirts emblazoned with the word "Constitution," the huge banner urged: "Do not surrender! We support the judges!" As I entered the air-conditioned hall early that morning, I saw more protestors inside, holding a huge banner with a similar slogan. A small number of security people treated the intruders gently, but firmly banned them from entering the inner sanctum of the hall, which contained elevators leading up to the judges' chambers.

I was lucky. The chief justice was already in her office, and when I called her from a reception downstairs, she let me in. Professor Małgorzata Gersdorf, my old friend from our studies at law school, received me in her large office on the first floor. From her energetic and friendly demeanor, it was hard to immediately gather that she was in a truly dramatic situation, best captured by one word: embattled. "I will not give in. I will not resign. They are trying all the tricks of the trade, but I will not help them, and I will not resign," she told me over a coffee.

"They," about whom Gersdorf was talking, were President Andrzej Duda and Minister of Justice Zbigniew Ziobro, plus the entire officialdom of PiS. After the CT had been disabled, the Supreme Court remained the main judicial thorn in PiS's side, and the intransigent, brave Gersdorf – the main bête noire of the regime. No wonder. The Supreme Court is the only court with the power to undo all judgments by all courts in the nation, either through a normal appellate procedure, or through an extraordinary appellate process ("cassation").

But the most important reason why the Supreme Court *had* to be captured to make the rulers feel safe was a seemingly minuscule function in the context of its other powers. It could consider electoral disputes and decide whether the officially announced result was correct. And such decisions also have consequences for the budgetary assignment of campaign expenditures by parties and candidates as well as party financing from the national budget between the elections. The aim of capturing the court was to have politicians elect judges who will in turn decide favorably on the same politicians' election results and party budgets. Małgorzata Gersdorf, along with a group of "older" judges all elected before the new KRS began appointing only party loyalists to the SC, stood in the way.

The politicians found a simple solution: They passed a law that lowered the retirement age for all Supreme Court judges. A new retirement age of 65 years would help get rid of about a third of judges of the court (to be replaced with PiS-friendly ones), including the chief justice. But there was a problem. The chief justice's term of office is specifically determined by the constitution as six years. And she still had two years to go. But PiS was in a hurry, and they wanted to overturn the constitutional term of office with a statute lowering the retirement age of judges.

The idea that you can purge an institution in such a vulgar way and in breach of express constitutional pronouncements is of course shocking. When President Duda was asked in a rare interview with independent TV station TVN: "How about if your opponents try to get rid of you by lowering the retirement age for President and so overturn your term of office," the 47-year-old Duda answered smugly: "I still have a long time to go before 65." Clearly, he did not understand the point of the question.

Gersdorf refused to announce that she would step down and insisted that she would continue until the end of her constitutional term of office on April 30, 2020. After some inept maneuvering, combined with pressure from EU institutions, the government had to give in. It was a spectacular defeat for PiS – and the death of the court was postponed. For two years, to be precise. Supported by a huge majority of her fellow judges, Gersdorf stayed until the end of her term. Eventually, her court was fully captured in the first half of 2020, later than PiS planned. Despite low support in the secret ballot for candidates to be presented to the president, Duda appointed Dr. Małgorzata Manowska as the new chief justice: a person fully loyal to the PiS leadership and a longtime collaborator and friend of Minister of Justice Ziobro. She was appointed, notwithstanding that the overwhelming majority of Supreme Court judges voted for a distinguished alternative, Professor Włodzimierz Wróbel. He was soon charged with disciplinary offenses. With a large influx of completely new judges appointed to the two new chambers (and to facilitate it, KRS lowered the threshold of qualifications required for nomination), the Supreme Court thus ceased to exist as an independent top court in Poland.

The Supreme Court of Hungary (renamed in 2011 as the Kúria) followed a slightly different trajectory, but it resulted in a similar outcome. Its current president was elected by the parliament in October 2020 – with votes cast exclusively by majority MPs – after the term of office of his predecessor, Mr. Péter Darák, expired. The ruling party's loyalist Zsolt András Varga (previously a Fidesz-appointed prosecutor) had long been groomed for the position – but he faced two problems. First, he did not have five years of legal practice as an ordinary judge, a statutory prerequisite, and second, at the time he applied, he was not an "ordinary" judge – another condition. A statutory change quickly removed these obstacles. First, practice as judge of the Constitutional Court (as Mr. Varga had) was allowed to count for the purpose of the five years requirement and, second, all judges of Constitutional Court were allowed to "register" as ordinary judges, by a simple application. These two quick changes in law paved the way for Mr. Varga to the top of the Kúria. The National Council of Judiciary (a representative body of Hungarian judges) issued a negative opinion about Mr. Varga's candidacy, but the parliament was not bothered about such details. Shortly after, at least seven other sitting judges of Constitutional Court were appointed in a fast-track procedure as ordinary judges – which will help them to move on to the Kúria once their constitutional court term expires. Their happy escape route from the CC to the Supreme Court will benefit the ruling party, without doubt. These judges are likely to provide support for the state in cases in which it will be a party. And it should not come as a surprise that shortly after Fidesz managed to place its trusted person at the top of the Kúria, the minister of justice submitted a new bill further increasing the Kúria president's powers. The law was adopted in December 2020.[36]

The happy outcome for Mr. Varga in 2020 stood in a stark contrast to one of the previous presidents of the Supreme Court, Mr. András Baka, who, at the time the Supreme Court was converted into the Kúria in 2011, had wished to continue as the president of the top court. At the time, he was prevented from maintaining the position by the same ruling majority because...he had not served a five-year tenure as a regular judge. (He had been a judge of the European Court of Human Rights in Strasbourg, on behalf of Hungary.) As an aside: Mr. Baka had had a disagreeable habit of criticizing the Orbán government's reforms of the judiciary.

Judicial Resistance

This leads us to the other side of the populists-versus-courts interaction – the conduct of the courts themselves, and in particular their responses to populist assaults and attempts (occasionally successful) at institutional capture. Again, there has been a wide range of responses, from overt and courageous resistance through to various strategies of accommodation,

---

[36] See Amnesty International, "Status of the Hungarian Judiciary," Amnesty International Hungary, Budapest (2021), pp. 26–27.

crisis control, or lying low, to willful and enthusiastic support for populist actions.

Polish judges have used various forms to signal their criticism of the "reforms" and their solidarity with embattled colleagues. During the campaign to oust Chief Justice Gersdorf before the end of her constitutional term of office in June 2018, the sixty-three sitting judges of the Supreme Court adopted a resolution of support for her and also a declaration of disagreement with the government's unconstitutional actions. The second declaration was quite grave in its tone. If the new provisions enter into force, the judges warned, it would "constitute an obvious violation by the legislature of one of the fundamental guarantees of the independence of the judiciary and will soon significantly disrupt the normal functioning of the Supreme Court." How prophetic they were.

Judges of lower courts also kept on signing various open letters and declarations. When the new Disciplinary Chamber threatened to remove judicial immunity for district court judge Igor Tuleya, 581 judges from all over Poland signed a letter of support for him in March 2021. Various provincial courts have also adopted similar declarations in defense of their colleagues. Judges have also utilized a more judicial method of protest, such as sending preliminary references to the European Union's top court in Luxembourg (the CJEU). When the Supreme Court took this step for the first time in August 2018, at the height of a crisis in which the government tried to force the judges to leave the Supreme Court, it was later described as "a cry for help from the president [chief justice] of the Court [Małgorzata Gersdorf] and another twenty-seven judges whom the government had moved to fire."[37] Many more similar preliminary references have since been sent to Luxembourg, to the great displeasure of the government, demanding the CJEU use EU law to provide an authoritative interpretation of the illegality of the Polish statutes establishing the extraordinary chambers in the Supreme Court as well as other elements of PiS's "reform" of courts. Some of these questions resulted in CJEU judgments that should have led to suspension of those pseudo-chambers. But they didn't. The government stood firm in defending the Star Chamber it had created and denounced the CJEU for playing politics.

---

[37] Kim Lane Scheppele and R. Daniel Kelemen, "Defending Democracy in EU Member States: Beyond Article 7 TEU," in Francesca Bignami (ed.), *EU Law in Populist Times: Crises and Prospects* (Cambridge: Cambridge University Press, 2020), pp. 413–456 at 453.

Taking a public stand against the executive and denouncing governmental interference with judicial independence is, for judges, a brave thing to do. If they are on the top court and enjoy strong guarantees against discharge, they may do so with relative impunity, and earn deserved fame. On January 12, 2018, four senior judges of the Indian Supreme Court held an unprecedented press conference raising concerns of "outside influences."[38] The protest was in response to the highly suspicious manipulation of the way sensitive cases were being assigned to particular judges; the protesting judges openly expressed suspicions about the political pressures placed upon Chief Justice Dipak Misra, who was in charge of assigning cases. It was not the hapless chief justice, but rather the Indian government, that was the real target of the judges' objections. And Misra's head (metaphorically speaking, I hasten to add) was saved by the politicians: Despite the publicity and attention that the Supreme Court judges' statements garnered, an impeachment motion against the chief justice on grounds of judicial misbehavior was rejected by the Indian parliament in April 2018, citing a lack of substantial merit.

Just like the way the justices of the India's top court used press conferences as a platform to denounce executive influence, Brazil's Supreme Court (STF) used informational means to respond to assaults by the top executive. After the outbreak of Covid-19, President Bolsonaro instituted special legislation preventing local governments from imposing mobility restrictions, to which the STF ruled that, while Bolsonaro had the power to institute health measures at the federal level, including lockdowns and mask mandates, it was ultimately up to the states and cities to decide whether they would institute more restrictive measures. The decision drew fury from the Bolsonaro administration. For the coming months, Bolsonaro attacked the court for "removing all powers from him" and for legitimizing what he described as attacks on the civil liberties of the Brazilian population by governors and mayors. Bolsonaro supporters have tirelessly repeated the same piece of false information in their attempts to defend the government. This disinformation campaign led the Brazilian Supreme Court to start a social media communication effort called "#Verdades do STF" (literally: "#Supreme Court Truths") to combat misinformation about its own rulings as well as other issues

---

[38] Gaurav Mukherjee, "Symposium: A Moment of Self-Reckoning for the Supreme Court of India? Reflections on the Judges' Press Conference," IACL-AIDC Blog (May 18, 2018), www.blog-iacl-aidc.org/blog/2018/5/17/a-moment-of-self-reckoning-for-the-supreme-court-of-india-reflections-on-the-judges-press-conference.

involving the judiciary. The war of words between Bolsonaro and top Brazilian judges has escalated recently: Chief Justice of the Federal Supreme Court Luiz Fux canceled a meeting with the president and the speaker of the two congressional houses at the beginning of the court's term in 2021, on the basis that any dialogue requires mutual respect. Likewise, the head of Electoral Superior Court, Justice Roberto Barroso (probably the best-known Brazilian judge internationally) has accused Bolsonaro of spreading fake news, which he characterized as antidemocratic conduct by the president.[39]

This goes to show that these forms of resistance go only so far. In the case of Poland, the authorities have disregarded judges' resolutions and ignored the CJEU judgments. What prevails, among judges, is a philosophical resignation, connected with the moral dilemma: What should I do? Is there such a thing as "judicial disobedience"? What are the legitimate forms of judicial resistance? What about speeches in public assemblies outside courts? Will they contribute to or undermine the judiciary's legitimacy in the eyes of the public? The president of the Polish Judges' Association *Iustitia*, Dr. Krystian Markiewicz, assessed that only about 3 percent of Polish judges have accepted the "reforms." But judges have had to find a modus vivendi in a bad system. Most judges would resist open political pressures for handing down this or that judgment. But should they accept the career advancement paths created by a deformed system? The only way of applying for a promotion to a higher court is through the new KRS, which is now a thoroughly politicized body, accountable to the ruling party. "This is a devilish alternative. I understand those judges who say: let us hold off on it, we shall not appear before *this* KRS, but on the other hand many judges definitely deserve the promotion. I do not know, what they should do," said Judge Jarosław Gwizdak of the district court in Katowice, in southern Poland.[40]

Judges are usually not heroes. The capacity for martyrdom does not figure in the job description, and judges are not socialized into a life of high risk and sacrifice. At the lower levels of the court hierarchy, when faced with increasing demands from an authoritarian state, judges escape into apathy and melancholic perplexity. "Everybody is laying low in their courtroom or office in silence, and happy not being bothered," said a Hungarian judge in a survey by Amnesty International in June 2020, responding to the growing powers of the government-appointed

---

[39] Meyer and Neto, "Courts Are Finally Standing Up to Bolsonaro."
[40] Quoted in Sadurski, *Poland's Constitutional Breakdown*, p. 104.

president of the National Judiciary Office in court appointments and administration. Another added, also anonymously: "[M]any judges have become uninterested and self-censorship has become automatic."[41]

Lying low in the face of the executive assault is something that judges are good at. A Hungarian law scholar, Eszter Bodnár, describes the various ways that the Constitutional Court has avoided conflicts with other branches – despite the fact that such conflicts are built into the court's very power to annul other branches' decisions (and note that this is the same court that a few decades earlier was considered one of the most activist constitutional courts in the world!).[42] The three doctrinal measures in its tool kit are: statements of legislative omission, declarations of constitutional requirements, and most simply, non-decisions. The first measure is used instead of annulling a problematic statute and involves the court merely determining that there has been a legislative "omission to act," but it cannot enforce its decision. As Bodnár states, it is "a soft instrument as the Constitutional Court does not have any tools to execute its decision and therefore, a lot of the omissions exist permanently."[43]

The second measure is a device well known in the world of constitutional courts as interpretive judgments or, in French, "*interprétation conforme.*" Rather than striking down a bad legal act, the court provides for a mandatory way of understanding it. Termed a "constitutional requirement" in Hungary, the court has used this measure often. Most notably, the court used it when called to review a truly shocking law introduced by the Orbán regime, namely the 2018 act that punished homelessness ("residing in public spaces as a habitual dwelling"). This act followed a special constitutional amendment (the Seventh Amendment) introduced by the Orbán-controlled parliament. In 2019, the Constitutional Court rescued the outrageous provision from the invalidation that it deserved but added a "constitutional requirement" that it could only be enforced if a homeless person would at that time have been offered a placement in a home.[44]

---

[41] Amnesty International, "Status of the Hungarian Judiciary," p. 24.
[42] See Gábor Halmai, "The Hungarian Approach to Constitutional Review: The End of Activism? The First Decade of the Hungarian Constitutional Court," in Wojciech Sadurski (ed.), *Constitutional Justice, East and West* (The Hague: Kluwer Law International, 2002), pp. 189–211 at 195–208.
[43] Bodnár, "Disarming the Guardians."
[44] Ibid.

The simplest escape route for the court is simply to avoid making decisions – procrastinating and postponing the decision ad kalendas Graecas. Or, more precisely, until such time that the matter is no longer relevant. The court applied this approach to the challenge against the law on billboards with political advertisements with which the Introduction to this book began. The challenge to the act enacted in the summer of 2017 was meant to result in the annulment of the statute prior to the 2018 elections, but the court did not deliver judgment until 2019. This was similar to a case involving a challenge to the act resulting in the expulsion of the Central European University from Hungary: The court kept postponing the decision on the politically sensitive issue until it became irrelevant, and the CEU moved to Vienna.[45]

The predicament of the Hungarian Constitutional Court is characteristic of many other courts in the regimes sliding into authoritarianism. Two eminent Indian legal scholars put it very well, concluding from the "lying low" tactic of their Supreme Court: "[J]udicial self-abrogation—whether adopted as a survival tactic in the face of an assertive new government, for reasons of ideological sympathy with that government, or on simple careerist grounds...The courts have, in other words, become participants in politics, even if they have also been victims of it."[46] But what is the boundary between a wise survival tactic ("lying low," waiting for a better day, holding off) and a complete surrender, which either renders the court irrelevant or, even worse, adds an honorific imprimatur to acts by the despots? On which side of the boundary a court finds itself will depend on a great number of factors: the actual motivations of the judges (honorable or self-serving?), the strength of the authoritarian assault (more carrots or sticks?), or the nature of the laws under challenge.

This last factor is particularly important. Consider again one of the cruelest Hungarian statutes (and constitutional amendments) that Orbán devised: the criminalization of homelessness. Does a court approving such a law still deserve a modicum of respect? "It depends" is not a great answer, just as it would not be a satisfactory answer to a question about the legal permissibility of torture. The following reflections by a Hungarian legal scholar, Viktor Kazai, are worth quoting in full, because they capture the dilemma just stated, better than anything else I have come across recently:

---

[45] Ibid.
[46] Madhav Khosla and Milan Vaishnav, "The Three Faces of the Indian State," *Journal of Democracy*, 32/1 (2021), 111–125 at 117.

It is clear that the Court operates in a very hostile political environment. I have been constantly arguing that a certain amount a self-restraint, the strategic avoidance of direct conflict with the ruling political parties is a normal reaction of a constitutional court in such a situation. However, self-restraint cannot lead to unconditional subservience to the government under any circumstances. The very aim of constitutional review is to exercise control over the political branches, not to help them undermine the established constitutional standards. Unfortunately, day by day the Hungarian Constitutional Court is getting closer to become nothing more than a sham institution, like those constitutional control mechanisms operating in authoritarian regimes.[47]

Democracy versus Judges?

There is a temptation to present the incapacitation of constitutional courts as a triumph of political democracy – best personified in representative institutions – over a government of judges, or "juristocracy" (a pathological system not of the rule of law but the rule of lawyers). A number of scholars around the world, but most notably in the United States, support views known as "political constitutionalism," which favors more democratic input into constitutional oversight. Some defenders of Jarosław Kaczyński and Viktor Orban have argued that this is what is happening in the countries they rule. This is, for instance, what was also claimed by several Hungarian judges of the constitutional court – some of them, constitutional law professors – as well as by Mr. András Varga, whom we have already met. These judges, in their extra-judicial appearances, have turned into apologists of the regime that has subjected them into compliance and rendered them a subservient court. Many of them, observes their knowledgeable critic Gábor Halmai, "acknowledge that the [Constitutional] Court hasn't been confrontational towards the current legislature and the government" and "characterize this behavior as a special approach within the system of separation of powers, best described as a partnership in a constitutional dialogue."[48]

---

[47] Viktor Z. Kazai, "No One Has the Right to Be Homeless...," *Verfassungsblog* (June 13, 2019), www.verfassungsblog.de/no-one-has-the-right-to-be-homeless.

[48] Gábor Halmai, "Populism or Authoritarianism? A Plaidoyer against Illiberal or Authoritarian Constitutionalism," in Martin Krygier, Adam Czarnota, and Wojciech Sadurski (eds.), *Anti-constitutional Populism* (in press).

But this temptation should be resisted. It would be an odd "dialogue" if one of the conversationalists were appointed by and is indebted for their position at the table to the other one. The so-called political constitutionalism strand in modern constitutional theory calls for a reduction of the role of judges when the subject-matter demands legitimacy endowed by electoral mandate. But it does not call for the incapacitation of judges in their own field of competence. Opposition to "juristocracy" should lead to judges becoming perhaps less *powerful*, but not more *dependent*.

"Political constitutionalism" does not call for the *unrestrained* exercise of legislative and executive power; it just calls for restraints other than those coming from a judge's discretionary decision. Political constitutionalism prefers the separation of powers as a checking device to that of judicial review in the process of articulating vague constitutional rights. But most importantly, "political constitutionalism" assumes a well-functioning political democracy, with fair and honest political institutions. In particular, it assumes the existence of a legislature in which elected members "deliberate and vote on public issues, and the procedures for lawmaking are elaborate and responsible, and incorporate various safeguards...and multiple levels of consideration, debate, and voting," whereby "these processes connect both formally (through public hearings and consultation procedures) and informally with wider debates in the society."[49] Nothing remotely like this idealistic vision of Jeremy Waldron (a scholar considered one of the leading representatives of "political constitutionalism") exists in the authoritarian populist states discussed in this book. Today's Poland, Hungary, or Venezuela are hardly paragons of elaborate deliberation in the process of law-making.

Clashes between an independent court and the legislature + executive tandem, the latter being strong by virtue of electoral support, is something written into the fabric of constitutional democracy. Yet there is no reason to believe that judges are necessarily on the side of angels: They may be wrong, and MPs or ministers may be right. When the executive grows stronger, however, and is not merely *irritated* by judicial activism but *angered* by their very independence – the political balance moves dangerously against the judiciary. And it is not so much dangerous for judges as it is for the citizens, whom they are supposed to protect in face of potentially arbitrary power.

---

[49] Jeremy Waldron, "The Core of the Case against Judicial Review," *Yale Law Journal*, 115 (2006), 1346–1406 at 1361, footnotes omitted.

No wonder that some constitutional scholars think hard about ways of preventing or minimizing this clash. Some believe that in states where democracy is still vulnerable to executive excesses, constitutions should adopt "weak judicial review" – constitutionalist jargon used to describe a system where courts can pass judgment on laws but without going so far as to strike it down.[50] They can only make a tentative observation that the law may be unconstitutional – but the last word rests with the parliament.

One can, of course, speculate that such a cautious design will limit the friction between strong political branches and weak courts. But it is just that – speculation. What we do know is that systems of "weak" or even no judicial review in a democratic setting exist only in consolidated, traditional democracies: in the United Kingdom, Australia, New Zealand, Japan, Canada, Scandinavia. In some of these countries judges have no power to invalidate statutes they find unconstitutional (United Kingdom, New Zealand), in some their judgments may be overridden by the parliament (Canada), in some there is no constitutional bill of rights under which a robust judicial review may flourish (Australia), and in some, courts are very deferential to the legislature (Scandinavia, Japan). On the other hand, we know that almost all "transitional" democracies – democracies only recently established and still vulnerable to internal assaults – have opted for a system of "robust review," in which constitutional judges have the powers to invalidate laws that fail (in the eyes of those judges) to meet constitutional muster. This cannot be mere coincidence. Robust review is seen as indispensable for keeping politicians in check and for imposing constitutional discipline where custom, convention, and culture fail to perform the role they play in more consolidated democracies. But if courts are disempowered, what is left to make sure that politicians then observe the constitution? Sure, friction between the branches will be lower, but this also lowers the benefits of having courts in the first place.

And, if we are in the realm of speculation, one may speculate that opting for "weak review" to save the courts may be useful in circumstances where tensions between the court and the executive (and/or the legislature) are at relatively low levels of intensity. When political branches are *moderately* hostile to constitutional review and insist on

---

[50] Stephen Gardbaum, "Are Strong Constitutional Courts Always a Good Thing for New Democracies?" *Columbia Journal of Transnational Law*, 53 (2015), 285–320.

having the last word on constitutional disputes, conferral of weak competences upon courts may make good sense.

When the conflict is intense, however, as when the executive is strongly determined to disregard constitutional restraints on its powers, and the government is energetically committed to dismantling all checks and balances, no amount of deliberately weak constitutional review will save the courts. In the already-quoted words of Mr. Kazai, "self-restraint cannot lead to unconditional subservience to the government under any circumstances." But in Hungary, it has.

"Blame Game" No More

The disarmament, capture, and transformation of courts into government allies is not an unqualified benefit to authoritarian rulers. Quite apart from all the other political costs, domestic and international, a fully dependent court (especially a constitutional court, with its special visibility and prominence) is of no use to the government in the "blame game" – a function that courts may otherwise perform, to the benefit of the executive or the party controlling the parliamentary majority.

Governments may often find it useful to dump certain decisions on courts. For example, when a government decision is politically costly and unpopular, the court may replace the government as the decision-maker while absorbing the political costs. This function is occasionally played by constitutional courts in both democratic and authoritarian systems. But in the latter, the plausibility of costs absorption depends upon the general belief that the court is *independent* of the government. If it is not, the blame game does not work because everyone knows that whatever the court decides is a consequence of political decisions by rulers.

When, for instance, the hapless, powerless, obedient Constitutional Tribunal in Poland announced its outrageous decision on abortion rights in October 2020 – effectively, extinguishing legal abortion in the country – tens of thousands of angry women (and men) went spontaneously to protest in the streets. Not in the central, office-filled Aleja Szucha in Warsaw, where the CT building is located, but in a quiet residential area of Żoliborz, in Mickiewicza Street, where Jarosław Kaczyński lives. Kaczyński is not a judge of the Constitutional Tribunal, but no one was fooled. The CT is just a puppet in his hands. Why would protestors waste their time and show their anger at marionettes playing a role written for them by the real ultimate Judge?

In Poland, Hungary, and Venezuela, the blame game does not work. The full dependence of judges on the leader and/or the ruling party has rendered it ineffective. It is general knowledge that actual decisions are being made elsewhere, and that the court is just a spokesperson for the ruling elite. The inability to benefit from shifting even part of the blame onto the court if the court is so dependent on the regime is a real cost to the regime.

But clearly, populist politicians believe that it is a cost worth incurring.

5

Paranoia

On the morning of April 10, 2010, an Tupolev aircraft carrying ninety-six leading Polish politicians, military commanders, and religious and civic leaders, including President Lech Kaczyński and his wife, crashed in a deep fog on its descent toward a military airport in Smolensk, Russia. No one survived.

The visit was fraught with symbolism: It was meant to commemorate the memory of over 21,000 Polish officers and soldiers murdered on Stalin's orders by the KGB in five killing fields, one of them the forest of Katyń, not far from Smolensk, in April 1940. Lech Kaczyński intended this visit to be the inauguration of his presidential campaign, less than three months before the election, and at a time when his ratings were at an all-time low. For this reason, his visit was separated from Prime Minister Donald Tusk's visit to Katyń, who came with a small governmental delegation three days earlier and was joined by Russian prime minister Vladimir Putin. Neither Tusk nor Kaczyński fancied a joint visit at a time when the relationship between the two leading politicians from parties bitterly opposed to each other (Tusk from Civic Platform [PO]; Kaczyński from Law and Justice [PiS] was particularly sour).

The causes of the crash were later comprehensively described by a state commission chaired by the minister for the interior, Jerzy Miller. They were a combination of extremely bad weather (heavy fog, getting worse by the minute), human error on the part of the Polish pilots (uncertainty as to the real altitude of the plane, wrongful efforts to attempt to land despite having no visual contact with the airstrip, etc.) and of the Russian airport personnel (failure to issue a firm prohibition on landing), bad training and organization in the military air force unit responsible for the flights of VIPs, interference in the cockpit by officials and commanders who distracted and distressed the pilots by urging them to land no matter what, insufficient advance planning of the visit, and the appalling condition of the airport itself. The state report confirmed what was clear from the beginning: The plane should have never taken off, knowing the weather situation on arrival; once it had taken off, it should have been redirected to an alternate airport; once it had approached Smolensk, it should have abandoned any attempt to land. The bottom line: On approach it flew too fast, too low, and with none of the required minima of horizontal and vertical visibility.

As one would expect, the disaster caused a great deal of emotion – anger, mourning, and distress – in Polish society. PiS (a party co-founded by Lech Kaczyński) quickly decided to play the "Smolensk card" in internal Polish politics, by rejecting outright the explanation of the causes of disaster by the Miller commission and transforming a tragic but avoidable aircraft crash into a political mass murder. Jarosław Kaczyński, Lech's twin brother and PiS leader, seized by personal trauma and additionally irritated by his own defeat in the presidential elections that took place in the shadow of the disaster, on June 20 and July 4, 2010, established "Smolensk" as his main platform for attacking the PO government and the newly elected president, Bronisław Komorowski, by shamelessly propounding conspiracy theories. In the strong version, blame was laid on the Tusk government for complicity with the Russians in masterminding the crash; in the weak version, the government was blamed for its alleged unwillingness to properly investigate the crash. One of the most (in)famous speeches by Jarosław Kaczyński on this topic referred to his late brother and his co-passengers as having been "betrayed at dawn," referring to a moving poem by great Polish poet Zbigniew Herbert.[1]

Jarosław Kaczyński found an enthusiastic executioner of this line of attack on the Civic Platform government in Antoni Macierewicz, an ex-head of military counterintelligence (in 2006–2007) and a hawk in PiS leadership. Macierewicz quickly set up an alternative commission for investigating the crash, which regularly kept coming up with new "revelations," all suggesting somebody's criminal intent and action, but none with even minimal plausibility. (Occasionally, even the absence of any available evidence was treated as evidence of how shrewd the wrongdoers were.) The workings of this commission, in conjunction with monthly rallies in the center of Warsaw on the tenth of each month, invariably culminating in front of the Presidential Palace with an angry speech by Kaczyński, formed the core of the "Smolensk ritual" that infused Polish

---

[1] Speech by Jarosław Kaczyński on April 10, 2011. *Gazeta Wyborcza online* (April 11, 2011), www.wyborcza.pl/1,76842,9417172,Kaczynski_podpala_Polske.html.

public life with a particularly toxic kind of paranoia and was an effective instrument for mobilizing the hard core of PiS supporters.

In fact, the ritual did not end with the PiS victory in 2015. To the contrary, with Macierewicz becoming minister of defense and deputy leader of PiS, and with his commission upgraded in status to an official governmental body, the "Smolensk conspiracy" became part of the political orthodoxy of Poland post-2015. Macierewicz required the names of Smolensk victims be read at all important public events with military participation (equating the death in a plane crash to killing in war), urged NATO involvement in a new investigation, and even proclaimed that the "Smolensk assault" was the first act in a war waged by Russia against Poland. As Timothy Snyder describes with only a little exaggeration, "After 2015, Smolensk became more important than the Katyn massacre that Polish leaders had wished to commemorate, more important than the Second World War, more important than the twentieth century."[2]

As the saying goes, "even paranoiacs have real enemies." But the air crash in which President Kaczyński died was decidedly not such a case.

"They Are Up to Something"[3]

Smolensk is only one among many conspiracy theories concocted by populist leaders. While it is perhaps unique because it attaches to such a terrible event, it is otherwise not necessarily the most fantastic nor the most intelligence-defying of the conspiracy theories out there. As David Runciman suggests, "the twenty-first century [can] begin to look like the golden age of conspiracy theories. They seem to be everywhere at present."[4] Hungary's Orbán built much of his rhetoric on a quasi-personal struggle with George Soros. He has not limited himself to imputing all sort of nasty motives to Soros – his alleged hatred for the national tradition, for Christian religion, for the patriotic feelings of Hungarians – but has actually ascribed to him a "Plan." The Plan was to undermine Orbán's government but also, more ambitiously, to change Hungarian society by supporting Muslim immigration and (somewhat

---

[2] Timothy Snyder, *The Road to Unfreedom* (New York: Penguin Random House, 2018), p. 206.
[3] With apologies to Bruno Castanho Silva, Federico Vegetti, and Levente Littvay, "The Elite Is Up to Something: Exploring the Relation between Populism and Belief in Conspiracy Theories," *Swiss Political Science Review*, 23 (2017), 423–443.
[4] David Runciman, *How Democracy Ends* (London: Profile Books, 2018), p. 63.

incongruously, but so what?) liberal ideas of an "Open Society" modeled on the ideas of the author of that concept, and Soros's teacher, the philosopher Karl Popper. The central object of the Plan was to promote settlements of a large number of Muslims in Europe, and more particularly, in Hungary.[5] As one commentator encapsulates his reading of Orbán's theory and its perception in Hungarian society (with the caveat that exaggeration is probably intended for rhetorical purposes): Soros is "leading an international cabal that included other Jews such as the Rothschilds, as well as Freemasons and Illuminati."[6] Another scholar who has analyzed a large number of official Fidesz messages on Facebook reports that the content of these messages frequently includes allegations that "civic organizations function as an interconnected system, backed by Soros, which assists immigration,...that Soros supports NGOs that help asylum seekers to get into Hungary,...[and that] Soros has political influence through the financing of oppositional politicians who would 'change our homeland into an immigration country.'"[7]

Virtually every populist leader has his (a gender in this case is accurate) favorite conspiracy. Brazil's Bolsonaro has repeatedly invoked the idea that the Amazon is under threat from foreign takeover,[8] that his political opponent, former president Dilma Roussef, had conspired with Fidel Castro to implant communism in Brazil,[9] that the minister of education during Lula's presidency intended to indoctrinate the country's youth into homosexuality,[10] or that the Covid-19 virus was

---

[5] For a good account, see Peter Plenta, "Conspiracy Theories as a Political Instrument: Utilization of Anti-Soros Narratives in Central Europe," *Contemporary Politics*, 26 (2020), 512–530.

[6] Ivan Kalmar, "Islamophobia and Anti-antisemitism: The Case of Hungary and the 'Soros Plot,'" *Patterns of Prejudice*, 54 (2020), 182–198 at 182.

[7] Tamas Toth, "Target the Enemy: Explicit and Implicit Populism in the Rhetoric of the Hungarian Right," *Journal of Contemporary European Studies* (2020). DOI: 10.1080/14782804.2020.1757415, p. 13.

[8] Luiz Romero, "How Brazil's Fear of Losing the Amazon Guides Bolsonaro's Policies towards the Forest," *CNN* (June 22, 2021), www.edition.cnn.com/2021/06/22/americas/brazil-amazon-fear-meme-bolsonaro-intl/index.html.

[9] Rafael Evangelista and Fernanda Bruno, "WhatsApp and Political Instability in Brazil: Targeted Messages and Political Radicalisation," *Internet Policy Review*, 8/4 (2019), 1–23 at 9.

[10] Vincent Bevins, "Where Conspiracy Reigns," *The Atlantic* (September 16, 2020), www.theatlantic.com/ideas/archive/2020/09/how-anti-communist-conspiracies-haunt-brazil/614665.

deliberately produced in a Chinese laboratory.[11] Venezuela's Chavez discovered numerous planned assaults on his life; by one count, there were sixty-three such assassination plots during his fourteen years as president.[12] Following the cancer diagnoses of several left-wing Latin American leaders (namely, Dilma Rousseff, Fernando Lugo, Luiz Inácio Lula da Silva, Cristina Kirchner, and Hugo Chavez), Chavez offered the theory that someone, who felt challenged by these leaders, had developed a "technology to inoculate cancer."[13] In India, Modi's BJP party, always happy to stir hatred of Hindus against Muslims, called a recent Muslim religious congregation in New Delhi "CoronaJihad" and "CoronaTerrorism," with appropriate hashtags going viral on social media.[14] Even more recently, the BJP took on the so-called Love Jihad – an alleged secret campaign by Muslim men to seduce young Hindu women into marriage, and hence bring about conversion to Islam.[15] And several human rights activists have been jailed, without trial, since June 2018 on trumped-up charges of being involved in the "BK 16 conspiracy" (BK is an acronym of Bhima Koregaon, the location of a historic 1818 battle of Indians against the British), allegedly aimed at assassinating Prime Minister Modi and imposing a Maoist regime in India.[16]

All these conspiracy theories fit the classic description of the paranoid style in politics offered by Richard Hofstadter in his 1964 essay.[17] The

---

[11] Carlie Porterfield, "Brazil's Bolsonaro Floats Conspiracy Theory That Coronavirus May Be 'Biological Warfare,'" *Forbes* (May 6, 2021), www.forbes.com/sites/carlieporterfield/ 2021/05/05/brazils-bolsonaro-floats-conspiracy-theory-that-coronavirus-may-be-bio logical-warfare/?sh=374800c32bb5.

[12] Rick Rockwell, "Populism and Modern-Day Conspiracy Theories," *Global Americans* (May 17, 2015), www.theglobalamericans.org/2015/05/populism-and-modern-day-con spiracy-theories.

[13] Castanho Silva, Vegetti, and Littvay, "The Elite Is Up to Something," p. 423.

[14] Jayshree Bajoria, "CoronaJihad Is Only the Latest Manifestation: Islamophobia in India Has Been Years in the Making," *Human Rights Watch* (May 1, 2020), www.hrw.org/ news/2020/05/01/coronajihad-only-latest-manifestation-islamophobia-india-has-been-years-making.

[15] Dexter Filkins, "Blood and Soil in Narendra Modi's India," *The New Yorker* (December 2, 2019), www.newyorker.com/magazine/2019/12/09/blood-and-soil-in-narendra-modis-india.

[16] Siddhartha Deb, "The Unravelling of a Conspiracy: Were the 16 Charged with Plotting to Kill India's Prime Minister Framed?" *The Guardian* (August 12, 2021), www.theguardian .com/world/2021/aug/12/bhima-koregaon-case-india-conspiracy-modi.

[17] Richard Hofstadter, "The Paranoid Style in American Politics," *Harper's* (November 1964), 77–86.

paranoid account perceives the world as composed of largely hostile forces, plotting against forces of the good, the latter personified in the Leader who knows that any compromises with the enemy are signs of weakness (or worse, of betrayal), which must lead to catastrophe. Paranoid discourse is based on the Manichean antinomy of Good and Evil, and a conviction that Good will not triumph if the forces of Evil are allowed to maintain their strongholds in the judiciary, media, or NGOs. Opponents display a curious combination of pathetic weakness (because they are not in tune with real society) and distressing power (which justifies constant mobilization against them). The Evil they represent is apocalyptic yet capable of being prevented, hence the need for continuous vigilance and struggle. Grotesque exaggerations, deep suspicion, and absurd conspiracy theories – all aspects Hofstadter had detected in the paranoid political style – are abundantly present in populist speeches today.

As should be clear, I am not attributing to populists "paranoia" in a clinical sense of the word but am borrowing it, just as Hofstadter did, for a political analysis. And I may repeat after Hofstadter, "I have neither the competence nor the desire to classify any figures of the past or present as certifiable lunatics."[18] (I should perhaps add that I share many people's misgivings about using clinical terms to depict reprehensible political attitudes – but I am using the word only to trace a generally accepted linguistic usage.) The dismantling of constitutional checks and balances is a consequence of the paranoid style of politics, and of the perception (so reminiscent of paranoia by Stalin) that the more crushed the enemies are (and crushed they *are* – otherwise the struggle launched by the Leader would turn out to be tragically misplaced, which is unthinkable), the more vicious and desperate, hence dangerous, they become. What better way of demonstrating the enemies' invidiousness and perfidy than by revealing to the people secret arrangements by powerful people, who attempt to conceal their role, and who are determined to violate the people's true interests? What better way of discrediting those machinations by evil people than by speaking to actual events that have (allegedly) occurred, or are (allegedly) occurring, or were meant to occur?

Hugo Pérez Hernáiz offers a helpful, sequential account of the construction of conspiracy theories, in seven steps.[19] His account is based on

---

[18] Ibid., p. 77
[19] Hugo Antonio Pérez Hernáiz, "The Uses of Conspiracy Theories for the Construction of a Political Religion in Venezuela," *International Journal of Humanities and Social Sciences*, 2 (2008), 970–981.

Chávez's Venezuela, but I find that it almost perfectly fits many other conspiracy theories produced by ruling populists, including in Poland and Hungary:

- First, the Leader propounds a conspiracy in very general terms while claiming to possess concrete evidence.
- Second, other officials echo the claim, which leads to the media frequently repeating those allegations. The allegations become a newsworthy event as a result of media saturation with claims about a plot.
- Third, while no evidence of a plot is made public, official actions (such as formal investigative commissions or approaches to courts) are undertaken.
- Fourth, public opinion is called upon to exercise its "common sense"-based knowledge, including attention to unrelated but uncontroverted facts. (In Venezuela, CIA interventions in Latin America were often mentioned; in Poland, the history of Russian hostile actions was invoked; in India, it was the five-decade long history of the Maoist insurgency in central and eastern states, which is now largely a spent force.)
- Fifth, an enemy is constructed as a multifaceted but relatively united conspirator.
- Sixth, official statements and the regime's propaganda reinforce a strong opposition between "us" and "them."
- Seventh, the conspiracies propounded are connected to a broader theory about a high level of institutional control by the conspirator, with the government's aim being to seize control of those institutions, in the interest of the people. "The aim of the revolution is to re-gain control of those institutions that before the revolution were, and even during the transformation process are, in the hands of the conspirators, and give them back to the people, so they may serve them in their struggle to reach the utopia."[20] Replace the word "revolution" with whatever self-description is favored by the local populist ruler (the rather anodyne "Good Change" in the case of Poland, for instance), and you have a good account of how a conspiracy theory is constructed.

It was nicely prefigured by a lovely aria, "La calunnia" (known in English translations as "Start a Rumour"), in the *Barber of Seville*, by Rossini. Except that Dr. Basilio's "calunnia" had less catastrophic consequences.

---

[20] Ibid., pp. 976–977.

It is understandable why there is such a strong connection between populism and conspiracy theories, though of course populists have no monopoly on the paranoid style. The basic idea going to the heart of populism – that a malicious establishment has appropriated democracy from the people to itself – itself *is* a generic conspiracy theory. "Conspiracy theory is the logic of populism," says David Runciman.[21] A number of important empirical studies have recently analyzed the relationship between support for populism and belief in conspiracies. And this connection makes sense: the principled "anti-elitism" of populism rests upon suspicion of those seen as "greedy actors who do evil, secret deeds for the sake of more resources or power."[22] At the same time, both conspiracy theorists and populists depict the general public as innocent victims of selfish elites. Hence, conspiracies confirm two main aspects of the populist outlook: glorification of the common people and dislike of political elites.[23] In one study, three US political scientists show how the endorsement of conspiracy theories, which attribute wicked intent to political opponents, can reinforce one's political views by impugning opposing viewpoints.[24] They also find strong traces of conspiracy endorsements among conservatives (though not liberals) in the United States who are highly knowledgeable about politics but lacking in trust: "[T]he combination of high knowledge and low trust is the perfect storm for ideologically motivated conspiracy endorsement *for conservatives, but not for liberals*."[25] It is difficult to say if similar patterns exist in societies other than the United States, but a generalized lack of trust is certainly a quasi-universal psychological background to populism.

Conspiracy theories satisfy many people's need for simple explanations for complex, multi-causal developments: Why bother to unpack the reasons for the massive rise in migration from North Africa to Europe after 2015 if a "Soros's plan" provides an easy-to-understand answer? Conspiracy theories provide people with easily achievable order, control, and certainty about their beliefs. Conspiracy beliefs also fulfill the urge to reconcile one's belief in the extraordinary value of one's own group (primarily, the nation) with the melancholy observation that other

---

[21] Runciman, *How Democracy Ends*, p. 65.
[22] Castanho Silva, Vegetti, and Littvay, "The Elite Is Up to Something," p. 433.
[23] Ibid., p. 436.
[24] Joanne Miller, Kyle Saunders, and Christina Farhart, "Conspiracy Endorsement as Motivated Reasoning: The Moderating Roles of Political Knowledge and Trust," *American Journal of Political Science*, 60 (2016), 824–844 at 826.
[25] Ibid., p. 837.

nations fail to properly recognize its virtues. Psychologist Agnieszka Golec de Zavala suggests that "populism has collective narcissism at its heart"[26] – collective narcissism being the belief that one's own group is exceptional and entitled to privileged treatment but is not sufficiently recognized by others. Golec de Zavala adds: "Conspiracy theories provide external reasons why others undermine the exceptionality of the in-group…[W]hen people's committed belief is violated (their group's exceptionality is not validated by others) they are motivated to search for new meaning. This makes them likely to seize on conspiracy theories, which offer coherent meaning systems often supported by elaborate arguments."[27] For Golec de Zavala, current and historical Polish beliefs endorsing the conspiracy stereotypes of the Jewish minority, the suspicions that gender-equality activists and scholars secretly plot to undermine family values, and yes, also the conspiratorial beliefs about Russian involvement in the Smolensk air crash – are all instances of "collective narcissism."[28]

This sets out the *demand* side of conspiracy theories propounded by populists. What about the supply side? It is enough to reflect upon the functions of such theories to understand the reasons populists have for spreading often grotesque and fanciful theories. For one thing, these theories provide excuses for inefficiencies, errors, and other failures of populists themselves. Consider Jarosław Kaczyński's Smolensk conspiracy theory. Much around the disaster points to tragic errors by his brother and his entourage: his insistence on having a huge crowd of officials accompany him in a political spectacle, his urging the pilots to try to land no matter what, as well as bureaucratic errors by the presidential office in the preparation of the trip (not checking if the airport was flight-worthy), and so forth. But if you have a simple explanation like a conspiracy, these mistakes pale into insignificance: Nothing could have protected President Kaczynski against a criminal plot. Ditto with Orbán contra Soros. Nothing could have avoided the influx of migrants into Budapest if a criminal mastermind, a sort of Ernst Blofeld character from

---

[26] Agnieszka Golec de Zavala, "Why Is Populism So Robustly Associated with Conspiratorial Thinking? Collective Narcissism and the Meaning Maintenance Model," in J. D. Sinnott and J. S. Rabin (eds.), *The Psychology of Political Behavior in a Time of Change* (Cham: Springer Nature, 2021), pp. 277-290 at 278.
[27] Ibid., p. 278.
[28] Ibid., p. 282.

James Bond movies, deliberately designed it that way. Conspiracies exculpate the populists.

More importantly, these theories are a powerful device for political mobilization. They denigrate opponents and strengthen the stature of the populist leader. If, as a target of the conspiracy the leader survives, his endurance despite all odds suggests a God-like character. If he falls victim to the conspirators (as was the case for Lech Kaczyński), his death renders him an instant martyr, and confers additional aura upon the survivors. Especially if the survivor happens to be the victim's twin brother. As Peter Plenta, an analyst of Orbán's narratives says, "conspiracy theories can serve as an effective instrument of political mobilisation, particularly when the 'villain' is connected with the opposition camp. Conspiracy theories possess a critical communicative function by helping to unite the audience."[29]

Further, conspiracy theories bolster political polarization, putting onto the political agenda items about which responses may be only yes or no. Either Prime Minister Tusk had conspired with Russians to murder the Polish president or he did not; *tertium non datur*. Either the Chinese deliberately manufactured Coronavirus in their labs or they did not. There is no room for "compromise" or trade-offs with such statements of alleged fact. Beliefs in alleged conspiracies do not lend themselves to balancing positions, which are the stuff of democracy. Hence, propounding conspiracy theories is deeply anti-democratic because it undermines the grounds for consensus and compromise, divides society further along non-negotiable dimensions, and strengthens preexisting cleavages by providing people with new and outrageous reasons to dislike their opponents.

It also erodes the epistemic basis of democracy, which requires a degree of common beliefs in the reality "out there." In the world of alternative realities or alternative facts, when any proposition *about facts*, even the most fanciful, enjoys equal status with any other set of beliefs, the epistemic grounds for social collaboration run out. A theory about the influx of migrants being caused by George Soros's perfidious plan is as good as an explanation related to the effects of wars in the Middle East or structural poverty. In such circumstances, working together for the public good is made less and less possible. It is not that people are divided about their conceptions of the public good – this is routine in a

---

[29] Plenta, "Conspiracy Theories," p. 516.

democracy – but that they are divided about the facts that establish objective parameters within which the public good is identified. And the facts invoked by conspiracy theorists are often unverifiable and unfalsifiable, because denials only confirm the suspicion of conspiracy. Evidence produced by opponents of conspiracy theories are invoked as additional proof of the conspiracy that deceives the public, either fabricated by the conspirators themselves or their advocates.[30] In this way, conspiracy theories have self-defending and self-perpetuating characteristics.

On the whole, conspiracy theories are fatal to democracy because they lower the levels of political trust and discourage people from participating in politics, including to vote, because such theories make people feel politically powerless. People lose the sense of political agency if anything of importance is ultimately produced by some shadowy machinations anyway. A natural consequence of the belief in conspiracies and plots is to strengthen the central executive: Only a unified, strong government, led by a strong leader, can face the power of dangerous, secretive plotters. The separation of powers, checks and balances, or the accountability of central institutions weaken and disarm those who have the will to resist conspiracies. So those in a non-populist camp who underestimate the force of conspiracy theories, on the basis that they are too absurd, silly, or fantastic to be taken seriously, do so at their peril.

Lies, Damn Lies, and Populism

Why do populist leaders lie so much? So ostentatiously, so shamelessly, with such impunity, and notwithstanding the huge fact-checking industries in their countries that prove them wrong again and again?

Why could Jarosław Kaczyński claim that there is hard evidence (in the form of traces of explosives) for an "explosion" in the air of the presidential aircraft on April 10, 2010, or that in some Western states there are spheres where sharia law is binding? Why could Orbán say that the European Commission wanted to bring in immigrants with a special migrant visa and that it wanted to establish a mandatory settlement quota?[31] Why could Bolsonaro claim that the former president Dilma

---

[30] See, similarly, Eirikur Bergmann, *Conspiracy and Populism: The Politics of Information* (Cham: Springer Nature, 2018), pp. 56–57.
[31] "'Fake News': EU Rejects Orbán's Migration Media Campaign," *Al Jazeera* (February 19, 2019), www.aljazeera.com/news/2019/2/19/fake-news-eu-rejects-Orbáns-migration-media-campaign.

Roussef had met with Fidel Castro (while at the time the photo that allegedly showed her with the Cuban leader was taken, Roussef was just 11 years old, meaning the photo was clearly a fake)?[32] Or why could Duterte say that some four thousand people had been killed in the "war on drugs" while independent media investigations showed that the number was closer to seven thousand?[33] And why could they tell all these and innumerable other lies, despite the fact that they have been proven false beyond doubt, and have never been required to retract or apologize, or pay any political price for telling them – why?

The simplest answer is: because they *could*. Changes in information and communication infrastructures brought about by social media have opened up enormous spaces for the dissemination of misinformation and plain lies. Traditional media, with their gatekeeping and mediating functions, have become relatively less important. As a result, there are no longer recognized and effective arbiters, umpires, or gatekeepers for information released to the general public. Media abundance makes it possible for everyone to find their own "truths," and truths are a function of prior political convictions and beliefs. The structural characteristics of social media – not being restrained by any scarcity of carriers of information, along with the low costs for entry into and distribution of news, resulting in an enormous supply of news and commentary, in the absence of any centralized editorial control or the like – in addition to all their other positive consequences, make it easy for politicians and propagandists to circulate information immediately and directly to their audiences. As a result, there are huge incentives to distribute disinformation and very few incentives for reviewing information for accuracy.

And yet, the mere availability of formidable carriers for lies and disinformation, and the pattern of incentives accompanying the overabundance of speech on social media, does not explain, in itself, why populist leaders are so enthusiastic in propagating lies, and their audiences so forgiving of even the most evident lies. Lying has some functions that go beyond and are indeed unrelated to convincing others of facts about public matters. Of course, part of the reason for sharing disinformation is that many people will actually *believe* in it, which advantages populists: the subject-matter of disinformation dispensed by populists is

---

[32] Evangelista and Bruno, "WhatsApp and Political Instability in Brazil," p. 9.
[33] Glenda Gloria, "War of Words: Rodrigo Duterte's Violent Relationship with Language," *World Policy Institute*, 35/2 (2018), 9–13 at 12.

of course such that it bolsters the populist cause. And even if fake news is not fully believed, it creates the phenomenon of a "belief echo" – false news about a political opponent may still harm and damage their image, by the sheer fact of something negative about them being repeated endlessly, even – ironically – in fact checks. "Belief echoes unfortunately show how fact checking has limited effect or perhaps sometimes even makes matters worse. Fact check needs to reiterate the false claim, which in and by itself makes the belief echoes stronger. And even if the fact check is taken at face value, the rumor still damages the reputation of its subjects."[34] Studies of the Brexit campaign show that, even if various claims made by proponents of "Leave" had been thoroughly discredited, the amplification of their arguments meant that public discourse around Brexit was shaped by the Leavers.[35]

But lies have functions that go well beyond deception. They create a special bond between leaders and their audience. When a populist leader lies, the lenient audience becomes part of a certain community, (a form of "dirty togetherness," as Polish sociologist Adam Podgórecki called it, although in a different context) in which everyone is involved in a special pact. These linkages bind the group, cemented by a common knowledge of a moral wrong – rather like the bond of partners in crime. Since, in contrast to fully authoritarian states, viewers and readers in populist regimes *have* access to respectable, accurate sources of information, where freedom of the media is by and large observed, their subsequent participation in the lie – even if only as minimal as passive reception of deceitful broadcast or by reading biased newspapers – has all the characteristics of voluntary complicity. As András Sajó says in his recent book, in a political system based on lies, "[t]he institutions fall in line first, but after a while, a growing number of citizens accept the lies and become accomplices of the regime..."[36] They all know that what is being told is a lie, and that others know that they know it is a lie. The result is a sort of Parade of Liars, in which no one pretends that the truth is being massacred – because the truth is not the point of the practice.

---

[34] Vincent Hendricks and Mads Vestergaard, *Reality Lost: Markets of Attention, Misinformation and Manipulation* (Cham: Springer Nature, 2019), p. 60.

[35] See Glenda Cooper, "Populist Rhetoric and Media Misinformation in the 2016 UK Brexit Referendum," in Howard Tumber and Silvio Waisbord (eds.), *The Routledge Companion to Media Disinformation and Populism* (London: Routledge, 2021), pp. 397–410 at 406.

[36] András Sajó, *Ruling by Cheating* (Cambridge: Cambridge University Press, 2021), p. 326, footnote omitted.

The point is to create a bond and mobilize the believers. It creates a specific test of loyalty: if you believe in an obvious lie propounded by the leader (for instance, in the Smolensk conspiracy), and are willing to publicly assert it with a straight face, then you are truly *in*. If you express any doubts, you are out. Acceding to a lie is a membership card carried by populist party members. That is why populist lies are public and are publicized unashamedly. Catherine Fieschi, a British public intellectual, put it well: "Populist lying...is designed to be seen – it is the opposite of a cover-up. In the populist playbook, lying itself is glorified; it is an instrument of subversion, its purpose to demonstrate that the liar will stop at nothing to 'serve the people.' The lies are signals that these politicians are not bound by the usual norms of the liberal democratic elite."[37] Hendricks and Vestergaard write about "blue lies" – a concept borrowed from cases where police officers lie out of loyalty to the group to cover for colleagues. And they add, more generally: "Blue lies are lies on behalf of a group that serve the group. The lies may strengthen the internal coherence of the group and loyalty among its members."[38]

Lies uttered with complete political (not to mention, legal) impunity also bolster the Leader's position as the most powerful actor: His power and agency extend upon the truth. "See," he seems to be telling his fans, "I lied. I know I lied, you know that I lied, and I know that you know that I lied – and the sky has not fallen." In a world where lying is wrong, according to the traditional orthodoxy impressed upon us by parents, schools, and churches, and where the doing of a wrong calls for a penalty, lying with impunity is a sign of extraordinary power. Ivan Krastev and Stephen Holmes put it well: "Paying no price for telling easily exposable untruths is an effective way to display one's power and impunity."[39]

The result is that there is no longer a common denominator of criteria for truth: Every "truth" is equally as good or bad as any other. The erosion of common tests for truth is greatly desired in a populist ecosystem and has been described as "epistemological fracture," with features including a bifurcated view of politics, where truths belong to political leaders and their followers, and where disinformation ("post truth") is

---

[37] Catherine Fieschi, "Why Europe's New Populists Tell So Many Lies – And Do It So Shamelessly," *The Guardian* (October 1, 2019), www.theguardian.com/commentisfree/2019/sep/30/europe-populist-lie-shamelessly-salvini-johnson.

[38] Hendricks and Vestergaard, *Reality Lost*, p. 83 (citations omitted).

[39] Ivan Krastev and Stephen Holmes, *The Light That Failed* (New York: Pegasus Books, 2019), p. 174.

embraced because there is no longer a common standard for evidence-based truth.[40] And even if the strong statement that there has been a total collapse in the standards of truth probably goes too far, the weaker observation, that standards have been greatly *relaxed* under populism, is probably true. And so too has been the severity of moral responses to lying.

Daniel Effron, professor at the London Business School, observed that for followers of President Trump, for example, the standard for the truth of his statement was not so much whether the facts he described happened but whether they *could have happened*. Or if not a standard for truth, then at least the harshness of the moral condemnation of his lying. "When a falsehood resonated with people's politics, asking them to imagine counterfactual situations in which it could have been true softened their moral judgments."[41] Writing about one of the most bizarre claims (I describe it as bizarre because it was so inconsequential and so self-evidently false), namely, about the size of crowds at Trump's presidential inauguration, Effron referred to the view of one of Trump's advisers that, if only the weather on the day was nicer, the crowd would have certainly hit record numbers. Ditto, and this time with more sinister consequences, the lies about Obama's birthplace (though not mentioned in Effron's article): No amount of evidence to the contrary would suffice for Trump's followers because, after all, Obama *could have been* born in Asia or Africa. The same goes for the Smolensk air crash (it could have been produced by an explosion from a bomb planted aboard) or Soros's plan to bring millions of migrants to Europe. When theoretical probability becomes a proxy for hard evidence of what has happened, populist audiences may find it easier to overcome their cognitive dissonance stemming from obvious lies by their favorite politicians. And that is all that populist leaders need.

Talking to People

"I have only one intention in speaking with you all. Come, let us serve our Mother India. Let us all take our nation to the new heights. Let us all

---

[40] See Howard Tumber and Silvio Waisbord, "Media, Disinformation, and Populism," in Howard Tumber and Silvio Waisbord (eds.), *The Routledge Companion to Media Disinformation and Populism* (London: Routledge, 2021), pp. 13–25 at 21.

[41] Daniel A. Effron, "Why Trump Supporters Don't Mind His Lies," *New York Times* (April 28, 2018), www.nytimes.com/2018/04/28/opinion/sunday/why-trump-supporters-dont-mind-his-lies.html.

take a step forward…Today, I have shared all the thoughts coming directly from my heart. I will meet you all next at 11 am on Sundays, but I trust our journey shall never end and will continue receiving love and suggestions from you."[42] This was how Narendra Modi addressed the people of India on October 3, 2014, in the first installment of his "Matters of the Heart" (Mann Ki Baat) monthly radio program.

When populist leaders speak directly to the people, their language has certain distinctive features. Each of these features, taken separately, may be found in the great (or not-so-great) speeches of perfectly democratic leaders: Charles de Gaulle, William Churchill, or FDR. But taken together, these features create a genre of their own, almost inimitable and unique. It is important to listen to populists. Their language – their rhetoric – tells us a lot about the nature of populism itself. Of course, we cannot take everything they say at face value. What they omit is often more important than what they say, and what they say is often used for strategic purposes, including calculated deceit. Kenneth Minogue warned with regard to "populism" in an essay published a long time ago that "[w]e must distinguish carefully between the *rhetoric* used by members of a movement – which may be randomly plagiarized from anywhere according to the needs of the movement and the *ideology* which expresses the deeper current of the movement"[43] – and this warning needs to be taken seriously. But the fact that populists "randomly plagiarize" some rhetorical devices rather than others is a significant clue to be picked up on when studying the nature of populism.

To start with, populist leaders like to use the first-person singular or plural when speaking about their in-group. This creates engagement, establishes a direct bond with the electorate, and cultivates a sense of community and togetherness, no matter how low in the social structure you are. In his first broadcast, Modi added: "I can reach the poorest homes, as mine, my nation's strength lies with the Mothers, Sisters and Youths; my nation's strength lies with the Farmers. I am expressing my trust towards the nation…I believe in your strength, hence, I believe in

---

[42] Anandita Bajpai, "'Matters of the Heart': The Sentimental Indian Prime Minister on *All India Radio*," in Barbara Christophe, Christoph Kohl, Heike Liebau, and Achim Saupe (eds), *The Politics of Authenticity and Populist Discourses* (Cham: Palgrave Macmillan, 2021), 105–126 at 116–117.

[43] Kenneth Minogue, "Populism as a Political Movement," in Ghita Ionescu and Ernest Gellner (eds.), *Populism: Its Meaning and National Characteristics* (London: Macmillan, 1969), pp. 197–211 at 198, quoted in Ernesto Laclau, *On Populist Reason* (London: Verso, 2018), p. 10.

our nation's future."[44] The Leader is a natural, irremovable part and parcel of that community: "[W]hen we sit with all our family members to listen to *Mann Ki Baat*, we feel that the head of our family is sitting with us and sharing his ideas with us... I am yours, I am one amongst you, I am with you, you elevated me in a way, and in this way I will continue to remain connected with you as a family member through *Mann Ki Baat*."[45] This sense of (almost) self-effacement, of modesty, and of being a man of the people was a favorite style employed by Chávez too. His manner was to constantly build ties with the poor, the excluded, and disadvantaged in Venezuela, as illustrated by the expression "I am a little of all of you," which Chávez included in his first speech as president-elect.[46]

While an insider within the group of common people, a populist leader is a constant outsider, rejected, and despised by the elite. This is one of the main themes of populism: the people versus the elite. The former is pristine and honest, the latter is self-serving and dangerous. Of course, the construction of the people is in itself a function of defining "the other," so its inclusion is necessarily accompanied by exclusion, both "horizontally" (of another ethnic, religious, or cultural group) or "vertically" (of the elite, which is corrupt, self-serving, and arrogant). The horizontal connects with the vertical by associations drawn between the elite and the Others, as we have seen already in Chapter 1. Liberal elites are denounced, for instance, as supporting an influx of refugees. In contrast to political elites, the Leader is marginalized, excluded, and ignored: This message strengthens cohesion within the in-group and fosters a sense of inclusion. In this way, the privileges and power enjoyed visibly by the leader are rendered insignificant, almost as the inevitable paraphernalia of his service to the People. This corresponds to (or even sometimes prefigures or imitates) the ideal template of "transferring power from [the elite in the capital] back to you the people," as announced in Trump's inaugural presidential speech.[47] And so, similarly, Bolsonaro promised that he was going to change Brazil because he was

---

[44] Bajpai, "Matters of the Heart," p. 109.
[45] Ibid., p. 119.
[46] Elena Block and Ralph Negrine, "The Populist Communication Style: Toward a Critical Framework," *International Journal of Communication*, 11 (2017), 178–197 at 185.
[47] Florian Hartleb, "Materializations of Populism in Today's Politics: Global Perspectives," in Barbara Christophe, Christoph Kohl, Heike Liebau, and Achim Saupe (eds.), *The Politics of Authenticity and Populist Discourses* (Cham: Palgrave Macmillan, 2021), pp. 31–52 at 37.

not part of the establishment,[48] while Jarosław Kaczyński, well into his second consecutive term of rule, could complain that the "mainstream" media representing the old elite was predominantly against him and his party. Orbán, responding to a question from the German newspaper *Bild* on press freedom in Hungary presented himself (in the words of an analyst) as "the alienated leader unable to influence the dominant private media sector partly in 'German hands.'"[49]

All this contributes to a populist cult of personality – which is natural, as the entire institutional structure of populism is highly personalized. While it is not exactly true, as Nadia Urbinati claims, that "[a]ll populist regimes take the name of their leader"[50] (this is not really the case in Poland or Hungary), nevertheless populist systems in power do build around the personality (or charisma, with all the complications related to the word)[51] of the leader seen as an essential condition for the maintenance of the system. "There is no alternative" is the usual mantra within the supporting constituencies of populists, which really means there is no alternative unless the leader dies, steps down or is overthrown in behind-the-scenes machinations. Missing in this is the scenario of a regular, ordered rotation of power.

Oddly perhaps, the Leader is painted as a hero of almost superhuman proportions, and at the same time as an ordinary person, "one of us." This allows "us" to identify with him and excuse his weaknesses (corruption, for instance) because we can easily put ourselves, in our imagination, in his shoes (Silvio Berlusconi is a good example). Hugo Chavez often likened himself to Simon Bolivar, the greatest hero in Venezuelan political tradition.[52] Narendra Modi projected an "image as a corruption-free politician who would 'clean' Indian politics."[53] Similarly, Jair

---

[48] Yago Matheus da Silva, "Bolsonaro and Social Media: A Critical Discourse Analysis of the Brazilian President's Populist Communication on Twitter" (Master's thesis, Uppsala Universitet, 2020), p. 60.

[49] Christian Lamour, "Interviewing a Right-Wing Populist Leader during the 2019 EU Elections: Conflictual Situations and Equivocation beyond Borders," *Discourse and Communication*, 15 (2021), 59–73 at 65.

[50] Nadia Urbinati, *Me the People* (Cambridge:Harvard University Press, 2019), p. 117.

[51] As Urbinati perceptively observes, "Since charisma is not a quality that can be detached from the people's faith, there is no outside perspective from which we can decide whether a leader is charismatic." Ibid., pp. 122–123.

[52] Anibal Gauna, "Populism, Heroism, and Revolution. Chávez's Cultural Performances in Venezuela, 1999–2012," *American Journal of Cultural Sociology*, 6 (2016), 37–59 at 45.

[53] *Mann Ki Baat* [Modi's radio show], October 3, 2014, cited in Bajpai, "Matters of the Heart," 108.

Bolsonaro painted "the image of [himself as] a savior capable of 'cleansing' the country from corrupt leaders, communists, and activists."[54] Prime Minister Orbán is described by his sycophantic intellectual, Professor András Lánczi, thus: "His first name 'Victor' really define[s] his character: someone who wins."[55] And not only victorious but also exquisitely virtuous: "In my understanding Orbán discovered the system of the meritorious moral relationships alleviating the development of this moral requirement [of mutual trust]."[56] Orbán describes himself in heroic terms, connecting with the long, tragic Hungarian tradition. In a radio interview (as with many other populists studied here, regular radio broadcasts are Orbán's favorite means of traditional communication) for the public Kossuth Radio, answering a friendly question regarding the condemnation of Orbán in the European Parliament, he said: "I always go wherever Hungarian national interests or the honour of the Hungarian people need to be fought for...I'm not afraid of my own shadow...In the course of Hungarian history we've faced worse odds when we've needed to fight. One accepts that if one is Hungarian, this is one's fate."[57] And to be fair, Orbán had had heroic episodes in the early stages of his political career, which in fact commenced with his speech at the reburial of Imre Nagy, a martyr of the 1956 revolution, on June 16, 1989, when he was the first political leader since 1956 to demand the withdrawal of Soviet troops from Hungary. Jarosław Kaczyński was hailed by fellow politicians, including President Duda and Prime Minister Morawiecki, as a political "genius," even though as an individual he is as far from the conventional image of a "charismatic Leader" as one can imagine. In the Polish version of the cult of personality, there is "cult" all right but without the "personality."

But at the same time, these nearly divine figures are down-to-earth, simple, and approachable. They emphasize this message often by things as trivial as their clothes: Chavez came to an important business forum

---

[54] Ricardo F. Mendonça and Renato Duarte Caetano, "Populism as Parody: The Visual Self-Presentation of Jair Bolsonaro on Instagram," *The International Journal of Press/Politics*, 2 (2021), 210–235 at 219.

[55] András Lánczi, "The Renewed Social Contract – Hungary's Elections, 2018," *Hungarian Review*, 9/3 (2018), www.hungarianreview.com/article/20180525_the_renewed_social_contract_hungary_s_elections_2018, p. 3.

[56] Ibid., p. 7.

[57] Lamour, "Interviewing a Right-Wing Populist Leader," p. 69.

wearing a casual shirt with sleeves rolled up,[58] while Bolsonaro likes to circulate photos of him wearing a football jersey;[59] Modi, in turn, wears a "Modi kurta," a long shirt with short sleeves, which became famous after Modi explained that it dates back to the time when he was an itinerant worker, had no time to wash his clothes, so decided to cut his sleeves in half. (Eventually, the "Modi kurta" became so popular that the company that designed it for him asked for his permission to sell it under his name.)[60] In speeches and talks to the people, these politicians project themselves as "common men." The tone of Modi's radio broadcasts has been described by an analyst as "informal, colloquial, and yet sentimental."[61] Populists occasionally – but quite deliberately – descend to low manners to establish themselves as ordinary people: Duterte made rape jokes and jokes about Viagra,[62] Bolsonaro depicted gay men by using a Portuguese language equivalent of the epithet fa*gots,[63] while Chavez likened media executives (who had complained about freedom of the press) to "a truck full of squealing pigs."[64] Jarosław Kaczyński shouted at opposition MPs from the parliament's lectern: "Shut your treasonous mugs," and his trusted collaborator, MP Joanna Lichocka, showed the opposition benches in the same parliament the middle finger sign.

Occasionally such statements and conduct may be just the effect of emotional exhaustion, but often such bad manners are perfectly controllable. They are meant to show the populists' authenticity, a liberating rejection of "political correctness" (a quasi-universal theme and slogan used by populists around the world),[65] and a spectacle reinforcing the message of plain-speaking honesty. This is meant to be an "ostentatious

---

[58] Nicole Curato and Jonathan Corpus Ong, "Who Laughs at a Rape Joke? Illiberal Responsiveness in Rodrigo Duterte's Philippines," in Tanja Dreher and Anshuman Mondal (eds.), *Ethical Responsiveness and the Politics of Difference* (New York: Palgrave Macmillan, 2018), pp. 117–132 at 126.

[59] Mendonça and Caetano, "Populism as Parody," 223.

[60] Christophe Jaffrelot and Louise Tillin, "Populism in India," in Cristóbal Rovira Kaltwasser, Paul Taggart, Paulina Ochoa Espejo, and Pierre Ostiguy (eds.), *Oxford Handbook of Populism* (Oxford: Oxford University Press, 2017), pp. 179–194 at 186.

[61] Bajpai, "Matters of the Heart," pp. 116–117.

[62] Curato and Ong, "Who Laughs at a Rape Joke?" p. 126.

[63] Thomas Bustamante and Conrado Hubner Mendes, "Freedom without Responsibility: The Promise of Bolsonaro's COVID-Denial," *Jus Cogens*, 3 (2021), 181–207 at 191.

[64] Eduardo Frajman, "Broadcasting Populist Leadership: Hugo Chávez and *Aló Presidente*," *Journal of Latin American Studies*, 46 (2014), 501–526 at 511.

[65] On Orbán's philippics against political correctness, see Kim Lane Scheppele, "The Opportunism of Populists and the Defense of Constitutional Liberalism," *German Law Journal*, 20 (2019), 314–331 at 324.

shift in the limits of what can be said" and an instance of allegedly authentic behavior.[66] In the same vein, populist leaders occasionally boast of their own moral defects – a device probably meant to generate a sense of commonality with their audiences, consisting as they do of less-than-perfect humans. Just as Italy's prime minister Berlusconi's tax evasions provoked an exceptionally low level of societal condemnation in a country where tax evasion is widespread, so could Duterte openly admit to his marital infidelity by talking about his "two girlfriends" while married.[67]

Touching the Heart

While we find lots of emotions in all great political speeches or discourses, populist discourse stands out for its intensity: both of positive emotions toward "us" and negative emotions against "them," that is, those against whom anger and fear are addressed. In particular, "emotionalized blame" against elites distinguishes populist speech from mainstream politics.[68] A study conducted by Dominique Wirz in 2018 confirmed the effectiveness of using highly emotional language to generate populist successes. She found that "populist appeals elicit stronger emotions than nonpopulist appeals and that these emotions mediate the persuasiveness of the appeals. The widespread assumption that populist appeals are persuasive because they are inherently emotional is thus supported."[69]

As mentioned above, those emotions may be negative or positive. Negative emotions are most often those of anger and fear, which lead to the attribution of blame. Such negative emotions stress a sense of urgency and signal a sense of danger and threat to the community. They normally rely on a sense of injustice: a dissonance between widespread

---

[66] Barbara Christophe, Christoph Kohl, Heike Liebau, and Achim Saupe, "Claims to Authenticity in Populist Discourses: General Introduction to the Volume," in Barbara Christophe, Christoph Kohl, Heike Liebau, and Achim Saupe (eds), *The Politics of Authenticity and Populist Discourses* (Cham: Palgrave Macmillan, 2021), pp. 3–30 at 7.
[67] Gloria, "War of Words," 11.
[68] See Michael Hameleers, Linda Bos, and Claes H. de Vreese, "'*They* Did It': The Effects of Emotionalized Blame Attribution in Populist Communication," *Communication Research*, 44 (2017), 870–900 at 871
[69] Dominique Wirz, "Persuasion through Emotion? An Experimental Test of the Emotion-Eliciting Nature of Populist Communication," *International Journal of Communication*, 12 (2018), 1114–1138 at 1114.

moral ideals and the reality out there. They are against whoever is depicted as the enemy, whether as rich and fortunate as a financial elite or as poor and desperate as refugees and migrants. And it is not necessary that populist leaders and their acolytes actually *hate* the objects of their negative propaganda; what matters is that they know that some in their audience are likely to hate them. As Bálint Magyar explains, the leaders of the ruling party in Hungary are not necessarily anti-Semitic or anti-Romani: "[T]hey just want to win over people who have racist inclinations to their camp, too."[70] This is all the more so in a situation where Fidesz had to compete for the votes of the more radical right-wing party, Jobbik, in the same way that Kaczyński's PiS in Poland has to compete with an openly racist Konfederacja. Negative, racist intimations (anti-Semitic, anti-Muslim, anti-Roma) in official propaganda in both these countries are not really addressed to those groups but are rather meant to capture target audiences that include anti-Semites, anti-Muslims, religious bigots, and the like. Orbán himself, when openly challenged on the possibly anti-Semitic nature of his anti-Soros posters, turned it into a joke, saying, "I can't do anything about the fact that George Soros in a Hungarian of Jewish origin: that is solely a matter for the Good Lord." And he immediately invoked one of the standard anti-Semitic tropes: "But in Hungary, it is Soros who embodies the worst face of globalism."[71]

But, contrary to the intuitive view, the *positive* emotions emphasized by populists – those of hope or virtue – may be as strong as or even stronger in populist discourses than negative ones. When populists stress their closeness to the "real" people, they present themselves as spokespersons for the people, fighting to improve their situation. This benign sentimentalism may be as useful as anger or fear and is frequently employed by populists. As one analyst of the Indian leader's broadcasts noted: "Modi not only makes frequent use of words like 'tears,' 'joy,' 'happiness,' 'touched the heart,' 'emotional,' etc.; he also intonates the emotions with his style of speaking."[72] This goes well with the "family" metaphor so gladly used by him. This account of the general message sent by Modi's radio programs is particularly instructive when it notes: "It...thus emerges that Modi relies on the show not for propagating

---

[70] Bálint Magyar, *Post-Communist Mafia State: The Case of Hungary* (Budapest: CEU Press, 2016), p. 235, emphases removed.

[71] Orbán interviewed by German *Welt*, cited by Lamour, "Interviewing a Right-Wing Populist Leader," p. 67.

[72] Bajpai, "Matters of the Heart," p. 115.

larger governmental schemes, plans, or technocratic truths but for proving his concern for people's everyday lives, for reiterating his emotional attachment to them, for recognizing their aspirations, achievements and everyday struggles, and finally for projecting himself as one among them."[73]

Speaking as "just one of us" goes hand in hand with populists' open disdain for experts, scholars, and intellectuals, whereby academic knowledge is replaced by "common sense," available to every person who wants to see the truth. This is truth undistorted by difficult jargon, hermetic vocabulary, and evidence based on complex research, inaccessible to common people. For a populist, a tweet from another committed populist is worth as much – or more – as an empirical study in a peer-refereed review (though, to be fair, non-populist politicians don't make much use of those either). This has been described as the "democratization of evidence," in which no piece of information is more valuable than any other.[74] Climate change is one of the preferred targets of populist denials (denial of climate change is, for instance, the foundation of Bolsonaro's environmental policy).[75] Pro-PiS Polish commentators like to poke fun at climate change theories whenever they can complain of a cold day. And a single episode of violence committed in Europe by migrants from the Middle East or Africa provides anti-immigration populists with stronger evidence of the dangers of immigration than tons of statistics on crime.

This disdain for objectively (though not always easily and instantly) verifiable truth is of course greatly facilitated and enhanced by social media. A false or offensive statement (for example, about Hillary Clinton or Rahul Gandhi or Dilma Rousseff or Maria Sereno,[76] or George Soros or Donald Tusk – pick your favorite target of populist ire), is made "true" through its reverberations in "retweets," "likes," "favorites," and so forth. At certain point, such fake news or defamatory statements commence a life of their own, go viral, and come to dominate public discourse, not as statements propagated by their political rivals for self-serving reasons but

---

[73] Ibid., p. 119.
[74] David Zarefsky and Dima Mohammed, "The Rhetorical Stance of Populism," in Ingeborg van der Geest, Henrike Jansen, and Bart van Klink (eds.), *Vox Populi: Populism as a Rhetorical and Democratic Challenge* (Cheltenham: Edward Elgar, 2020), pp. 17–28 at 25.
[75] Rafael Mafei, Thomas Bustamante, and Emilio Peluso Neder Meyer, "Brazil: From Antiestablishmentarianism to Bolsonarism," in András Sajo, Renata Uitz, and Stephen Holmes (eds.), *The Routledge Handbook on Illiberalism* (in press).
[76] See Chapter 4.

rather by concerned citizens participating in the most democratic speech platforms ever invented.

Such speech requires simple explanations of complex phenomena. As already mentioned, populist explanations usually are monocausal, refer to easy-to-understand statements (conspiracy theories are an example), and see complexity as a strategy aimed at obfuscation, and so immediately to be regarded as suspect. Ambiguities, skepticism, "on the other hand"-types of arguments are rejected as unnecessary muddying. Historical analogies or analogies from other countries are liked, while depictions of distinguishing factors between cases claimed to be analogous are ignored. Invocation of stereotypes – that is, unjustified generalizations – are a preferred mode of argument: Muslims are terrorists, atheists are amoral, people of color are untrustworthy, and so forth. Populism "simplifies cases and circumstances, cherry-picking facts, and framing topics as well as information according to the stereotypical opposition between us-versus-them."[77] Policy elucidation is replaced with simple slogans especially in electoral debates. Thus, in relation to Bolsonaro, João Feres Júnior and Juliana Gagliardi write: "Throughout the electoral campaign Bolsonaro and his followers did much to oversimplify the political agenda...His official government plan, a document that all presidential candidates must publicize in order to run, is nothing but an inchoate set of simplistic and poorly explained ideas."[78]

Single-factor explanations lend themselves to grotesque exaggerations, another characteristic of the paranoid style depicted long ago by Richard Hofstadter.[79] Exaggeration and hyperbole usually apply to what is *at stake* in the maintenance of the populist's power: It is nothing less than the survival of society or of the Nation or of fundamental human goods. Eduardo Frajman quotes Chávez: "We are in the time of the Apocalypse, says the Bible; that is, a time in which one cannot be with God and the Devil at the same time. No, either you are with God or you are with the Devil."[80] As Jarosław Kaczyński diagnosed in 2014: "[I]n our [social] life a lot of evil has appeared, evil which is more and more insolent, more and

---

[77] Hendricks and Vestergaard, *Reality Lost*, p. 89.
[78] João Feres Júnior and Juliana Gagliardi, "Populism and the Media in Brazil: The Case of Jair Bolsonaro," in Christoph Kohl, Barbara Christophe, Heike Liebau, and Achim Saupe (eds.), *The Politics of Authenticity and Populist Discourses* (Cham: Palgrave Macmillan, 2021), pp. 83–104 at 98.
[79] Hofstadter, "The Paranoid Style," pp. 77–86.
[80] Frajman, "Broadcasting Populist Leadership," p. 511.

more aggressive, and enjoying more and more impunity."[81] To protest EU "interference" in the Polish system of justice, editor-in-chief of pro-PiS newspaper and a leader of pro-PiS NGOs, Tomasz Sakiewicz, announced "We are defending Polish sovereignty, we are not going to sell our sovereignty and freedom for any price."[82]

These lamentations over threats to the greatest goods of the nation have been aptly labeled by scholars as akin to a "melodramatic jeremiad": "Jeremiad as a rhetorical tactic demands conversion to the 'true' ways indicated by the 'chosen' who lead the national reformation... The populist rhetoric emphasizes the privileged status of those within the nation vigilant enough to see that its greatness is no longer recognized by others."[83] At the gathering of pro-PiS NGOs from which Sakiewicz's quote comes, PiS's then deputy leader Antoni Macierewicz said: "Those who attack the Constitutional Tribunal these days are not worthy of the title of Polish citizen, they do not deserve to be treated as Poles."[84]

Denying their opponents the status of "true" Poles is not an unusual rhetorical device in Poland, and in other populist regimes for that matter (Hungary, Brazil, etc.). Polish sociologist Andrzej Zybertowicz, who is well placed in the PiS establishment, in a TV discussion announced that the Polish nation consists only of those who endorse what he considers to be a "patriotic minimum," and whoever fails to meet any of these threshold conditions, Dr. Zybertowicz added, "signs off on Polishness."[85]

Oversimplifications, exaggerations, or disregard for scholarly knowledge do not mean that populists themselves and their acolytes are necessarily unintelligent. These are all studied attitudes, adopted for theatrical purposes. And regardless of their own brain power, they

---

[81] For Kaczyński's speech on December 10, 2017, to commemorate the April 10, 2010, air crash, see "Kaczyński: Nasi wrogowie nie spoczną" (TVN24 online, 10 10 2017), www.tvn24.pl/wiadomosci-z-kraju,3/jaroslaw-kaczynski-92-miesiecznica-katastrofy-smolenskiej,797515.html.

[82] Agata Kondzińska, "'Neomarksizm, śmierć, niszczenie cywilizacji chrześcijańskiej': Kluby 'Gazety Polskiej' bronią Trybunału i rządu PiS," *Gazeta Wyborcza* (July 31, 2021), www.wyborcza.pl/7,75398,27393867,neomarksizm-smierc-niszczenie-cywilizacji-chrzescijanskiej.html.

[83] Golec de Zavala, "Why Is Populism So Robustly Associated with Conspiratorial Thinking?" p. 281.

[84] Kondzińska, "Neomarksizm."

[85] "Plemię to za łagodne określenie. Plemiona mogą współistnieć," *TVN24* (November 12, 2017), www.tvn24.pl/wiadomosci-z-kraju,3/arena-idei-czy-polacy-to-jeden-narod-a-dwa-plemiona,789533.html.

usually embrace, for their support groups, scholars and intellectuals willing to provide them with expertise (though in clearly determined confines) and provide a degree of legitimacy through sycophantic applause. As Nadia Urbinati observes, "The creation of a populist leader is a strategic enterprise that requires the work of 'politico-intellectuals.' These intellectuals 'help' the *incarnatus* widen the categories for shaping the narrative and help him devise effective symbols."[86] Her own example is that of Ernesto Laclau, who helped Kirchnerism in Argentina. Viktor Orbán has his courtier-philosopher, András Lánczi (head of the main pro-Fidesz think tank and rector of Corvinus University in Budapest), and Kaczyński has Ryszard Legutko and Zbigniew Krasnodębski – both professors of philosophy, and both Members of European Parliament. . They all offer strategic advice to their masters but also produce a degree of respectability, especially within intellectual elites.

Bad Media and Good Media

"When there are no problems in the government, most of the media create something to talk about and manipulate. Always inform yourself through alternative media, because unfortunately, many of the usual ones do not want the best for Brazil, only for themselves!"[87] This tweet by Jair Bolsonaro is symptomatic of populists' approach to "traditional" (or "mainstream") media. They follow in the footsteps (as in so many other ways) of President Trump and his angry attitude toward the "MAINSTREAM MEDIA" (caps in original).[88] His war on the *New York Times* and the *Washington Post* prefigured Bolsonaro's animosity to *Folha de São Paulo*,[89] Duterte's successful war on the *Philippine Daily Inquirer* and the ABS-CBN broadcaster, Kaczyński's anger at the daily *Gazeta Wyborcza*, the weekly *Polityka*, and the broadcaster TVN-24, or Orbán's colonizing of basically all traditional media in Hungary (as described in some detail in Chapter 2). Depicting traditional media as vehicles of elite domination suits the populist narrative of "Us vs. Them" well. Populists avoid and treat with disdain both the mainstream media, which may ask them uncomfortable questions, and journals, which may publish critical editorials. Narendra Modi is "highly wary of whom he

---

[86] Urbinati, *Me the People*, p. 120.
[87] Da Silva, "Bolsonaro and Social Media," p. 76.
[88] Hartleb, "Materializations of Populism," p. 42.
[89] Da Silva, "Bolsonaro and Social Media," p. 73.

speaks to and when," so much so, we are told by an expert from India, that "during his first term of five years as Prime Minister, Modi officially organized only one press conference with all media houses."[90] And his preference for a radio-based "conversation of the month" is understood as a "modus operandi that allows him to sidestep more combative questioning by interviewers."[91] This is typical. In the entire period after the 2015 electoral victories, Poland's ultimate leader, Jarosław Kaczyński, has not once met with a journalist from any other publication than the flattering, pro-PiS media, and his rare press conferences do not include Q and As, concluding immediately after his statements.

In contrast, populist leaders just love *social* media – and are very good at it. That is why they gain in Twitter or Facebook what they lose in *Folha de São Paulo* or *Gazeta Wyborcza*. "For the populist, reaching out directly to the electorate and building momentum through the collaborative action of citizens retweeting messages strengthens the politician's normative claim to legitimacy."[92] Social media removes journalists, editors, and publishers as intermediaries between the leader and the people. "In the specific case of socially mediated populist communication, the network media logic means that populist leaders' linkage with their constituencies or sympathisers is entirely disintermediated: that is, the production of contents is free from being filtered by journalists or other types of gatekeepers."[93] It is where populist actors find an unmediated, unspoiled "people's voice": The only actors are the populists and their fans. Twitter is their medium of choice (personal disclosure: I am an enthusiastic user of Twitter myself). "Twitter facilitates the kind of horizontal, interactive communication praised by populist rhetoric. It offers a flattened communication structure in contrast to the top-down structure of the legacy media. It is suitable for unmediated exchanges between politicians and citizens."[94]

---

[90] Bajpai, "Matters of the Heart," p. 123.
[91] Jaffrelot and Tillin, "Populism in India," p. 188.
[92] A'ndre Gonawela, Joyojeet Pal, Udit Thawani, Elmer van der Vlugt, Wim Out, and Priyank Chandra, "Speaking Their Mind: Populist Style and Antagonistic Messaging in the Tweets of Donald Trump, Narendra Modi, Nigel Farage, and Geert Wilders," *Computer Supported Cooperative Work*, 27 (2018), 293–326 at 299.
[93] Gianpietro Mazzoleni and Roberta Bracciale, "Socially Mediated Populism: The Communicative Strategies of Political Leaders on Facebook," *Palgrave Communications*, 4 (2018). DOI: 10.1057/s41599-018-0104-x, p. 3.
[94] Silvio Waisbord and Adriana Amado, "Populist Communication by Digital Means: Presidential Twitter in Latin America," *Information, Communication and Society*, 20 (2017), 1330–1346 at 1332.

Social media, and in particular Twitter, have structural characteristics that make it eminently suited to populist purposes. It is unmediated: whatever comes to your mind, subject to the condition that it is simple and brief (simple *because* brief), finds its way to your fans instantly. Social media enables a populist "echo chamber" (as already described above). The combination of the horizontality and ubiquitousness of social media allows "a vast circulation of populist content with high potential impact, thanks to a viral diffusion."[95] Social media enhances the personalized and emotive communication style of populists: It contributes to "dramatising populist communication because they are platforms suited to producing emotional, controversial, even violent contents typical of much populist activism."[96] It enables populists to use simple and provocative language, with terse messaging that is rewarded for its uncomplicatedness and impulsivity. And, perhaps most importantly, social media is a far more interactive means of communicating with the public, resulting in the public feeling closer to the populist. When messages are quickly disseminated, users can publicly signal their reactions in their "retweets" or "likes," which create an illusion of a direct and active rapport with politicians who are then seen as the ordinary persons' interlocutors. (The fact that many such likes, retweets, endorsements, or favorites are now driven by commercial enterprises is conveniently disregarded, for the sake of maintaining the pleasant fiction of direct interaction). "Whatever the medium," Ruth Ben-Ghiat observes, "a paradoxical truth holds: the more skilled the leader is at this mediatized politics, the more his admirers see him as authentic and feel a personal connection with him."[97]

All this creates a quasi-symbiotic relationship between social media and populist leaders. No wonder that the latter take such full advantage of the former. Bolsonaro is particularly apt at WhatsApp: Messages from his presidential campaign were distributed through at least 1,500 groups.[98] Duterte was no less professional in exploiting social media. A central reason that Duterte's messages in 2016 campaign went viral on social media was the use of paid "informal actors, including paid trolls and influencers" liking, sharing, and commenting on his posts.[99] Chávez on Twitter reached more than 4 million followers (and we are talking

---

[95] Mazzoleni and Bracciale, "Socially Mediated Populism," p. 3.
[96] Ibid., p. 3.
[97] Ruth Ben-Ghiat, *Strongmen* (New York: W. W. Norton, 2020), p. 94.
[98] Mendonça and Duarte Caetano, "Populism as Parody," p. 220.
[99] Aim Sinpeng, Dimitar Gueorguiev, and Aries A. Arugay, "Strong Fans, Weak Campaigns: Social Media and Duterte in the 2016 Philippine Election," *Journal of East Asian Studies*, 20 (2020) 353–374 at 367, 369.

about the early 2010s) and he apparently even "appointed six ministers via Twitter, demanding 'efficiency.'"[100]

When Conservative Intellectuals Meet in Paris

"In March 2017, a group of conservative scholars and intellectuals met in Paris" – reads the first sentence.[101] Admittedly, not the most arresting announcement, but don't yawn: What follows is worth reading. It is a manifesto called, appropriately enough, "The Paris Statement," signed by twelve intellectuals from nine countries (the French are overrepresented), including Chantal Delsol, András Lánczi, Ryszard Legutko, Pierre Manent, and Roger Scruton – all recognizable names of the European intelligentsia.[102]

The statement has not made a big impact – if anything, it was greeted by a deafening silence in European media and public discourse. It is not particularly interesting philosophically; rather, it is a predictable lament about the liberal, cosmopolitan left that is threatening European Christian traditions, and so forth. Each of its thirty-three numbered paragraphs has a helpful summary at the margins, so one can get the general impression just by reading those headings, for instance: "A false Europe threatens us" (para. 2), "The false Europe is utopian and tyrannical" (para. 3), "The nation-state is a hallmark of Europe" (para. 7), "Christianity encouraged cultural unity" (para. 9), all the way down to "Only empires are multicultural" (para. 28), "A proper hierarchy nourishes social well-being" (para. 29), and "Marriage and family are essential" (para. 33). Considering the combined brainpower of the signatories, not earth-shattering discoveries.

What *is*, however, both striking and fascinating is the particular rhetorical manner used consistently throughout the statement. It is all built on a dichotomy between "the false Europe" and "the true (real) Europe." For example, "the false Europe" espouses superstitions of progress, stifles dissent, and is utopian, all of which puts "the true Europe" at risk "because of the suffocating grip that the false Europe has over our imaginations" (paras. 3 and 4). Also, "the true Europe" encourages public

---

[100] Block and Negrine, "The Populist Communication Style," p. 188.
[101] The Paris Statement, "A Europe We Can Believe In" (Introduction), www.thetrueeurope.eu.
[102] The Paris Statement, "A Europe We Can Believe In" (Full text), www.thetrueeurope.eu/a-europe-we-can-believe-in.

participation (para. 5), is a community of nations (paras. 7 and 12), "has been marked by Christianity" (para. 9), affirms the equal dignity of every individual (para. 10), draws inspiration from the national tradition" (para. 11), and so forth. In contrast, "the false Europe" has a one-sided commitment to human liberty (para. 14), boasts commitment to equality but in a utopian version of multiculturalism (para. 17), is fragile and impotent (para. 20), and for all these reasons must be resisted: "Breaking the spell of the false Europe and its utopian, pseudo-religious crusade for a borderless world means fostering a new kind of statesmanship and a new kind of statesman" (para. 26.) It is notable that the antinomy is *not* that of a "good Europe" and "bad Europe," not between reasonable, attractive, plausible, coherent, and the like, visions and the unreasonable, unattractive, incoherent, and implausible ones. It is between "true" (or "real") and "false." The views being criticized and rejected by the signatories are not merely incorrect: they are not real. They are defined out of existence. The good conceptions are the only real or true ones.

This striking dichotomy *may* be perhaps seen to be borne of the linguistic idiosyncrasies of the English language. But no. Other translations of the statement confirm this reading. In French it is "L'Europe veritable" versus "fausse Europe"; in Italian "L'Europa vera" versus "La falsa Europa"; in German "Das wahre Europa" versus "Das falsche Europa"; and in Polish it is "prawdziwa Europa" versus "fałszywa Europa." So, it is not an error in translation, or a misuse of a word. It is a conscious, deliberate, consistent dichotomy between what is real (true) and what is unreal (false). The views with which the conservative philosophers disagree are not criticized but dismissed as not "real." And a Europe the vision of which they do not like is false, unreal, nonexistent.

At one point the statement asserts, "We must recover an abiding respect for reality" (para. 25), and this is an important clue to its puzzling language. Reality is not what is *out there* (because the exponents of all those ideas they dismiss as false are definitely *out there*; indeed, it is their ubiquity that has triggered the alarmist tone of the statement). Reality is what is correct. Just as for political populists, the opponents to their rule are not real members of the people but place themselves beyond the pale (not "true Poles," "true Hungarians," etc.), so the views opposed by the signatories of the statement are beyond the pale of the European universe of ideas. They just do not exist, even if our sense and minds tell us that these ideas *are* being shared, endorsed, and defended by many.

And yes, there is a point at the end of the manifesto where its authors engage with the concept of populism (para. 34) – and thus build a connection between the general theme of this book and the Paris Statement. "There is great anxiety in Europe today because of the rise of what is called 'populism' – though the meaning of the term seems never to be defined, and it is used mostly as invective," they say with disapproval, not of populism but of the anti-populists using the term. What follows is particularly warm toward the right-wing populist movements in Europe today, though none is identified by name. But the statement's use of code words helps us recognize them rather precisely: "[W]e acknowledge that much in this new political phenomenon can represent a healthy rebellion against the tyranny of the false Europe, which labels as 'anti-democratic' any threat to its monopoly on moral legitimacy. The so-called 'populism' challenges the dictatorship of the status quo, the 'fanaticism of the centre,' and rightly so." And they conclude with a statement: "It is a sign that even in the midst of our degraded and impoverished political culture, the historical agency of the European peoples can be reborn. Populism should be engaged." This sounds to me like a huge approval of the movements of Matteo Salvini, Marine Le Pen, Jarosław Kaczyński, or Viktor Orbán.

They are not false. They are real.

6

Democracy Diseased

Populism in the Time of Covid

"I have no idea what's awaiting me, or what will happen when this all ends. For the moment I know this: there are sick people and they need curing," says Dr. Bernard Rieux in *The Plague*, a novel by Albert Camus that naturally enough comes to one's mind in these pandemic days. "They need curing" – the task at hand is self-evident, and apparently easy to ascertain, as a measure of the quality of a government. Whether it be democratic or authoritarian, populist or liberal, open to globalization or closed and inward-looking – a government faced with a disaster of this size must be able to deliver quick and efficient solutions. Just like a war, the pandemic trumps many nuances and distinctions, bringing to the forefront the essential criterion of a good government: whether it gets things done when the question is the life or death of its subjects.

It also provides citizens with a seemingly simple and easy test for their government, and for comparing it to others facing the same tragedy. There is no room for subtle trade-offs between incommensurate goods ("More efficiency or more liberty?"), for philosophical deliberations about the proper functions of a government ("But should the government be in the business of supplying this public good rather than relegating it to the market of private goods?"), for endless controversies about the criteria and currencies of values ("How do you really measure the infringement upon this or that right?"), and so forth. The dominant purpose, the role of the government, the measure of achievement – are there for all to see. And compare. And judge. As Ivan Krastev noted: "The paradox of this crisis is that it has given governments extraordinary powers, while also empowering every citizen by allowing them to judge whether their government is doing better or worse than others."[1]

How are we to judge whether populist-authoritarian governments, such as those discussed in this book, are "doing better or worse than

---

[1] Ivan Krastev, *Is It Tomorrow Yet?* (London: Allen Lane, 2020).

others"? Any response must be of course bracketed by the proviso "so far." These words are being written in the midst of the crisis: up to now (late February 2022), nearly 6 million people around the world have fallen victim to Covid-19. The size of this number is as if the population of a country the size of Ireland or Liberia was wiped out, although some estimates place it much higher, up to 16 million (think of the populations of Cambodia or the Netherlands). On the day this book is read, the number will be sadly much higher. And even once the worst of the pandemic is over, its aftershocks – including political and legal ones – will reverberate for a long time, perhaps until the end of the lives of the generations currently inhabiting this planet.

Another caveat is needed. Even if (and it is a big If) we believe that we have a simple, easily measurable criterion for how well a government has coped with the pandemic, the matrix being the number of deaths or cases or measurable economic effects of the pandemic, these outcomes are largely affected by matters outside political control, and thus cannot be said to be a source of blame or praise for the government. There are simply too many contingent, uncontrollable factors in the pandemic. As Guido Alfani, professor of economic history at Bocconi University in Milan notes: "The local economic consequences of a pandemic depend upon unpredictable epidemiological factors and not only upon the quality of the health institutions and of the policies for pandemic containment (for Covid-19, it might turn out that within Europe, Italy suffered more simply because it was affected first)."[2] Alfani is a good historian and draws analogies with various past pandemics. For instance, writing about a great plague in the early seventeenth century in Europe, he notes: "in 1629–30, plague entered north Italy with infected armies coming from France and Germany to fight in the War of the Mantuan Succession – and nobody has ever been able to impose a quarantine on an enemy army."[3] So even the best, most rational anti-pandemic policies do not always prove successful, and vice versa, a state with an incompetent, chaotic leadership may get away from the calamity relatively scot-free.

For these reasons at least, I only have moderate ambitions here: I do not intend to present a comprehensive scorecard for how various types of

---

[2] Guido Alfani, "Pandemics and the Asymmetric Shocks: Lessons from the History of Plagues," VoxEU/CEPR (April 9, 2020), www.voxeu.org/article/pandemics-and-asymmetric-shocks, p. 4.
[3] Ibid., p. 3.

governments have coped with the pandemic (and note that authoritarian countries' statistics are not quite reliable anyway, which renders comparisons uncertain), but rather aim to assess whether populism is emerging from this world-scale disaster as a "winner" compared to liberal democracy. And I believe that some tentative, provisional judgments can be already offered.

The Populist Dividend?

At the outset of the pandemic, conventional wisdom had it that Covid-19 would strengthen populist appeal, deepen the populist grip on power, and threaten democracies worldwide. Populists, it was feared, would exploit its means of social control, unconstrained by checks and balances, and display the weaknesses of liberal democracy unforgivingly at a moment when time and authority are in dramatically short supply. Faced with an existential threat, people would naturally rally behind a strong government and a decisive leader and disrespect politicians who favored deliberation and consultation prior to taking decisions. People also, naturally enough, in times of such danger have a higher tolerance for restrictions of their rights and liberties, and greater appetite for the lifting, temporarily, of usual democratic processes.

An argument was that authoritarian governments that had been successful in taking people out of poverty – in particular, China – would carry on their efficiency dividend into a more efficient struggle against the pandemic, thus consolidating their attractiveness in a world in which the popularity of liberal democracy was diminishing. The outcomes for traditional liberal values may be disastrous: "[A]uthoritarian regimes may see the crisis as an opportunity for consolidation. Political and legal tools developed to control the spread of the virus may become tools simply to control us," fear Miguel Maduro and Paul Kahn.[4] The "authoritarian advantage" brought into sharp relief by the pandemic would consolidate the populists' grip on power where they are in government, and at the same time bolster their political attractiveness in places where they are still challenging democratic governments. In addition, when entire states are locked down, domestic political and constitutional excesses of populists are less visible externally, any oversight by

---

[4] Miguel Maduro and Paul Kahn, "Introduction: A New Beginning," in Miguel Maduro and Paul Kahn (eds.), *Democracy in Times of Pandemic* (Cambridge: Cambridge University Press, 2020), pp. 1–18 at 7.

supranational agencies and by world public opinion is meeker, and authoritarians can get away with much more than they would in times when their mischiefs are highly visible.

One could be excused for thinking along these lines. In addition to all the veto points, checks and balances, and procedures that slow down decision-making (instruments that may be partially lifted or even withdrawn in times of emergency), liberal democracies have a fundamental and non-negotiable feature going to their very essence, which is that politicians are restricted by public opinion in how they act. In the words of Michael Ignatieff, an age-old dilemma of democratic leadership is:

> How far ahead of their electorate can leaders afford to be? How can they secure consent if they act before there is demonstrable evidence of a threat? "Better safe than sorry" is hard to sell and may make a politician look skittish and weak. Even if the Italian Prime Minister's advisors were warning him of the likely consequences of the epidemic, he still faced the unenviable task of justifying restrictive measures in the absence of direct consequences.[5]

The conventional wisdom seems partly vindicated by historical experience. Some scholars claim (but others deny, it should be added) that the Spanish flu was a factor (though certainly not *the* factor!) contributing to the rise of right-wing political extremism after the First World War, for instance in Germany.[6] Going much further back in history, the Black Death in Europe in 1347–1351 unleashed pogroms against the Jews, believed to be guilty of poisoning wells and food supplies.[7] Plagues, pandemics, epidemics – these calamities brought about (the argument goes) by-and-large harmful political changes, contributing to fear, violence, hysteria, and scapegoating. Why would it be different today?

---

[5] Michael Ignatieff, "The Reckoning: Evaluating Democratic Leadership," in Miguel Maduro and Paul Kahn (eds.), *Democracy in Times of Pandemic* (Cambridge: Cambridge University Press, 2020), pp. 89–103 at 94.

[6] For such a claim, see Kristian Blickle, "Pandemics Change Cities: Municipal Spending and Voter Extremism in Germany, 1918–1933," *Federal Reserve Bank of New York Staff Reports* (2020), at 13. For a rebuttal, see Allison Sommer, "Did the Spanish Flu Pandemic Really Lead to the Rise of Nazism?" *Haaretz* (May 16, 2020), www.haaretz.com/us-news/.premium-did-the-spanish-flu-pandemic-really-lead-to-the-rise-of-nazism-1.8825631. For a sustained scholarly rebuttal, see also Daniel Gingerich and Jan Vogler, "Pandemics and Political Development: The Electoral Legacy of the Black Death in Germany," *World Politics*, 73 (2021), 393–440.

[7] Samuel Cohn, "Pandemics: Waves of Disease, Waves of Hate from the Plague of Athens to A.I.D.S.," *Historical Research*, 85 (2012), 535–555 at 536.

The same features that lead democracies to overall better policies may be seen to present obstacles in coping with events that are simultaneously unpredictable, global, and all-encompassing. These three features of the pandemic – just like a world war (of course, with some caveats as to its unpredictability) – put democracies to a crash test that is very difficult to pass successfully, and create an impression of the superiority of authoritarianisms, at least at the *beginning* of the pandemic (as is usually the case at the beginning of the war). As one Chinese political scientist notes,

> The entrenchment of authoritarianism is first and foremost reflected by the durability of authoritarian regimes during the pandemic. To the disappointment of those seeking cracks in the authoritarian regimes hit hard by the pandemic, the autocrats around the world have largely survived the tests resulting from the pandemic. In particular, the resilience of communist regimes, such as China and Vietnam, has provided clear examples of entrenched authoritarianism during the pandemic...[T]he evidence so far suggests that the [Chinese] regime has not only managed to survive the crisis but also boosted its legitimacy.[8]

Oh My Göd

The pandemic has been a powerful accelerator of many of the preexisting trends, both negative and positive, in business, culture, and politics. It has also revealed and accelerated trends in populist-authoritarian politics. As a local expert said about Turkey, "Coronavirus was used as an excuse for the already oppressive government to do things that it has long planned to do, but had not been able to."[9] This applies to a number of populist regimes described in this book.

In Hungary, Viktor Orbán declared a "state of danger" on March 11, 2020. This is a constitutionally ordained procedure under the Hungarian Constitution and lasts for fifteen days unless extended by the parliament – so it duly expired on March 26. Four days later the parliament approved what was described as the "Enabling Act," effectively granting Orbán

---

[8] Qingming Huang, "The Pandemic and the Transformation of Liberal International Order," *Journal of Chinese Political Science*, 26/1 (2021), 1–26 at 11.

[9] Anonymous respondent quoted in Sarah Repucci and Amy Slipowitz, "Democracy under Lockdown," *Freedom House Special Report* (2020), at 3, www.freedomhouse.org/sites/default/files/2020-10/COVID-19_Special_Report_Final_.pdf.

emergency powers.[10] The enabling act had no sunset provision and entitled Orbán to rule by decree without any parliamentary oversight. Such oversight is provided, as compulsory, only in a constitutional state of emergency. So Orbán effectively gave himself all the powers of a state of emergency – minus all the constitutional guarantees of parliamentary control that are attached to such a status.

While Orbán enjoys a comfortable parliamentary supermajority, the point of this trick was to further sideline the opposition and deny them any resources – including any argumentative ones – to expose the government's failures. This is perfectly consistent with Orbán's refusal to treat the opposition as a legitimate political force, and to reject any consensus-seeking in politics, even in such matters as public health. More parliamentary safeguards certainly "would have helped build public trust, which is a prerequisite for successfully combatting a pandemic"[11] – but inter-party consensus is low on Orbán's list of priorities. When the opposition opposed the Enabling Act, Fidesz's president of the parliament, László Kövér, said in an interview, "[t]his opposition is not part of the Hungarian nation."[12]

Orbán enthusiastically used his enhanced powers to strengthen the government's grip on the Hungarian society, for instance by placing military commanders in "strategic companies" and hospitals (these commanders further exfiltrated sensitive data to government for no apparent health reason), sacking members of several companies and replacing them by government cronies,[13] and creating "special economic areas" under Decree No 135/2020. What does this last matter have to do with the pandemic and Orbán's grab for power? – you may ask. The folk in Göd, a small city of 20,000, just north of Budapest, can answer. The decree allowed the government to create "special economic areas" and then transfer real-estate from the municipal to the county level. This

---

[10] Péter Krékó, "The World Must Not Let Viktor Orbán Get Away with His Pandemic Power-Grab," *The Guardian* (April 1, 2020), www.theguardian.com/commentisfree/2020/apr/01/viktor-Orbán-pandemic-power-grab-hungary.
[11] Márta Pardavi and András Kádár, "Hungary Should Not Become Patient Zero," *Just Security* (April 22, 2020), www.justsecurity.org/69780/hungary-should-not-become-patient-zero.
[12] Giorgos Katsambekis, Yannis Stavrakakis, Paula Biglieri, and Kurt Adam Sengul, "Populism and the Pandemic," *Populismus* (June 2020), at 30.
[13] Kim Lane Scheppele and David Pozen, "Executive Overreach and Underreach in the Pandemic," in Miguel Maduro and Paul Kahn (eds.), *Democracy in Times of Pandemic* (Cambridge: Cambridge University Press, 2020), pp. 38–53 at 41.

decree was used in the town of Göd to strip it of its industrial area and thus one-third of its tax revenue. "The main purpose of this was to punish the town, for the fact that it is opposition-led, and its mayor belongs to the opposition party Momentum," explains a Hungarian lawyer, and adds that it was "one of the most blatant misuses of extraordinary power vested on the Hungarian Government in the context of the fight against the pandemic."[14]

The trajectory of responses to Covid-19 in Poland was quite different; in fact it was the opposite. The government strenuously resisted – against the facts – the need to introduce any state of emergency or other special measures. The reason was simple and entirely party-political. In the middle of 2020, presidential elections were coming up – with PiS's candidate Andrzej Duda poised for reelection – and PiS strategists calculated (correctly, in my view) that the earlier the election was held, the better. As the crisis developed, any backlash would affect Duda's chances of reelection. And here is the catch: A formal announcement of a state of emergency (in this case, the most obvious match would be the constitutionally defined "state of natural calamity") must automatically result in the postponement of any elections until ninety days after the state of emergency is lifted. So the leader of the ruling party, Jarosław Kaczyński, kept reassuring the public day after day in the first months of the pandemic that there was no cause warranting the declaration of a state of calamity. Various successive restrictions (face masks, social distancing, travel prohibitions, etc.) were imposed in an apparent violation of the constitution – the very constitution that supplied an obvious avenue for lawfully introducing such measures.

In the end the presidential elections *were* delayed (under the pressure of a junior coalition partner), with some 20 million euros wasted on ballot papers, printed for the aborted postal vote of May 10, 2020. The elections eventually took place on June 28 and July 12, 2020, even though the public health situation had not improved (if anything, it had further deteriorated), despite all the PiS leaders and, most prominently, Prime Minister Morawiecki reassuring citizens that going to vote would be perfectly safe. He addressed this call especially to Poland's seniors – the cohort most vulnerable to Covid-19 but also the most supportive of PiS. Following these cynical and manipulative actions, which included

---

[14] Dániel Karsai, "The Curious and Alarming Story of the City of Göd," *Verfassungsblog* (May 15, 2020), www.verfassungsblog.de/the-curious-and-alarming-story-of-the-city-of-goed/.

candidate Duda's open banalization of the pandemic threat and his failure to endorse vaccinations during public campaign TV appearances ("I don't like needles being put in my arm"), Duda marginally won reelection. As Alan Greene put it, the Polish case demonstrates that "de jure states of emergency can actually better protect constitutional norms in exceptional crises than pressing ahead with business as usual. In this instance, the Polish government sought to circumvent the extra protections in place during an emergency, by not declaring an emergency at all."[15]

No emergency measures were adopted in places like Poland, where the leaders openly defied reality, regardless of the tragic situation, by following President Trump's lead and minimizing and ignoring the situation. This was certainly the case in Brazil, where President Jair Bolsonaro infamously (and repeatedly) compared Covid-19 to "a little flu," while, as a critic who called out his behavior noted, "coughing into the crowd." It was not a metaphor: the article by Jocelyn Kestenbaum is illustrated by a photo of the mask-free president actually coughing into his hands (the same hands with which he happily shook hands with others) at a packed anti-quarantine rally in Brasília.[16] Bolsonaro consistently refused to call for lockdowns or the use of face masks. As an American expert on Brazil put it, "Bolsonaro has treated the pandemic as less a public-health crisis than a public relations challenge."[17]

Covid Casualties

The more typical response by authoritarian populists has been the opposite: to declare constitutional states of emergency and push them well beyond the limits of the necessary. On March 8, 2020, in the Philippines, Duterte declared a state of emergency in accordance with the constitutionally ordained procedure.[18] Soon after, a law was adopted giving the president "special temporary powers" (initially for three months, but later extended), under which he ordered the police and

---

[15] Alan Greene, *Emergency Powers in a Time of Pandemic* (Bristol: Bristol University Press, 2021), p. 211.
[16] Jocelyn Kestenbaum, "Coughing into the Crowd: Bolsonaro's Botched COVID-19 Response," *Just Security* (May 1, 2020), www.justsecurity.org/69960/coughing-into-the-crowd-bolsonaros-botched-covid-19-response/.
[17] Amy Erica Smith, "Covid vs. Democracy: Brazil's Populist Playbook," *Journal of Democracy*, 31/4 (2020), 76–90 at 81.
[18] Maria Atienza, "Emergency Powers and COVID-19: The Philippines as a Case Study," *Melbourne Forum on Constitution Building* (2020), p. 1.

the military to shoot violators of his "enhanced community quarantine" if they were unruly or threatened law enforcement officers. The law quickly showed its bite: In April 2020, the Philippine police arrested activists distributing food assistance north of Manila and charged them with violating emergency laws. They were indicted with inciting sedition after anti-government newspapers were found in their vehicle.[19]

Similarly, on March 13, 2020, in Venezuela, President Maduro declared a state of emergency, which has subsequently been extended on five occasions *despite the parliament not approving it*, as is constitutionally required. Tortures, mass arrests, and extra-judicial killings have intensified. As Human Rights Watch reported in late 2020, "The government has used the Covid-19 state of emergency as a pretext to repress dissent, arbitrarily detaining and prosecuting dozens of political opponents, including legislators, journalists, health-care workers who criticize the government's handling of the pandemic, and lawyers who provide legal support to demonstrators protesting lack of access to water, gasoline, or medicines."[20]

In India, a national lockdown ordered at the end of March 2020, imposed with a mere four hours' notice, was so chaotic, disproportionate, and brutal that in addition to failing to contain the virus, it led to unspeakable human tragedies. The police-enforced curfew left more than 40 million migrant workers without access to any support or pay. Many of them set out for home on foot or bicycle, having been stranded away from their homes and without resources. The government responded by attempting to use police to restrain their movement.[21]

The first casualty of the Covid-related restrictions has usually been freedom of speech. Orbán's government introduced decrees that provided for the prosecution of "*any untrue fact or any misrepresented true fact*" regarding the pandemic.[22] The Hungarian police detained persons who posted comments critical of the government online, while the

---

[19] Murray Hiebert, "COVID-19 Threatens Democracy in Southeast Asia," *East Asia Forum* (May 25, 2020), www.eastasiaforum.org/2020/05/25/covid-19-threatens-democracy-in-southeast-asia/.

[20] Human Rights Watch, "Venezuela, Events of 2020," www.hrw.org/world-report/2021/country-chapters/venezuela.

[21] Rahul Mukherji, "Covid vs. Democracy: India's Illiberal Remedy," *Journal of Democracy*, 31/4 (2020), 91–105 at 97.

[22] Péter Cseresnyés, "New Law Granting Enhanced Powers to Orbán Gov't Garners International Outcry," *Hungary Today* (April 3, 2020), https://hungarytoday.hu/new-law-granting-enhanced-powers-to-orban-govt-garners-international-outcry/.

opposition denounced this as evidence of government intimidation against critics.[23] Repression under the guise of combating "fake news" related to Covid-19 has become quasi-universal in the populist world. In India, several journalists and doctors have been charged for their public criticism of the authorities' response to Covid-19. In Mumbai, the police went so far as to pass an order prohibiting "any person inciting mistrust towards government functionaries and their actions taken in order to prevent spread of the Covid-19 virus and thereby causing danger to human health or safety or a disturbance to the public tranquility."[24] Censorship also reached social media: Twitter deleted several tweets critical of Indian government tweets, at the request of the Indian government, on the basis that it was misleading information. According to Vox Recode, some of the tweets, such as satirical cartoons about Modi's uncaring attitude to outbreaks, did not seem to contain misleading information.[25] Similarly, in the Philippines, Duterte signed a law that criminalized spreading "false information" about Covid-19. This law has been subsequently used to subpoena at least one Facebook user for making a critical post, and also to prosecute journalists and a local mayor for causing a "covid scare." Human Rights Watch claims the law is being used for "politically motivated" arrests.[26]

Covid-19 has been frequently used as an excuse to restrict rights of freedom of assembly, giving the authorities an easy pretext to silence their opponents on matters entirely unrelated to the pandemic. In Poland, police were used to conduct mass arrests at abortion protests, under the guise of Covid-19 restrictions, which, as already mentioned, in the absence of state emergency were of dubious constitutionality.[27] In May 2020, Indian police shut down a group of protesters protesting a

---

[23] Policy Department for Citizens' Rights and Constitutional Affairs, "The Impact of Coronavirus Measures on Democracy, Rule of Law and Fundamental Rights in the EU," *European Parliament* (2021), at158.

[24] OHCHR, "Asia: Bachelet Alarmed by Clampdown on Freedom of Expression during COVID-19" (June 3, 2020), www.ohchr.org/EN/NewsEvents/Pages/DisplayNews.aspx?NewsID=25920andLangID=E.

[25] Shirin Ghaffary, "A Major Battle over Free Speech on Social Media Is Playing Out in India during the Pandemic," *Vox Recode* (May 1, 2021), www.vox.com/recode/22410931/india-pandemic-facebook-twitter-free-speech-modi-covid-19-censorship-free-speech-takedown.

[26] Carlos Conde, "Philippine Activists Charged with Sedition, 'Fake News,'" *Human Rights Watch* (April 22, 2020), www.hrw.org/news/2020/04/22/philippine-activists-charged-sedition-fake-news.

[27] Jacek Kucharczyk, "The Pandemic as a Catalyst for Populist Authoritarianism in Poland," in Sophia Russak (ed.), *The Effect of Covid on EU Democracies*, European Policy Institutes Network (2021), pp. 27–28 at 27.

controversial citizenship law citing Covid-19 restrictions. This was described by some activists as a misuse of power.[28]

Covid-19 has also provided an engine for populist xenophobia and hatred of "Others." As in so many other ways, Donald Trump became the model to emulate, with his China-bashing ("Chinese virus") and WHO-bashing. Other populists followed suit, replacing China and WHO with their own favorite targets. Viktor Orbán has directly linked the coronavirus to immigration, stating: "There is a clear link between illegal migration and the coronavirus epidemic, as many immigrants come from or through Iran, which is one of the focal points of the infection."[29] The leader of the Italian populist party Lega, Matteo Salvini, linked the spread of Covid with the disembarkation of refugees in Italian harbors. In India, officials of the ruling Bharatiya Janata Party likened Muslims to suicide bombers for protesting against the new citizenship law, and the ruling party and media have singled out Muslims as "supercarriers."[30] Jair Bolsonaro claimed that Covid-19 was deliberately engineered as a bioweapon, implying the Chinese produced it in a lab.[31]

Covid-related discourse has occasionally prompted populists to make grotesque, nationalist boasts about their own country's alleged success in handling the pandemic. One example was on March 24, 2020, when Polish prime minister Morawiecki announced on Facebook, as his government showed a great deal of incompetence and corruption toward the worsening crisis: "Today, Poland is at the absolute top of the world when it comes to the speed and efficiency of decisions [related to the pandemic]. We prefer to prevent than cure...Economic powers such as the United Kingdom, Germany and the United States have followed the path we have set out."[32] No need to add that all these three states would be

---

[28] Murali Krishnan, "Citizenship Law: Is India Using COVID-19 Emergency to Arrest Protesters?" *DW* (May 28, 2020), www.dw.com/en/citizenship-law-is-india-using-covid-19-emergency-to-arrest-protesters/a-53603260.

[29] Ágnes Kövér, "Civil Society and COVID-19 in Hungary: The Complete Annexation of Civil Space," *Nonprofit Policy Forum*, 12/1 (2021), at 121.

[30] Florian Bieber, "Global Nationalism in Times of the COVID-19 Pandemic," *Nationalities Papers* (2020), at 6.

[31] Carlie Porterfield, "Brazil's Bolsonaro Floats Conspiracy Theory That Coronavirus May Be 'Biological Warfare,'" *Forbes* (May 5, 2021) hwww.forbes.com/sites/carlieporterfield/2021/05/05/brazils-bolsonaro-floats-conspiracy-theory-that-coronavirus-may-be-biological-warfare/?sh=556060aa2bb5.

[32] Artur Lipiński, "Poland: 'If We Don't Elect the President, the Country Will Plunge into Chaos,'" in Giuliano Bobba and Nicholas Hubé (eds.), *Populism and the Politicization of the COVID-19 Crisis in Europe* (Cham: Palgrave Macmillan, 2021), pp. 115–130 at 122.

surprised, perhaps amused, by this information, but of course *they* were not the audience to which the message was addressed.

Democracy's Covid Dividends

And yet, the "authoritarian dividend" has not placed populists ahead of liberal democracies in handling Covid-19. Without going into the excesses described above – transcending the necessary measures related to states of emergency, wherever imposed, or harsh repression of freedom of speech about the pandemic – many liberal democracies have addressed the pandemic better than many authoritarian populist governments. True, there have been some autocracies (Vietnam, China, after an initial period of chaos and suppression of truth, the United Arab Emirates) or openly populist regimes (Israel under Prime Minister Netanyahu) that have handled Covid better than some liberal democracies (Italy or the United States). However, the converse is also true: there have been many liberal democracies (Australia, New Zealand, the Baltic states, or Germany) that have handled the problems much better than many populist authoritarian states (Brazil, Turkey, or India). The least that can be said is that the *weak* statement is true: Populism per se is no advantage in addressing the health crisis. Whether the strong statement is also correct – that populisms are at a disadvantage in the struggle against Covid – is hard to tell. As the cliché goes: The jury is still out.

But even the weak thesis is interesting enough: Why would populism, with its power to mobilize the masses around the leader and not incapacitated in its quick reactions by the dispersal of powers, not prove intrinsically superior in the face of such challenges? There must be something about liberal democracy that provides it with a degree of resilience against such catastrophes that overrides the forces of the conventional wisdom outlined at the opening of this chapter. Let us survey some of these factors. Each of them is a coin with two sides: A positive liberal side also has a negative populist side. What is a source of strength for liberal democracy is, when absent, a source of weakness for populism. In this manner, this section continues to survey the characteristics of populism, as revealed by Covid-19.

A core element of populism is the pitting of the morally virtuous "people" against the corrupt "elites." The complexity of modern government has elevated technocratic experts such as scientists to a position of significance, placing them in the class of "elite" villains of populism. In much the same way that populists seek to dismantle democratic institutions that mediate what they perceive as the expression of the voice of the people, they also seek to attack the authority of scientific elites.[33] As Richard Hofstadter had noted some time ago: "Once the intellectual was gently ridiculed because he was not needed; now he is fiercely resented because he is needed too much." This resentment is caused by the achievements of intellectuals, and the growing dependence of societies upon their skills. Hofstadter added: "Intellect is resented as a form of power or privilege."[34]

The word "expert" in the populist language has become invective. For example, former UK Secretary of State for Justice Michael Gove claimed that the British people "have had enough of experts...from organizations with acronyms saying that they know what is best."[35] Rising GOP star and potential 2024 presidential contender Kirsti Noem stated "We are not and will not be the subjects of an elite class of so-called experts. We the people are the government."[36] Pitting arrogant experts against the pure people has become a favorite populist rhetorical device.

Even prior to the pandemic, ruling populists' "anti-science" disposition was evident in their approach to policy. De-funding and abolishing scientific institutions is a hallmark of populist regimes.[37] Bolsonaro cut the budget of the Ministry of Science in half. In Venezuela, "at all levels of the national scientific establishment, inexperienced professionals with little scientific or technical knowledge or background have been assigned to positions of authority."[38] Orbán directed funding away from the Hungarian Academy of Sciences, which it had accused of "engaging in politics."[39] And when the crisis hit, some populist leaders (such as

---

[33] Niels Mede and Mike Schäfer, "Science-Related Populism: Conceptualizing Populist Demands toward Science," *Public Understanding of Science*, 29 (2020), 473–491 at 482.

[34] Richard Hofstadter, "On the Unpopularity of Intellect," in *Uncollected Essays, 1956–1965* (New York: Library of America, 2020), pp. 28–50 at 39.

[35] Mede and Schäfer, "Science-Related Populism," p. 474.

[36] Steve Inskeep, "GOP Rising Star Kristi Noem Addresses Republican Convention," *NPR* (August 27, 2020), www.npr.org/2020/08/27/906592669/gop-rising-star-kristi-noem-addresses-republican-convention.

[37] Eunjung Lee and Marjorie Johnstone, "Resisting Politics of Authoritarian Populism during COVID-19, Reclaiming Democracy and Narrative Justice: Centering Critical Thinking in Social Work," *International Social Work*, 64 (2021), 716–730 at 722.

[38] Jim Daley, "Venezuela Is Unraveling – So Is Its Science," *Scientific American* (February 15, 2019), www.scientificamerican.com/article/venezuela-is-unraveling-mdash-so-is-its-science/.

[39] "Hungarian Researchers Rally against Government 'Attack on Science,'" *France 24* (February 12, 2019), www.france24.com/en/20190212-hungarian-researchers-rally-against-government-attack-science.

Bolsonaro) exacerbated public distrust of science and continued to criticize scientific authorities.

In this assault on science, populists were greatly helped by counter-science, advanced not as a rejection of the scientific method itself, but rather an attack on the scientific establishment and a questioning of its objectivity.[40] In dismissing the severity of Covid-19 or in presenting alternative cures, populist leaders frequently embraced the language and paraphernalia of science. Writing about President Trump's "skeptical" response to the virus, Ari Shulman observed Trump's "embrace of scientific expertise of a sort" by relying on findings that the real infection fatality rate might be lower than the roughly 0.1 percent that accompanies the seasonal flu (the prevailing estimates were between 1 and 2 percent), noting that "Fox News hosts glommed on to a viral Medium post by a Silicon Valley entrepreneur arguing along the same lines."[41] The case of hydroxychloroquine is a particularly instructive case-study. Based on an eccentric French researcher, Didier Raoult, who claimed to offer evidence that hydroxychloroquine and azithromycin, two widely available drugs, might be highly effective in treating coronavirus, President Trump proclaimed the treatment a possible miracle cure.

Armed with this alternative knowledge, based either on unreliable or fragmentary findings, populist leaders could challenge the scientific mainstream by questioning its objectivity. This was made explicit by supporters of Bolsonaro, who claimed: "If chloroquine was called [former President] Lula's drug, not Bolsonaro's or Trump's, I assure it would be a successs."[42] Similarly, right wing publications in the United States have repeatedly claimed that the medical establishment deliberately suppressed evidence of hydroxychloroquine's effectiveness in order to injure Trump's electoral prospects, for example by claiming that National Institute of Allergy and Infectious Diseases director Dr. Anthony Fauci lied about hydroxychloroquine.[43]

---

[40] Mede and Schäfer, "Science-Related Populism," 478.
[41] Ari Schulman, "The Coronavirus and the Right's Scientific Counterrevolution," *The New Republic* (June 15, 2020), www.newrepublic.com/article/158058/coronavirus-conservative-experts-scientific-counterrevolution.
[42] Guilherme Casarões and David Magalhães, "The Hydroxychloroquine Alliance: How Far-Right Leaders and Alt-Science Preachers Came Together to Promote a Miracle Drug," *Brazilian Journal of Public Administration*, 55/1 (2021), 197–214 at 206.
[43] Jim Hoft, "Smoking Gun: Fauci Lied, Millions Died – Fauci Was Informed of Hydroxychloroquine Success in Early 2020 but Lied to Public Instead Despite the Science #FauciEmails," *The Gateway Pundit* (June 3, 2020), www.thegatewaypundit.com/2021/06/

The shifting advice of the WHO and epidemiologists made it easier for populists to question the scientific consensus.[44] A clear example is the early guidance on masks, which suggested they were ineffective in combating the virus. This guidance was later overturned on the basis of new evidence. And of course, the fact that there are theories and counter-theories, mainstream positions and eccentric views, challenges to scientific conventional wisdoms, and the like – is in itself a good thing. It is the stuff of science. Orthodoxy kills progress. Today's eccentricities become tomorrow's mainstream, and today's challenges become tomorrow's conventional wisdoms. But when dramatic, *practical* policies of life and death crucially rely on scientific evidence, the quality of evidence, as judged by today's dominant standards of the academic community, is of utmost importance. By placing pseudo-science (again, judged by today's contingent and provisional academic standards) on par with serious and sound evidence, populists may gain short-term popularity but render it difficult, often impossible, to find solutions for the existential crisis of their countries.

But in their assault on science, populists often go a step further and rather than producing suspicious evidence from "alternative science," go beyond the scientific framework altogether. Science is then countered with "common sense," available to all, except those contaminated with scientific viewpoints, which unnecessarily blur and distort what can be seen by every reasonable person.

The valorization of "common sense" over expert opinion produces individuals – heroes of populist worldviews, nicely described by Ari Shulman: "We might describe such figures as representative of a very specific sort of authority, long revered as a cultural hero on the business-minded right: the back-of-the-envelope expert, the autodidact bootstrapper who claims to cut through the baloney and show you how simple it all really is."[45] Donald Trump demonstrated this clearly in a meeting discussing the coronavirus where he said: "So what do I know? I'm not a doctor. I'm not a doctor. But I have common sense."[46]

---

smoking-gun-fauci-lied-millions-died-fauci-informed-hydroxchloroquine-worked-lied-public-instead-despite-science-fauciemails/.

[44] Maduro and Kahn "Introduction," p. 5.
[45] Schulman, "The Coronavirus."
[46] Daniel Politi, "Trump Keeps Promoting Unproven Drug for the Coronavirus: 'I'm Not a Doctor. But I Have Common Sense,'" *Slate* (April 5, 2020), www.slate.com/news-and-politics/2020/04/trump-promoting-unproven-drug-hydroxychloroquine-coronavirus.html.

Populists are uncomfortable to admit errors (following an immortal line delivered by John Wayne, "Never apologize, mister, it's a sign of weakness") and are also uncomfortable about sharing the podium with scientists. For example, Trump grew increasingly uncomfortable about the presence – physically and intellectually – of Dr. Anthony Fauci next to him; he accused Dr. Fauci of being a "self-promoter" given his public exposure during the Covid-19 outbreak.[47] After Fauci gained prominence for his coronavirus briefings and congressional testimony, there was a real smear campaign by the White House, which compiled a list of comments and advice by Dr. Fauci, clearly to serve as evidence of his allegedly flawed perspective. This caused "many Trump supporters to oppose the medical establishment by spreading distrust of medical advice."[48] The Trump/Fauci debacle was echoed in Brazil by the relationships between Bolsonaro and his successive health ministers. After Bolsonaro's technocratic appointee, Luiz Henrique Mandetta, became popular for his willingness to endorse public-health guidelines in opposition to the president, he was replaced in April 2020 by the oncologist Nelson Teich, who in turn resigned four weeks later due to disagreements with the president. In his place Bolsonaro appointed Eduardo Pazuello, a general in the Brazilian Army.[49]

In Hungary, health officials weren't exactly smeared but they were sidelined. As we are told by two Hungarian observers, "[w]hile Orbán and other pro-government actors often referred to the importance of embracing scientists' knowledge and opinions, these experts were hardly visible in front of the public."[50]

The greater autonomy and independence that experts hold in democracies is one of the primary reasons that democracies take more competent and effective measures in response to the pandemic. Research by a Swedish political scientist into the politics of school closures around the world (one of the nearly consensually accepted policies to minimize

---

[47] Graig Graziosi, "Trump Says He Didn't Listen to Fauci 'Because I Was Doing the Opposite of What He Was Saying' in Fox Interview," *The Independent* (March 26, 2020), www.independent.co.uk/news/world/americas/us-politics/trump-fauci-fox-news-coronavirus-b1823118.html.

[48] Kristin Hedges and Gideon Lasco, "Medical Populism and COVID-19 Testing," *Open Anthropological Research*, 1/1 (2021), 73–86 at 81.

[49] See Smith, "Covid vs. Democracy," 82.

[50] Márton Bene and Zsolt Boda "Hungary: Crisis as Usual – Populist Governance and the Pandemic," in Giuliano Bobba and Nicholas Hubé (eds.), *Populism and the Politicization of the COVID-19 Crisis in Europe* (Cham: Palgrave Macmillan, 2021), pp. 87–100 at 98.

health risks) shows that "other things being equal, democratic countries are likely to implement school closures sooner than those with a more authoritarian regime."[51] Democracy has the edge over authoritarian populism in that it can rely on science and experts without the need to kowtow to "common sense," untainted by knowledge.

Sunlight Is the Best Disinfectant

Controlling a virus requires transparency, while restrictions on information ultimately limit the effectiveness of the response by preventing rational responses. Such restrictions – especially when associated with criminal punishments and other reprisals for warnings about the crisis – impede the flow of information about what is really going on, and thus prevent taking rational decisions. As Thomas Carothers and David Wong say, "[t]hese crackdowns impede effective health responses, given that civil society can be a crucial partner to governments...in terms of collecting and distributing accurate and timely health-related information and delivering resources and care."[52] It is clear that a culture of secrecy and censorship contributed to the spread of the pandemic in Wuhan in the very early days of the crisis. In December 2019, Chinese authorities silenced and arrested Dr. Li Wenliang of Wuhan Central Hospital, who had warned of the outbreak. (Dr. Li died from the virus in February 2020.) This official approach surely must have facilitated the uncontrollable spread of the virus: suppression of information about the contagion squandered precious time when the virus might have been contained.

Transparency and effective communication of risks is not only essential for governments in order to quickly find remedies but also is necessary to allow individuals and organizations to act rationally during a pandemic. Hence, democracies have an informational dividend in coping with the crisis. For example, communication about lockdown supplies can prevent panic-buying, whereas a failure to ascertain what is included

---

[51] Axel Cronert, "Democracy, State Capacity, and COVID-19 Related School Closures," APSA Working Paper (April 28, 2020), www.preprints.apsanet.org/engage/apsa/article-details/5e80bf4c6a2482001a4c1b9f.

[52] Thomas Carothers and David Wong, "Authoritarian Weaknesses and the Pandemic," *Carnegie Endowment for International Peace* (August 11, 2020), www.carnegieendowment.org/2020/08/11/authoritarian-weaknesses-and-pandemic-pub-82452, p. 2.

and excluded from lockdowns can lead to confusion and loss of trust.[53] Populist governments' main instinct is to cover up failures rather than find rational solutions, and this can hinder the effectiveness of the pandemic response. Their central concern about crises such as these is how to frame the situation in a way that makes them look as good as possible rather than help them decide what to do to stop its escalation.

The worldwide tendency, almost exceptionless, of populist authoritarians to underestimate the true size of the tragedy – to lie, to put it in a less euphemistic way – is at the same time understandable and disastrous. Restrictions on information may serve partially to deny the extent of the outbreak, such as when Donald Trump did not push for increased testing in order to keep the cases of Covid-19 low.[54] Bolsonaro followed a similar approach in stopping daily case number reports amid what he claimed was media sensationalising of "a bit of a cold."[55] In Venezuela, only tests conducted at public labs are recorded in national data and private labs claim "the government has sidelined these facilities in an effort to centralize control over testing as well as the flow of information about infections."[56] Employees at a top private lab in Venezuela say (as paraphrased by Reuters): "[T]he lack of transparency on case counts and fatalities means even top public health officials don't know how far or how fast the virus is spreading in Venezuela. Authorities have detained medical workers and opposition politicians who publicly criticized the readiness of their local hospitals."[57]

The highest performing *authoritarian* state in terms of its pandemic response as of January 9, 2021, according to the Lowy Institute's Covid

---

[53] Laurence Freedman, "Muddled Messages as Britain Seeks to Stay Alert," *Lowy Interpreter* (May 14, 2020), www.lowyinstitute.org/the-interpreter/muddled-messages-britain-seeks-stay-alert; see also Rachel Kleinfeld, "Do Authoritarian or Democratic Countries Handle Pandemics Better?" *Carnegie Endowment for International Peace* (March 31, 2020), www.carnegieendowment.org/2020/03/31/do-authoritarian-or-democratic-countries-handle-pandemics-better-pub-81404.

[54] Anne Applebaum, "The Coronavirus Called America's Bluff," *The Atlantic* (March 15, 2020) www.theatlantic.com/ideas/archive/2020/03/coronavirus-showed-america-wasnt-task/608023/.

[55] Tom Phillips and Caio Briso, "Judge Orders Bolsonaro to Resume Publishing Brazil Covid-19 data," *Guardian* (June 10, 2020), www.theguardian.com/world/2020/jun/09/judge-orders-bolsonaro-to-resume-publishing-brazil-covid-19-data.

[56] Angus Berwick and Vivian Sequera, "In Run-Down Caracas Institute, Venezuela's Coronavirus Testing Falters," *Reuters* (April 17, 2020), www.reuters.com/article/us-health-coronavirus-venezuela-tests-in/in-run-down-caracas-institute-venezuelas-coronavirus-testing-falters-idUSKBN21Z1BR.

[57] Ibid.

Performance Index, was Vietnam.[58] Yet Vietnam has been notable for its transparency during the Covid-19 outbreak. Some have suggested: "Vietnam's COVID-19 success has been possible because of the full transparency of information and close coordination among government authorities."[59] Their policy approach of contact tracing, quarantines, reliance on voluntary compliance, and lockdowns was only possible with both external transparency and transparency between national and local governments.

This may lead to a virtuous cycle of creating more demands for transparency. After the pandemic, the regime may face increased pressures for freedom. As some observers note, the success of its Covid-19 strategy has, so far, bolstered trust in the ruling Communist Party of Vietnam, but is likely to segue into demands for transparency on other issues in the long run. "The success of COVID-19 is a double-edged sword that, if not handled very well, will likely haunt the party in the long run. If increasing expectations are not handled skillfully, the trust that the party has gained from its COVID-19 achievements may evaporate."[60] This may be an unexpected benefit of having knowledge-based policies for fighting Covid-19.

The Center Cannot Hold

Authoritarian regimes struggle to manage the crisis due to their "lack of coherence and flexibility in the hierarchy of government," and their tendency to scapegoat local governments rather than act cooperatively with them.[61] This may be disastrous for pandemic policies that require integration of regional and local authorities in a coherent plan. After all, the local level is where the action is: where testing, vaccinations, hospitalization, and so forth, occur. Doctors, nurses and ambulance drivers are not usually guided by the central government, and where they are, efficiency loss is visible. The disastrous slowness of Chinese authorities in its initial response to the outbreak in Wuhan was due to the inability of

---

[58] Lowy Institute, "Pandemic Performance Index," *Lowy Institute* (2021) https://interactives.lowyinstitute.org/features/covid-performance/.
[59] Mai Truong, "Vietnam's COVID-19 Success Is a Double-Edged Sword for the Communist Party," *The Diplomat* (August 6, 2020), www.thediplomat.com/2020/08/vietnams-covid-19-success-is-a-double-edged-sword-for-the-communist-party/.
[60] Ibid.
[61] Carothers and Wong, "Authoritarian Weaknesses and the Pandemic," p. 3.

decisions in today's China to be made without Xi's approval.[62] As Carothers and Wong observe, generally, "[e]ffective national public health responses to the pandemic require not just clear, consistent mandates from the top, but integrated approaches in which regional and local authorities can take initiative, adapt responses to local conditions, and report critical information up the line."[63]

Tell that to Mr. Péter Marki-Zay, mayor of Hodmezovasarhely, a city of 45,000 in southeast Hungary. In his own words, "[t]hey really tie your hands and feet together, and throw you into the water," he said. "And then you have to swim."[64] "They" are the central government in Budapest, and just like mayors in many other cities, he had struggled to get up-to-date information *about his own city*; they all knew only how many active cases there were in the whole county, not specifically within their cities. They had to make their own decisions about reopening of shops and markets. Over the Easter weekend, Mr. Marki-Zay decided to open farmers markets and playgrounds while the mayor in nearby Szeged chose to close the markets. Both were blasted for their decisions in the Orbán-related media. And yes, you guessed: both Mr. Marki-Zay and his colleague, mayor of Szeged, Mr. László Botka, are aligned with the opposition to Orbán's government.

As is Budapest's mayor, Gergely Karácsony. In response to the Orbán government's cuts to the business tax, which is collected by municipalities, allegedly to help Covid-19 response, Mr. Karácsony argued that stripping municipalities of funds would only deepen the crisis: "[H]alving this tax does not manage this crisis, but deepens it."[65] This tax is a vital source of revenue for local authorities. The cuts, under a Covid-related pretext, are widely seen by the opposition in Hungary as part of Orbán's war on the cities where the opposition dominates.

In Brazil, we see the opposite phenomenon of the central government actively seeking to prevent local governments from taking steps to control outbreaks. In response to state lockdowns, Bolsonaro issued Provision Act 926, preventing lockdowns from affecting certain activities

---

[62] Minxin Pei, "China's Coming Upheaval: Competition, the Coronavirus, and the Weakness of Xi Jinping," *Foreign Affairs*, 99/3 (2020), 82–95.
[63] Carothers and Wong, "Authoritarian Weaknesses and the Pandemic," p. 3.
[64] Emily Schultheis, "Viktor Orbán Has Declared War on Mayors," *Foreign Policy* (July 28, 2020), www.foreignpolicy.com/2020/07/28/viktor-Orbán-has-declared-a-war-on-mayors/.
[65] Krisztina Than, "Hungarian PM Cuts Local Business Tax, Budapest's Opposition Mayor Cries Foul," *Reuters* (December 20, 2020), www.reuters.com/article/us-hungary-econ omy-Orbán-idUKKBN28T0TW.

deemed essential.[66] This has been used to interfere with internal travel restrictions by categorizing all interstate travel as essential activity. Further, a Bolsonaro decree to classify churches and lottery houses as essential was overturned by a federal court. Bolsonaro also publicly criticized locally ordained lockdowns: "A small number of state and municipal authorities must abandon their scorched-earth ideas: the banning of public transport, the closing of commerce and mass confinement," and said that he would not use "his" troops to enforce them.[67] This critique became a federal campaign with the hashtag "Brazil cannot stop," which encouraged Brazilians to ignore local restrictions. A federal judge ordered the campaign to cease as it contradicted the health ministry's recommendations.[68]

In the Philippines, despite Duterte supporting decentralized government and the empowerment of local authorities (given his political origin story as a former mayor), he has taken a centralized approach to the pandemic. Under the Bayanihan Act, Local Government Units (LGUs) were required simply to follow presidential orders. Early in the pandemic, Duterte said (about mayors): "You just obey because I do not want a quarrel with you...If the worst happens, it is the government who takes control – the national government."[69] However, orders by Duterte were confusing and contradictory, leaving local officials to act on their own only to encounter problems later on, when clashing with different national government policies. There was little coordination with local government about national restrictions, and no consultation. "It was a top-down style. They [the national government] would get mad at people who would innovate, or look for other ways," said political science expert

---

[66] Emilio Meyer and Thomas Bustamate, "Authoritarianism without Emergency Powers: Brazil under COVID-19," *Verfassungsblog* (April 8, 2020), www.verfassungsblog.de/authoritarianism-without-emergency-powers-brazil-under-covid-19/.

[67] Tom Phillips, "Bolsonaro Says He 'Wouldn't Feel Anything' If Infected with Covid-19 and Attacks State Lockdowns," *Guardian* (March 15, 2020), www.theguardian.com/world/2020/mar/25/bolsonaro-brazil-wouldnt-feel-anything-covid-19-attack-state-lockdowns; Jon Anderson, "Brazil's COVID-19 Crisis and Jair Bolsonaro's Presidential Chaos," *The New Yorker* (April 13, 2021), www.newyorker.com/news/daily-comment/brazils-covid-19-crisis-and-jair-bolsonaros-presidential-chaos.

[68] Human Rights Watch, "Brazil: Bolsonaro Sabotages Anti-Covid-19 Efforts,"*Human Rights Watch* (April 10, 2020), www.hrw.org/news/2020/04/10/brazil-bolsonaro-sabotages-anti-covid-19-efforts.

[69] Pia Ranada, "Mayor of the Philippines' Leaves LGUs Blind amid COVID-19," *Rappler* (June 9, 2020), www.rappler.com/newsbreak/in-depth/mayor-of-the-philippines-leaves-lgus-blind-amid-covid-19.

Ela Atienza of the University of the Philippines.[70] Centralization went to absurd lengths. At a certain point, Duterte ordered local chiefs to "stand down" and obey national directives after Pasig City mayor Vico Sotto appealed for tricycles to be allowed to ferry workers, the sick, and the elderly. Duterte's hyper-centralized approach effectively made much of the remedial action impossible.

In India, despite health falling within the powers of the states under the constitution, the central government took a leading role in the Covid-19 outbreak and failed to cooperate with states. For example, the central government based its decisions on a Covid-19 database by Indian Council of Medical Research (ICMR) that seems to have been rife with errors. Rahul Mukherji believes that "it might have gained a more accurate sense of local hotspots had it instead relied on established collaboration between the states and a disease-surveillance program run by the National Centre for Disease Control."[71]

This all illustrates how populist governments, bent on utmost centralization, are incapable of finding the most effective remedies, tailored to local conditions and responding to local knowledge. They engage in a blame game, laying responsibilities for failures at local administration while taking credit for successes. In that, populists all followed the example of Donald Trump. Early on he had made it clear that for states to get any assistance from the federal government, they would have to "show appreciation."[72]

"Trust Me"

One of the greatest predictors of success in combatting Covid-19 is institutional trust: trust of individuals in government. Trust in each other, too: "[H]orizontal" trust is important to the sense of empathy and solidarity that help enforce common solutions. This is one of the paradoxes of the pandemic predicament: separated from each other by self-isolation and quarantine, rendered anonymous by face masks in public spaces, individuals are paradoxically more together than ever before, even if the togetherness is mediated by a laptop or smartphone screen. But from the point of view of combating Covid-19, "vertical" trust is even more important. This form of social trust is critical to

---

[70] Ibid.
[71] Mukherji, "Covid vs. Democracy," p. 95.
[72] Hedges and Lasco, "Medical Populism," p. 80.

voluntary compliance with low-cost Covid-19 measures such as social distancing. "Hard" enforcement mechanisms such as security forces, are no substitute for voluntary compliance. As Spain's chief epidemiologist put it,"we do not have enough police officers as to put one in each corner of each park."[73]

An Oxford University study found that a greater governmental ability to enforce the restrictions does not seem to matter for mobility related to shops, pharmacies, and workplaces. Indeed, as the authors of the study argue, "countries with democratically accountable governments introduced less stringent lockdowns but experienced approximately 20% larger declines in geographic mobility at the same level of policy stringency," even accounting for state capacity.[74] Similarly, research in the United States indicates that counties with higher social trust had greater rates of compliance with social-distancing requirements.[75] In Australia, a government-designed and managed contact-tracing app called CovidSafe has been used since the beginning of the pandemic and yet millions of citizens have voluntarily downloaded and used it, seemingly without any concerns for potential breaches of privacy by the government, or that the information collected may be used for any other purpose than to contain the virus. When I go to a shop or an office or a take-out restaurant in Sydney, I see everyone scanning a QR code at the entrance collecting information necessary to assist contract-tracing, without being compelled to do so or being denied entry for not doing so.

Populists damage institutional trust by fomenting polarization and distancing themselves further from their political opponents and their electorates. If they have solid electoral support, they do not reach out to those who did not vote for them. Institutions they inhabit are highly politicized, in a party-political sense, and the top offices are deeply personalized, as a result of which those who do not admire the charismatic leader have no reasons to trust the office the leader holds. Pugnacious polarization weakens society's capacity to deal with a public threat of these proportions.

---

[73] Nicholas Charron, Victor Lapuente, and Andrés Rodriguez-Pose, "Uncooperative Society, Uncooperative Politics or Both?," University of Gothenburg QOG Institute, Working Paper 12 (2020), p. 9.

[74] Carl Benedikt Frey, Chinchih Chen, and Giorgio Presidente, "Democracy, Culture, and Contagion: Political Regimes and Countries' Responsiveness to Covid-19," Oxford Martin School, Working Paper (May 13, 2020), p. 3.

[75] Abel Brodeur, Idaliya Grigoryeva, and Lamis Kattan, "Stay-at-Home Orders, Social Distancing and Trust," *Journal of Population Economics*, 34 (2021), 1321–1354.

The often-militaristic language used by populists in combating the virus can further emphasize division and prevent a popular buy-in for pandemic restrictions.[76] In the Philippines, Duterte used the same rhetorical style as he applied to the war on drugs and his anti-terrorism bill when discussing the Covid response. Although it is a health crisis, for Duterte it was still a matter of peace and order, and "the troublemakers" (*"yung mga pasaway"* in Tagalog) are targeted as a problem. No wonder that such a heavy-handed approach did little to inspire confidence during a crisis that requires cooperation, consensus-building, and consultation.

There is a significant correlation between how democratic a country is and how high the levels of institutional trust are. But the correlation is not absolute: While statistically, democratic states have higher social capital than authoritarian ones, there may be democratic countries with relatively low levels of trust (Greece, Portugal, Bulgaria) and non-democratic states with high degrees of institutional trust (China, United Arab Republic). As such, factors other than democratic nature of the regime may be determinative of trust. In China, this may be a result of a combination of factors: the Confucian tradition emphasizing social networks and community, the institutional and economic performance of the leadership of the Communist Party, and the popularity of spectacular anti-corruption drives. Another potential factor is the shrewdness of central authorities that control the "blame game," that is, successfully imposing blame for failures on local governments, resulting in relatively high trust in the government in Beijing and low trust in local institutions.[77] Similar factors, and in particular the good economic performance of the ruling Communist Party and its popular anti-corruption campaigns, explain high levels of institutional trust in Vietnam. All this may convince people "that the [Communist Party of Vietnam] does care about the well-being of its citizens."[78]

---

[76] Daniel Innerarity, "Understanding, Deciding, and Learning: The Key Political Challenges in the Pandemic," in Miguel Maduro and Paul Kahn (eds.), *Democracy in Times of Pandemic* (Cambridge: Cambridge University Press, 2020), p. 131.

[77] For similar explanations of the phenomenon of high institutional trust in China, see Dan Chen, "Local Distrust and Regime Support: Sources and Effects of Political Trust in China," *Political Research Quarterly*, 70/2 (2017), 314–326; Christoph Steinhardt, "How Is High Trust in China Possible? Comparing the Origins of Generalized Trust in Three Chinese Societies," *Political Studies*, 60 (2012), 434–454.

[78] Mai Truong, "Explaining Public Trust in Vietnam," *Asia Times* (October 7, 2020), https://asiatimes.com/2020/10/explaining-public-trust-in-vietnam/.

As it happens, neither China nor Vietnam are "populist" regimes in the sense adopted in this book. Populism is probably more destructive of social trust than authoritarian-paternalistic or authoritarian-technocratic political systems both because of its trajectory (many populist systems have a path dependence originating in democracies) and because they more openly violate what they preach than overtly authoritarian governments with high output legitimacy. It is hypocrisy that is devastating to trust. In the discipline of gaining and maintaining institutional trust, populists lose both against democrats and against (at least some) authoritarians.

No Country Is an Island. Unless It Is

The virus knows no borders, and so remedies must transcend particular nation-states, even the most powerful. This, in turn, prompts the increased internationalization of health policies, and a higher degree of supranational oversight. Populists like national sovereignty, not globalization. Liberal democracy has nothing to hide and basks in international scrutiny.

The above may be thought to be false, if not outright absurd. After all, the first reaction of nation-states to Covid-19 was to order border closures, hoard scarce medical supplies and personal protective equipment, and blame one another for the spread of the virus. I am writing these words in a middle-sized liberal democracy that has been as hermetically sealed off from the rest of the world as it is humanly possible (a feat facilitated by the fact that it *is* an island) since the beginning of the outbreak, with virtually no foreign arrivals or departures overseas allowed to and from Australia.

But while an instinctive isolation is an immediate effect of the pandemic, it has many invidious effects from the point of view of the struggle against the very pandemic isolationists want to contain. So-called vaccine nationalism, meaning the prioritization by countries of their domestic needs for vaccines at the expense of others, is ultimately counterproductive. "Without equal vaccine distribution [around the world], experts warn, the pandemic could continue to live on residually for years, bringing with it even more death or further economic collapse."[79] So even if we put to one side all the idealistic and altruistic arguments (as so

---

[79] Yasmeen Serhan, "Vaccine Nationalism Is Doomed to Fail," *The Atlantic* (December 8, 2020), www.amp.theatlantic.com/amp/article/617323/.

many governments do) and look only at the pragmatic policies driven by the wealthy countries' self-interest, autarchy is self-defeating. "If the virus remains endemic anywhere, it will continue to pose a threat everywhere."[80] This is confirmed by some number-crunching modeling that shows that more equitable distribution of vaccines worldwide both will save lives and also bring considerable benefits to the global economy.[81]

Hoarding of scarce medical resources has strong precedents. All supplies of a vaccine developed in 2009 to deal with swine flu (which killed nearly 300,000 globally) were bought up entirely by the wealthy countries, and only then was a small percentage shared with poor states, after determining that the remaining supplies would be sufficient to meet domestic needs. Regarding Covid-19, some health administrators, including those at the US Food and Drug Administration under Trump, defended vaccine nationalism based on an analogy with the use of oxygen masks dropping inside a depressurized airplane in an emergency: The instruction is that you put on your own first, and only then help those in your care (something that, by the way, to some people comes naturally). But the analogy is misleading. Prioritizing vaccines to supply wealthy vaccine-producing countries (or those able to afford purchasing vaccines by outbidding others) is rather like providing oxygen masks for the first-class passengers only.[82] A "my country first" approach, abstaining from coordinating efforts at a regional and global scale, leads to vastly sub-optimal outcomes, both economically and in terms of human lives.

This is, indeed, a paradox of the pandemic. On the one hand, it triggers national autarchy, which is instinctively seen as a prerequisite for effective countermeasures; but on the other hand, it necessitates a higher degree of international collaboration. The paradox is illusory. Sealing off the national territory is a technical measure to limit movement of people, not necessarily across national borders, but the latter form is the easiest to implement. It is not necessarily rational: after all, the movement of an infected person from northern to southern Poland is just as bad as the movement of that person from southern Poland to the neighboring region in Slovakia. "[M]ost things that went wrong actually went wrong

---

[80] Ibid.
[81] Ibid.
[82] See Thomas J. Bollyky and Chad P. Bown, "The Tragedy of Vaccine Nationalism," *Foreign Affairs* (September/October 2020), www.foreignaffairs.com/print/node/1126225.

inside countries, not between them," says Fareed Zakaria.[83] But to find effective solutions, international collaboration at an unprecedented scale is necessary. As Ivan Krastev has put it, COVID-19 "has synchronized the world and brought us together in a way no previous crisis could."[84] Krastev is right: The pandemic has been a great agent of globalization, stronger than other transnational crises, including the global financial crisis and the refugees emergency. Unable to leave their countries as tourists, as businesspeople, or as frequent-flyer-miles-accruing professionals, people took to social media as never before, connecting with their networks and support groups in other countries. And governments and public opinion in nation-states sought supranational sources of help with eagerness, reinvigorating various much-maligned global and regional institutions.

Both the WHO and the European Union are cases in point. They both share a predicament noted by Neil Walker about many international organizations: "Too strong, and their willingness and ability to dictate matters to the [member] states is feared and resented. Too weak, which is the likely outcome of persistent underfunding and rhetorical undercutting, and they may be criticized by these same states for their susceptibility to domination by rival strong states."[85] The WHO has a lot of things to be blamed for. It was too slow to declare a public health emergency after learning about the outbreak, which warranted accusations by some observers and politicians that it was unduly influenced by the Chinese authorities. (But then, the WHO is largely at the mercy of notifications by states that must report disease outbreaks, and China failed to do so when it should have.) It failed to promptly issue recommendations for such measures as travel bans and stay-at-home orders on time, while many states already implemented such measures, and in retrospect, were justified in doing so. But at the same time, the WHO turned out to be important, and much of the criticism matched the account by Neil Walker of a self-fulfilling prophecy whereby states failed to collaborate with each other (as the International Heath Regulations of 2005, under which the WHO functions, now demand), by coordinating

---

[83] Fareed Zakaria, *Ten Lessons for a Post-Pandemic World* (New York: W. W. Norton, 2020), p. 218.
[84] Krastev, *Is It Tomorrow Yet?* p. 10.
[85] Neil Walker, "The Crisis of Democratic Leadership in Times of Pandemic," in Miguel Maduro and Paul Kahn (eds.), *Democracy in Times of Pandemic* (Cambridge: Cambridge University Press, 2020), pp. 23–38 at 34.

medical, logistical, and legal responses to public health regulations. As Oona Hathaway and her collaborators at Yale Law School claim, "[t]he [WHO] serves an invaluable role as a center of scientific expertise and a champion for global health. Yet it is too often powerless in the face of its biggest funders, unable to criticize them when they violate the WHO's rules for fear of retaliation."[86] Both sentences in this quote are equally important, and they exemplify nicely the general paradox of re-nationalization and globalization in the face of the pandemic. Up until now, the WHO had undertaken several important actions: While slow to declare the pandemic, it nevertheless quite early on (on January 23, 2020) urged countries that the disease would spread beyond China, it worked with social media to combat the spread of misinformation about the virus, and it played a major role in trials of potential treatments and then in distribution of billions of vaccines in 2021.[87]

Similarly, the member-states of the European Union came to realize that a supranational polity in Europe would be indispensable in handling the crisis, despite all its weaknesses, often exaggerated as in part of a traditional blame game that the European member-state governments have engaged since the very beginning. To be sure, at the outset of the pandemic, EU institutions were indecisive and slow to act. In particular Italians (being among the first Europeans to be hit) felt let down, both by European institutions and by their fellow member-states, which displayed shamefully low levels of solidarity in response to pleas for medical equipment. The European Commission advisory panel on Covid-19 was set up by the EU member states as late as March 16, 2020. And even though a strategic medical stockpile had been approved by the Commission in March 2019, well before the pandemic, it was only implemented after the WHO declared the outbreak a global pandemic on March 11, 2020, and several member-states had difficulties purchasing medical equipment. This was perhaps due to the fact of the quick re-nationalization of EU architecture resulting from the outbreak: closed borders, sealed-off national economies, panic-driven solutions at a national level. Lockdowns were determined in national capitals, not in Brussels. This new architecture was not a context to which EU decision-makers had been habituated: it was deeply antithetical to the Europeans

---

[86] Oona A. Hathaway, Preston J. Lim, Alasdair Phillips-Robins, and Mark Stevens, "The COVID-19 Pandemic and International Law," Yale Law School, Public Law Research Paper (March 30, 2021), www.ssrn.com/abstract=3815164, p. 75.
[87] See ibid., pp. 81–82.

Union's modus operandi. And, more importantly, member-states are very much the "masters" of the EU institutions, and at the beginning of the crisis in early 2020, they did not see any special need for cooperation due to the general underestimation of the size of the outbreak.[88]

As Jonathan White notes, it was only when "economic dimensions of the crisis became more pronounced, [that] executive activity in Europe became overtly transnational."[89] From activism by the European Central Bank, new cross-national arrangements for loans and grants, the adoption of a pathbreaking system of collective borrowing and common debt in mid-2020, through to a gigantic Recovery Fund agreed upon in December 2020, EU member-states pooled their actions and resources under the aegis of the European Union, and within the existing institutional setup. This was largely prompted by pressure from European public opinion. While national governments had not conferred any authority for establishing a common health policy upon the European Union, nevertheless by July 2020, over two-thirds of EU citizens expected the European Union to have a more active role in protecting their health, particularly in protecting them from health threats that transcend national borders.[90] As is usual within the European Union, nothing was particularly frictionless, and in particular the adoption of the Recovery Plan was marred by resistance from two populist governments, Poland and Hungary, against tying the dispensation of the funds to the rule of law and non-corruption guarantees. In the best (or the worst, depending on one's point of view) EU tradition, a compromise was found, with important ambiguities relegated to a decision to be made by the Court of Justice. But the primacy of the joint EU solution over unilateral "each for themselves" remedies was not publicly questioned by any government. Covid-19 turned to be an agenda-setter for novel supranational solutions within the European Union, and the dominant view (naturally, tentative) among EU scholars seems to be that the Union has coped well with the Covid-19 crisis, managed to adapt its conduct

---

[88] Jordana Jacint and Juan Carlos Triviño-Salazar, "Where Are the ECDC and the EU-Wide Responses in the COVID-19 Pandemic?" *The Lancet*, 395/10237 (May 23, 2020), 1611–1612.

[89] Jonathan White, "Emergency Europe after Covid-19," in Gerard Delanty (ed.), *Pandemics, Politics, and Society: Critical Perspectives on the Covid-19 Crisis* (Berlin: De Gruyter: 2021), pp. 75–92 at 78.

[90] Alberto Alemanno, "Towards a European Health Union: Time to Level Up," *European Journal of Risk Regulation*, 11 (2020), 721–725 at 722.

flexibly to the requirements, and showed a high degree of institutional resilience.[91]

Connections between multilateralism, as reflected in institutions such as the WHO or the European Union (different though they are) and liberal democracy are not an inherent but a contingent matter. Theoretically one *can* think of populism bolstering global or regional organizations. But in the world as we know it, globalization favors supranational oversight under democratic norms while insistence on sovereignty helps local autocrats. This is certainly the case of the European Union: a polity strongly attached to liberal rights and democratic governance, often rhetorically but occasionally also in practice. So if the result of the pandemic is that global or regional institutions will be enhanced, a net advantage for liberal democracies and a net disadvantage for populist rulers is likely to occur.

Democracy Reinvigorated?

"The virus has undermined the messianic image of many populist leaders; the pandemic has shown that all were vulnerable, more so if they did not follow social distancing (defying scientific advice)."[92] In contrast to the projected image of strength and decisiveness, many populist leaders showed weakness, hesitation, and the predilection to fall back on prejudice, paranoia, and deception. Indeed, the two most pandemic-denialist leaders, Donald Trump and Jair Bolsonaro, presided over the countries with the highest death numbers in the world (at the time of writing these words, late February 2022, respectively -940,000 and 646,000; during Pesident Trump's term of office the death toll was over 750,000). And they too caught the virus.

Earlier in the chapter I have ventured a deliberately *weak* proposition: that populism, notwithstanding some apparent "advantages," is not more successful in coping with the disaster than liberal democracy. But this prudence may perhaps be set aside, and a stronger proposition made instead: that democracies have many built-in advantages that equip them *better* to handle the pandemic. In comparison to populism, as understood

---

[91] See Sarah Wolff and Stella Ladi, "European Union Responses to the Covid-19 Pandemic: Adaptability in Times of Permanent Emergency," *Journal of European Integration*, 42/8 (2020), 1025–1040.

[92] Sergei Guriev and Elias Papaioannou, "The Political Economy of Populism" (February 21, 2020), www.ssrn.com/abstract=3542052, p. 83.

in this book, and not in a global democracy-versus-authoritarianism battle of political models, liberal democracies acted faster and more effectively than populist regimes. I had already cited a case study on school closures. More generally, studies have been conducted that show that populist governments have been slower in their response to the pandemic than non-populist states. In particular, populists implemented fewer protective health measures in the early days of the pandemic, in the first half of 2020.[93] The better performance of democracies, if sustained throughout the crisis to its end, may lead the public to prefer "prudent leaders operating in the light of evidence-based policies rather than populist leaders who act whimsically and impulsively and prefer 'common sense' over science."[94] If the main source of populists' legitimacy is that they get things done, then their failure in coping with the pandemic may adversely affect their "output legitimacy."

"This microscopic foe has exploited flaws in our society"[95] – this observation by Scott Galloway, professor at New York University's Stern School of Business, applies not only to his country – the United States – but to every country affected by the virus, and hence the entire world. And it may be added that the pathogen has also extracted the *best* in the people – and their political institutions. Democracies have been no less willing to restrict the rights of their citizens (e.g., of movement and public assembly) when preserving life was essential, but they were usually carefully calibrated, non-discriminatory, with sunset clauses, oversight, judicial review, and so forth. If they occasionally tried to exceed reasonable limits, the force of civil society prevented such excesses. This is the mechanism of self-correction in a well-functioning democracy. When in January 2021, the Norwegian government proposed to add a curfew clause (a rather meek one, I should add) to existing emergency legislation, the outrage was so strong (nearly 1,500 submissions protesting the proposal) that the government quickly shelved the bill.[96] One of the

---

[93] Ibid., 83.
[94] Tamar Brandes and Yaniv Roznai, "Can COVID-19 Save Democracy from Populism?" in Tom Gerald Daly and Wojciech Sadurski (eds.), *Democracy 2020: Assessing Constitutional Decay, Breakdown, and Renewal Worldwide*, IACL-AIDC Global Roundtable E-book (December 2020), pp. 41–44 at 43.
[95] Scott Galloway, *Post Corona: From Crisis to Opportunity* (London: Bantam Press, 2020), p. 209.
[96] See Kristin Bergtora Sandvik, Hans Petter Graver, and Peter Sharff Smith, "The Pomp of Popular Constitutional Outrage," *Verfassungsblog*, March 2, 2021, www.verfassungsblog.de/the-pomp-of-popular-constitutional-outrage/.

submissions, by the Norwegian Bar Association, stated that during the pandemic, the Norwegian population has demonstrated that we trust the government – "the authorities should also show that they trust us."

No such trust has been displayed by populist governments; it is not in their DNA. Excessive restrictions, such as the ones evidenced above, and in particular those that constrained speech and prevented the media from spreading (allegedly) fake news about governmental actions in the face of the pandemic, did not necessarily help save lives. Gag laws adopted in Hungary, India, or the Philippines were disproportionate and unnecessary. They were ultimately directed at the regime's survival rather than at identifying the most rational public health solutions.[97]

---

[97] See, similarly, Innerarity, "Understanding, Deciding, and Learning," p. 130.

7

Antidotes, Remedies, and Miracles

A few years ago, Stephen Holmes observed, pessimistically: "When a politically adroit counter-elite has gained sufficient power to control the country's media, neutralize the courts, and undermine the capacity of the opposition to contest the next election, as it has in Hungary and Poland, liberal democracy will need some kind of miracle to help it back to life."[1] Control of the media, the neutralization of the courts, and the marginalization of the opposition *have* taken place, to higher or lower degrees, in all ruling populisms, as evidenced in this book. But will it take a "miracle" to undo the toxic deformations of democracies in these states?

Hopefully not. Some opponents of populism hope that populism will collapse under the weight of its own dysfunctionalities and inefficiencies, especially now that so many people have seen how inept and irresponsible some populist rulers are in responding to Covid-19. But the jury is still out on the overall balance sheet when it comes to handling the pandemic (see Chapter 6). More generally, however, liberal democrats like to think that populist political systems carry a seed of self-destruction: that they are, in the long run, ineffective and counter-productive, relying upon the knowledge (imperfect) and charisma (doubtful and not easy to maintain) of a single person. With its paranoid excesses and narrow epistemic base, populism may be seen to have a low capacity for effective governance. And by disconnecting the real center of political power from constitutionally established institutions and procedures, populist regimes seem to reduce the likelihood of self-correction facilitated by inter-institutional accountability.

In the essay just quoted, Stephen Holmes also observed: "[P]opulist leaders almost always prefer a personally loyal to a professionally competent staff. This makes it somewhat less likely that a cornered populist president will be able to design and implement a truly shrewd and

---

[1] Stephen Holmes, "How Democracies Perish," in Cass R. Sunstein (ed.), *Can It Happen Here? Authoritarianism in America* (New York: HarperCollins, 2018), pp. 387–427 at 420.

effective survival strategy."[2] The main legitimating ground of populism, namely that it effectively delivers goods to its electorate, seems to have a long-term tendency to decline. The major instrument by which populists maintain their popularity – mass clientelism – may become unsustainable. But a dramatic worsening of the economic situation may not lead to political reversal. As the famous Polish economist Leszek Balcerowicz observes, "the worsening economy may not be sufficient to stop and reverse a bad transition if forces of intimidation are already strong."[3] And yet, traditional remedies used by elected authoritarians in such circumstances, that is, intimidating their political opponents, may be counterproductive in Poland or the Philippines, Brazil or India, as it would clash with the strongly libertarian, occasionally perhaps even anarchistic, social attitudes in those countries.

Further, populism in power runs into a universal paradox: How to reconcile *being* the establishment with the anti-establishmentarian appeal that fuels populism's popularity? Ben Stanley notes that populist parties "often fell victim to the same public scepticism they had sought to cultivate when attacking established parties."[4] There is no reason to believe that, in the long run, any of the populisms in power will escape the force of this "scepticism" espoused by their electorates, which are, at the same time, most conducive to anti-establishment attitudes. The day that populist leaders such as Bolsonaro or Modi, Kaczyński or Orbán appear to them as the new establishment, even more nefarious than the establishment of old because they are less subject to routine rotations in power, will mark the beginning of the political end for those leaders. This may be precipitated by the departure of the Leader, caused by old age, bad health, death, or splits in the ruling group. By relying so strongly on one person, the system as a whole also shares his (this gender used advisedly) vulnerabilities, whereas a democratic system that incorporates simple mechanisms of self-correction and alternation in power is more resilient.

But none of these "miracles," to repeat Holmes's formula, can be a substitute for vigorous political action by opponents of populism. None

---

[2] Ibid., 422–423.
[3] Leszek Balcerowicz, "Recent Attacks against Freedom," unpublished manuscript (April 2015), p. 2.
[4] Ben Stanley, "Populism in Central and Eastern Europe," in Cristóbal Rovira Kaltwasser, Paul Taggart, Paulina Ochoa-Espejo, and Pierre Ostiguy (eds.), *The Oxford Handbook of Populism* (Oxford: Oxford University Press, 2017), pp. 140–160 at 157–158.

of the populist ruling elites will do the democrats a favor and politely step down, humiliated by their failures to deliver the goods, or embarrassed by the ineptness of the ultimate leader.

Winning against the Populists

The most obvious advice which may be given to anti-populists is: "Win elections." Easier said than done. True, contemporary populist authoritarianism has yielded examples of states where a ruling group with autocratic tendencies has conceded elections – for example, Macedonia in 2016 or Sri Lanka in 2015. But we know, as was shown in Chapter 2, that populists often tilt the electoral playing field to their favor, and in some populist regimes, the democrats will face an uphill battle to replace populists through electoral victory.

The hill is steeper in some countries than in others. To the question: "Is there a realistic opportunity for the opposition to increase its support or gain power through elections?" Freedom House ranks all countries on the scale from 0 (the least democratic) to 4 (the fairest electoral playing field). Its 2021 Report gives Hungary and the Philippines 2 points each, while India, Brazil, and Poland get 4 points each. (In Venezuela, under Maduro, it is 0.) The 4 points allocated to India must be however modified downward in view of the report's answer to a different question: "Do various segments of the population (including ethnic, racial, religious, gender, LGBT+, and other relevant groups) have full political rights and electoral opportunities?" which is only 2 out of 4 points (for Brazil, the Philippines, and Hungary, it is 3; and for Poland, 4.)[5]

In all these countries (except for Maduro's Venezuela, of course), electoral strategy should be the pathway of choice to restoring liberal democracy. The electoral mandate of populists needs to be countered with the electoral mandate of liberal democrats. Of course, in anti-populist political battles there will be also radical *non*-democrats, such as the extreme right-wing Jobbik in Hungary or Konfederacja in Poland. Whether their votes can help by adding to the democrats' numbers or hinder by splitting the opposition is a thoroughly context-specific matter. The best strategy by which to win elections in a field biased in favor of the incumbents will vary from country to country, but three propositions seem to be of quasi-universal applicability. First, the higher the voters'

---

[5] Freedom House, "Countries and Territories," www.freedomhouse.org/countries/freedom-world/scores.

turnout, the better the chances for the anti-populist opposition. Second, the more unified the opposition, the higher its chances of victory. Third, and most importantly, the more the opposition can convince society that its program is not merely *anti*-populist, but that it is a positive platform that goes well beyond return to the pre-populist status quo, the higher its chances of attracting moderate, undecided, and hesitant voters (including within the hitherto pro-government electorate), which will be decisive for a final electoral victory.

The most contingent and uncertain of these three propositions is the first one. In the abstract, one may speculate that bringing in additional voters (those who would go to the ballot boxes reluctantly and those who, in non-mandatory voting systems, would stay at home in "normal" times) may benefit *either* the incumbent or the opposition. The pool of undecided or non-committed may include people who espouse low-intensity interests and hence are the real targets of any pro-turnout campaign. But empirical studies seem to bear out the thesis that high turnouts in less than fully democratic systems are on balance beneficial to democrats.[6] For one thing, some of the countries discussed in this book have societies with an overall high rate of support for democracy (for instance, Brazil's population has the third highest commitment to democracy in South America, with Venezuela, the second highest),[7] so the existing pool of reluctant voters would likely bring more votes to democrats. And while populists may present themselves as mega-democrats before coming to power, their first term(s) in office may disabuse many voters of this illusion, and as a result those voters will have a choice between staying at home or voting for the anti-populist opposition. For another thing, populists in power have better means by which to mobilize their supporters to go to the ballot, either through propaganda or generous handouts, than the regime opponents who are often demoralized and convinced that "there is no alternative" – so why bother? This may suggest that democrats have a larger pool of non-voting supporters than populists do. For all these reasons, any marginal increase in turnout seems to disproportionately benefit opponents of ruling populists.

---

[6] Erica Frantz, "Voter Turnout and Opposition Performance in Competitive Authoritarian Elections," *Electoral Studies*, 54 (2018), 218–225.
[7] Richard Wike, Katie Simmons, Bruce Stokes, and Janell Fetterolf, "Globally, Broad Support for Representative and Direct Democracy but Many also Endorse Nondemocratic Alternatives," *Pew Research Center* (October 6, 2017), p. 5.

The second proposition, about the importance of unified anti-government coalitions in states governed by populists, is perhaps more self-evident. Populist governments rely as much on the captivating force of their programs as on the weakness of the opposition, usually fractured and flawed by infighting. Electoral systems, translating raw votes into seats in parliaments, unless they are perfectly proportional usually strongly favor big parties and coalitions and penalize small and medium parties running on their own. As the cliché goes: Oppositions do not win the elections; rather governing parties lose them. And so populists occasionally *lose* elections when confronted with a unified opposition, as was the case of the victory of Zuzana Čaputová in the Slovak presidential elections in 2019 against a left-populist candidate, or the mayor of Istanbul, Ekrem İmamoğlu, elected twice in 2019 (the first election was unceremoniously annulled), or the mayor of Budapest, Gergely Karácsony, and mayors of several other Hungarian cities, including in Hódmezővásárhely, a Fidesz stronghold in 2019, or the anti-Netanyahu coalition in Israel in 2021. Among the electorate, a fragmented opposition strengthens the message that there is really no feasible alternative to the ruling populists. It also diminishes the opposition's resilience to governmental coercion and fraud. And it makes it easy for rulers to use a "divide and rule" strategy, to play one opposition party off the other. With respect to the importance of an opposition coalition, this proposition is supported, mutatis mutandis, by older findings made by Marc Howard and Philip Roessler that in the context of "competitive authoritarianism," a united coalition is by far the most important factor bringing about liberalizing electoral outcomes. "The more divided the opposition parties, the more susceptible they are to governmental manipulation, cooptation, and repression."[8] To defeat the ruling populists, the democratic oppositions should present themselves as a united front.

Or should they really? The price to be paid for a united coalition is the thinning out of the opposition's program: the more parties it embraces, the narrower the common denominator on which they can agree. The anti-Netanyahu coalition of 2021 is perhaps the most extreme case of this, bringing together both right-wing and left-wing parties, as well as, for the first time ever in an Israeli coalition, an Arab party. One commentator has observed: "[T]he range of issues that the new government can

---

[8] Marc Morjé Howard and Philip G. Roessler, "Liberalizing Electoral Outcomes in Competitive Authoritarian Regimes," *American Journal of Political Science*, 50 (2006), 365–381 at 371.

address will be extremely limited and circumscribed...[T]his government came into being with one fundamental objective, and that was to remove Benjamin Netanyahu. It will do that."[9] If a united opposition has no other common goals beyond the negative task of removing a populist, *and voters know this*, then it may weaken its electoral appeal. Related to this is the real risk of clearly ideological parties losing some of their devoted voters when they are compelled to water down their electoral platform in order to match their coalition partners. They are, after all, "united" only with respect to a single goal: defeating the incumbents. So even if they win, they may be unable to be anything else than an election-winning machine. This is what happened in Venezuela, after the opposition's success in the 2015 parliamentary elections (preceded by their near success in the 2013 presidential elections), when, as one observer noted, "there [was] little underlying comity, ideological affinity, or shared policy consensus to hold the member parties [of the winning anti-Maduro coalition] together."[10] Comity, ideological affinity, policy consensus...These resources are scarcely found among anti-populist opposition parties, often demoralized following years of marginalization in the parliament and the media. As a result, there are difficult trade-offs to make.

Which brings me to the third proposition: anti-populist electoral platforms, that is, anti-populist political programs. Here, the main dilemma is that on the one hand, the platform should not merely be "anti," but on the other hand, the reality is that in populist states, the "anti" claims of democrats prevail, in importance and salience, over positive policy proposals. In the run-up to the Israeli elections, Yair Lapid said: "The real political fight is between populists and responsible leaders."[11] But "responsibility" without more is not much of a political program: Every leader claims this virtue. It may be difficult to convince

---

[9] Christina Pazzanese, "Will a Historically Diverse New Coalition Bring Big Changes to Israel?" *The Harvard Gazette* (June 7, 2021) (quoting Robert M. Danin), www.news.harvard.edu/gazette/story/2021/06/harvard-analysts-discuss-israels-historically-diverse-new-coalition.

[10] Harold Trinkunas, "Why Venezuela's Opposition Has Been Unable to Effectively Challenge Maduro," *Brookings* (January 8, 2018), www.brookings.edu/blog/order-from-chaos/2018/01/08/why-venezuelas-opposition-has-been-unable-to-effectively-challenge-maduro.

[11] Ruth Margalit, "The Defeat of Benjamin Netanyahu," *The New Yorker* (June 13, 2021), www.newyorker.com/news/dispatch/the-defeat-of-benjamin-netanyahu.

voters that the program of anti-populists goes beyond the negative, which in itself rarely leads to victory.

That is one dilemma. But a deeper dilemma is how to take on board the real concerns that had triggered the popularity of populism in the first place without at the same time absorbing populism's toxic remedies? This has happened to some democratic leaders, such as center-right Dutch prime minister Mark Rutte, who successfully employed populist slogans in the 2017 parliamentary elections and subsequently adopted populist policies on immigration and multiculturalism. But the success is Pyrrhic: the strategy of absorbing populism does not defeat populism in the long run – rather, it legitimizes it. And at the end of the day it really does not matter *who* proclaims populist policies. A proper reminder of this can be found in Australia. The populist right-wing party One Nation led by an arch-demagogue, Pauline Hanson, was disarmed when its ideas transferred into the political mainstream and were adopted by the governing center-right coalition. The result is one of the most punitive detention systems for asylum seekers in the world. As a result, the absorption of populism results in a lamentable race to the bottom by parties competing for the populist vote.[12]

There must be a better way. What such a program might look like will be sketched at the end of this chapter.

Cordon sanitaire?

Considering that polarization is the ecosystem in which populism flourishes, anti-populists would do well to use depolarizing strategies, thus reducing the exclusionary, divisive appeal of populists. One depolarizing guideline is to deescalate the personal character of the electoral competition and run it on issues rather than the character of an Orban, a Modi, or a Bolsonaro. On the eve of the election of President Trump in 2016, one commentator drew lessons from successful anti-populist strategy used in Italy, and observed that the only two politicians who had won electoral competitions against Silvio Berlusconi were Romano Prodi and Matteo Renzi, both of whom had focused on issues rather than on their opponent's character (even if their opponent's character was not all that

---

[12] See, similarly, Benjamin Mofitt, "The Trouble with Anti-populism: Why the Champions of Civility Keep Losing," *The Guardian* (February 14, 2020), www.theguardian.com/politics/2020/feb/14/anti-populism-politics-why-champions-of-civility-keep-losing.

saintly).[13] Discourses that are programmatic and flexible have anti-polarization effects, and may weaken populists' power. The mayor who won the 2019 Budapest elections is sometimes presented as an exemplar of an "active depolarizing strategy," in that he won on a platform of "representing the people against the seat of power, a pro-Europe and green agenda, and a willingness to work in a partnership with the national government."[14] The new Slovak president is also praised for her "messages of inclusion and a refusal to engage in the reciprocating discourse of denigration and disinformation from her populist rivals."[15]

But anti-polarization strategies have their limit, and there comes a time when anti-populists must call a spade a spade, no matter how "polarizing" it is. This is yet another dilemma in strategizing how to deal with populists. Polarization-promoting populists often compel their opponents to engage in a tit-for-tat; to respond differently may seem meek and passive. Depending on the nature of their rhetoric and program, it may be tempting – which is not necessarily to say wise – to apply a sort of "cordon sanitaire" – a political equivalent of social distancing – and if populist leaders cannot be ignored or delegitimized (when they are in the government, it obviously would not work), to try a stigmatizing strategy. (No doubt, this is much more difficult in our current world of social media than in times where traditional mainstream media was dominant and to some extent framed and regulated the national conversation.)[16] A cordon sanitaire may be particularly effective if combined with a seemingly opposite strategy, that of seeking dialogue with moderate elements of the governing populist parties and potential/actual defectors from ruling parties. There has been a good deal of empirical work in political science done that shows that stigma occasionally works – that people feel negatively about supporting parties they know many others feel negatively toward. According to some scholars, this emotion influences the way some people *vote*. Though of course the vote itself is secret, "voters are deterred from supporting a party when there is a social stigma

---

[13] Luigi Zingales, "The Right Way to Resist Trump," *The New York Times* (November 18, 2016) www.nytimes.com/2016/11/18/opinion/the-right-way-to-resist-trump.html.
[14] Murat Somer, Jennifer L. McCoy, and Russell E. Luke, "Pernicious Polarization, Autocratization and Opposition Strategies," *Democratization*, 28 (2021), pp. 929–948 at 941, footnote omitted.
[15] Ibid., p. 942, footnote omitted.
[16] Mark Little and Matthew Feldman, "Social Media and the Cordon Sanitaire," *Journal of Language and Politics*, 16 (2017), 510–522 at 513.

around it."[17] The results of such experiments are tentative only – and perhaps anecdotal evidence may provide illustrations showing the opposite effect, that a general opprobrium around a given party or politician often mobilizes extra support for them, by conferring upon them an aura of martyrdom. Donald Trump is one such example. When connected with conspiracy theories about the deep state and liberal plots against a given politician, Orbán, Bolsonaro, or Duterte are able to skillfully use the "stigma" addressed against them in a sort of boomerang effect. Stigmatization might backfire, in addition to contributing to a downward spiral of tribalism and hyper-polarization.

It may be thought, and is occasionally flagged,[18] that the ultimate manner of delegitimizing authoritarian populism would need to borrow from the toolbox of a doctrine known as "militant democracy": restrictions on freedom of parties or of political speech on the basis of protecting democracy against its internal enemies. But with regard to populists in power, these tools are certainly inapplicable. Quite apart from the usual problems and conundrums around "militant democracy" itself (that is, the medicine may be more harmful than the disease it is supposed to cure), such instruments may make sense when used against marginal, radical, obviously anti-democratic groups, often related to the ancien régime they seek to restore (Nazism, Communism, apartheid), and should be prevented from increasing their social popularity and support. But populist parties and leaders do not fit this picture. *They* control law-making and the enforcement of law: Why would they use it against themselves? They are not embedded in the ancien régime nor do they seek to restore it: Orbán is not a neo-Communist nor is Duterte a new Marcos. (Bolsonaro's sympathy toward the military regime of pre-1985 is a more questionable case.) And their anti-democratic character is questionable: in the eyes of many of their followers, *they* are truly democratic. Militant democracy in a state governed by populist rulers will certainly be used as a device to silence anti-populists.

"Out on the streets and in with the foreigners"

But *electoral* victory against populist rulers is not just about *elections*. It is about social resistance in the long period between election days; it is

---

[17] Eelco Harteveld, "Social Stigma and Support for the Populist Radical Right: An Experimental Study," *Scandinavian Political Studies*, 42 (2019), 296–307 at 304.

[18] Anna Lührmann, "Disrupting the Autocratization Sequence: Towards Democratic Resilience," *Democratization*, 28 (2021), 1017–1039 at 1028.

about civil society, NGOs, students and academics, trade unions, and of course demonstrations in streets and squares. "Protest may weaken the legitimacy of the incumbent and provide signals to the electorate that the incumbent is vulnerable to defeat."[19] In this sense, social resistance during the electoral cycle is important for electoral victory too. It mobilizes the opposition, helps it gain confidence, and sends a message to the outside world that ruling populists, for all their claims to represent the entire People, enjoy only the support of a majority, or sometimes a plurality, never a near-consensus. At least some societies where populists rule today have a vibrant and proud tradition of direct action – such as People's Power in the Philippines or Solidarność in Poland. In Bertelsmann's civil society participation index, Poland and India score a high 7/10, Brazil scores 6/10, and the Philippines, 5/10.[20] The challenge for opposition parties is to liaise with these movements, which are often single-issue, episodic, decentralized, spontaneous, and hostile to established political parties, including democratic opposition parties (Poland's pro-rule of law movement after 2017 and Women's Strike post-2020 are cases in point). But the best strategy for democratic opposition parties in the states where populism rules is to build a synergy with social non-partisan movements.

Likewise, with foreign supporters. This has particular relevance to Poland and Hungary, both members of the European Union. (Polish populists have highlighted the connection between the opposition's reliance on mass demonstration and foreign support, and summarize their strategy as the nicely rhyming though sarcastic slogan *"ulica i zagranica"* or "out on the streets and in with the foreigners.") This is because, in practice, the only possibly effective sites for external intervention in populist-authoritarian states in Europe are EU institutions (in particular, the Court of Justice of the European Union [CJEU]) with the capacity to influence legal developments in EU member states. The other pan-European structure – the Council of Europe (CoE) with the European Court of Human Rights (ECtHR) at its epicenter – has a much weaker effect on its member states, both due to its limited subject-matter and the merely indirect effect of its judgments upon the law of CoE member states. In contrast, the European Union has a relatively sophisticated tool

---

[19] Howard and Roessler, "Liberalizing Electoral Outcomes," p. 372.
[20] The World Bank, GovData360 "Civil Society Participation," *World Bank*, www.govdata360 .worldbank.org/indicators/hab8090ea?country=BRAandindicator=28738andviz=line_char tandyears=2006,2020#table-link.

kit for enforcing legal standards enshrined in EU treaties upon EU member-states moving along a path of disturbing populism.

This distinguishes some of the countries discussed in this book, such as Hungary and Poland on the one hand, from Brazil, Philippines, India, or Venezuela on the other. The latter governments need not be concerned about external intervention other than by nebulous and rarely effective "international public opinion" or pressures exerted by strong democratic countries in their bilateral relations with populist regimes. (To be sure, both Brazil and Venezuela have ratified the American Convention of Human Rights. but the judicial arm of the Convention, the Inter-American Court of Human Rights, has an even lesser impact on the national law of ratifiers than the ECtHR has on the law of CoE members, not to mention the European Union.)

The actual effectiveness of the European Union's tool kit upon rogue EU member-states is usually summarized in the expression "too little, too late." This skepticism applies in particular to judgments of the CJEU, but also to various interventions by the European Union's top technocratic body, the European Commission, its inter-governmental political body, the European Council, and (to a lesser degree) to its political-representative body, the European Parliament. The mood of scholarship on the European Union is that of a growing disappointment with the political will and effectiveness of each of these bodies to police clear departures from the standards of the rule of law, democracy, and human rights in countries governed by increasingly authoritarian populists. As three leading students of the European Union put it, the "failure to confront emerging autocracies in the EU threatens to make a mockery of the EU as the 'union of values' that Hungarian and Polish citizens sought to join in the first place."[21] Noting the overall pro–European Union public attitudes in these two countries, they ask: "[H]ow much longer can this popular support last, given the EU's overly cautious approach in rule of law enforcement?"[22]

Theirs is representative of the disenchantment with the European Union felt by friends and supporters of this supranational entity. And to remedy the seeming ineffectiveness of the current institutional setup,

---

[21] R. Daniel Kelemen, Tomasso Pavone, and Cassandra Emmons, "The Perils of Passivity in the Rule of Law Crisis: A Response to von Bogdandy," *Verfassungsblog* (November 26, 2019), www.verfassungsblog.de/the-perils-of-passivity-in-the-rule-of-law-crisis-a-response-to-von-bogdandy.

[22] Ibid.

some innovative ideas for new institutional designs have been put forward by other scholars, for instance in the form of a "Copenhagen Commission" – so called to refer to the famous Copenhagen Criteria, which had codified, on the eve of the Eastward enlargement, the principles of democracy, human rights, and the rule of law as prerequisites for membership in the European Union.[23] And it is perhaps not a coincidence that one scholar who has made important contributions to the study of populism in the last few years (Jan-Werner Müller) also authored this proposal.

Skepticism about the incapacity of the European Union to enforce standards of the rule of law and human rights in its member-states (as opposed to *candidate* states through the conditionality mechanism) may be occasionally exaggerated. For my part, I have argued that the tool kit can be to some degree effective, especially if, first, it is seen in its totality and, second, it is measured by realistic standards about what a supranational polity such as the European Union can do about its recalcitrant member-states in any case.[24]

The first point is about the need to see the tool kit holistically. An accurate image of what the European Union is doing emerges by taking together: (1) its measures that have a primarily *judicial* character – CJEU judgments, both in response to questions of preliminary reference and to the commission's infringement actions; (2) its measures that have a primarily *political* character – such as the Article 7 procedure, leading to the symbolic condemnation of a state breaching the Union values, and in some circumstances, even suspending the voting rights of that state in the council; (3) the whole range of various measures *in between* – such as the rule-of-law framework that compels governments at least to explain themselves, with the consequent reputational costs attached to that; and finally (4) possible *financial* sanctions related to the so-called rule-of-law conditionality, resulting in the refusal to transfer funds to a rogue state. One may conclude that the cumulative effect of all of this is not insignificant.

---

[23] Jan-Werner Müller, "Protecting the Rule of Law (and Democracy!) in the EU: The Idea of a Copenhagen Commission," in Carlos Closa and Dimitry Kochenov (eds.), *Reinforcing Rule of Law Oversight in the European Union* (Cambridge: Cambridge University Press, 2016), pp. 206–224 at 220.

[24] See Wojciech Sadurski, *Poland's Constitutional Breakdown* (Oxford: Oxford University Press, 2019), pp. 199–241.

The second point is that expectations must, unfortunately, be realistic, hence low. The tool kit of the European Union is but a function of the nature of the European Union as a whole. It must not be judged, for instance, by the standards of the effectiveness of a central government toward its component parts (states, provinces, Länder, etc.) in a federal state – because the European Union is not a federation. The baseline for any assessment we make of the European Union, in the field of its impact upon its member states, must be determined by what the European Union *is*, not what it *ought* to be in the dreams of the most idealistic Euro-enthusiasts.

The upshot for our discussion in this chapter is that international or regional "intervention" may be significant, but it does not have an autonomous value and must be seen as supporting and enhancing pro-democratic trends *inside* states. To put it bluntly, Brussels will not restore democracy and the rule of law in Warsaw or Budapest, just as the "international community" will not restore democracy in Venezuela or Brazil. But they can make a difference – mainly by providing argumentative, legal, and financial assets to democrats, and by making it more costly (in the broad sense of costs) for authoritarians to carry out their policies. By well-calibrated policies of pressure – court judgments, political declarations, sanctions – foreign actors may change the structure of incentives within populist states to the advantage of democrats. So, in the end it is a question of subsidiary assistance rather than intervention per se that may result in the restoration of liberal democracy. At the end of the day, what really matters is the collective decision in ballot boxes – so long as the ballot is not rigged.

Community without Populism

As emphasized before, the true challenge that lies before anti-populist democrats is not their electoral strategy but their program. The issue is not one of political technology but of political philosophy. Their task is to work out a program that responds to the local, context-dependent anxieties that triggered a populist response, but without populist aberrations: disregard for the rule of law, separation of powers, pluralism, minorities, and for the neediest, including migrants.

While I do not have a blueprint for such a program, what is key will be attempts to address the true concerns that led to the demand for populist solutions with policies that do not sacrifice liberal-democratic principles. Populist voters need to be respected, and so their concerns and fears must be taken seriously. The status anxieties of people voting for liberals is a real societal concern, though the intensity and character of those fears as represented by populist politicians and ideologists are toxic, especially when they are targeted against the most vulnerable groups. Fears related to globalization and consequent pathologies must be addressed in a way that does not pander to racism and xenophobia, which is the populist way of dealing with them.

Liberalism, in my view, has ample resources to respond to the *demand* for populism with an inclusionary and egalitarian *supply* of programs and policies. The starting point is to diagnose the sources of populist demand. As suggested in Chapter 1, this is very much context-specific, and in different places there are different configurations of anxieties and concerns that generate an aggregate populist demand. But the main ingredients form a relatively limited list: (1) a sense of economic insecurity and status anxiety; (2) xenophobic attitudes toward "Others," in particular migrants and refugees; (3) disenchantment with incumbent political elites, combined with the perception that the establishment is arrogant, remote, and insensitive to the needs of "real people"; (4) resentment against globalization, internationalism, and renewed support for nationalism (economic and other); (5) cultural and religious resentment, expressed in anti-modernist, anti-Enlightenment and anti-secularist views; and (6) impatience with liberal constraints upon government, with checks and balances viewed as an institutional obstacle to "getting things done" and to the expression of the will of the People. These factors come in different configurations, and the intensity of different anxieties will vary from place to place. This must be understood and taken seriously by liberal democrats. But precisely because the specific mix of anxieties is country-specific, so too are the responses to be offered.

In one of the best articles on the subject I have read, Jean Cohen, a professor of political philosophy at Columbia University, raises the question: "[H]ow can the status resentments of the religious, white, working class traditionalists (wherever they are) be framed and addressed without sacrificing allegiance to gender and racial equality, cultural modernity, political secularism, and democratic norms in a globalized society?"[25] This way of framing the question, originating as it does from US-specific experience, provides a fine template for our thinking about

---

[25] Jean L. Cohen, "Populism and the Politics of Resentment," *Jus Cogens*, 1 (2019), 5–39 at 31.

such a program, though the indicators of the usual constituency of populism may be replaced, depending on the specific context.

Only the most general contours may be suggested in abstract terms. in abstracto. Cohen again: "Only by devising effective counter-narratives and projects that address the social, political, and economic deficits people of all races, religions, ethnicities face, can we beat authoritarian populism based on scapegoating and polarization, reinforce democratic norms and further social justice."[26] It means that liberal democrats must reflect upon the deficits in our policies and narratives that left a gap for populists, demagogues, and authoritarians to fill. When people are concerned about their status, it should not be looked down upon as a reprehensible self-serving impulse of relatively well-off people who feel an irrational sense of threat from the poor or from strangers, because concerns about relative deprivation of one's group and one's own job insecurity is an indelible part of human society under capitalism, in particular in times of rapid change. "Identity" is not a bad word to be left to populists to exploit – being sensitive to people's attachment to their identities, whether ethnic, religious, or professional, does not have to be exclusionary or based on despising others. "Patriotism" is not an ugly word, insofar as for many people their sense of self-respect is undergirded by their pride in belonging to a particular nation- or state-bounded culture and history. "Community" should not be anathema for liberal democrats, insofar as for many people, self-fulfillment, and happiness is inextricably related to other people, even if only in their most proximate space. Religion should not be treated with condescension because for many people it is the main way of meeting their spiritual needs. Status, identity, patriotism, community, religion – liberal democrats have to pick up those objects of human love and concern, and turn them into non-exclusionary, non-hateful programs. Populists should not have the monopoly on those ideals.

Whether articulated in the language of Rawlsian "public reason," with its eminently inclusionary potential, or Dworkin's "equal concern and respect," or any other liberal-democratic vocabulary, liberalism has ample egalitarian and communitarian resources with which to counter the populist *supply* of exclusionary nativism. We should retrieve what is best in this tradition and incorporate it into a better-than-the-populists program. Cohen calls for "an inclusive politics of solidarity, one that

---

[26] Ibid., p. 32.

recovers the best normative impulses in political liberalism, democracy, and social democracy."[27] Others will disagree with her mix of political conceptions (for my part, I like it), but may nevertheless endorse her aspiration. This or a similar type of "counter-narrative" is needed to oppose populists by depleting the social *demand* for their policies. Viktor Orbán or Jair Bolsonaro do not warrant our respect, but their electors do.

[27] Ibid., p. 32.

Annex: Country Selection Explanation

My selection of six countries (Poland, Hungary, India, Philippines, Brazil, and Venezuela under Chávez, i.e., 1999–2012) is based on a combination of the following broad criteria:

1. The current leaders (or Chávez) came to power as a result of by-and large free and fair elections.
2. The state maintains to some extent certain political and civil rights (even if they are limited and protected in a discriminatory way).
3. There is still a degree of electoral competitiveness, that is, it is possible for the current opposition to win elections, even if the electoral playing field is tilted to favor the populist incumbents.
4. There has been a marked decline compared to the status quo ante (hence a democratic backsliding).

In other words, while the six countries I have selected are not liberal democracies, with the rule of law, separation of powers, and vertical or horizontal accountability in the period between elections, none could be characterized as authoritarian regimes with heavy violations of civil/political rights, and elections not constituting a viable opportunity for transfers of power.

There are doubtless other countries beyond the six I have selected that would meet the four criteria above. I am not making any pretense to comprehensiveness.

In support of my selection of these six cases (initially selected on anecdotal grounds), I am using three credible, generally recognized rankings.

1. The *Economist* ranking[1]

The *Economist*'s Democracy Index began in 2006, so it cannot give a full historical perspective of Venezuela's backsliding, which began when Chávez came into office in 1999.

---

[1] The *Economist* Intelligence Unit, "Democracy Index 2020," www.eiu.com/n/campaigns/democracy-index-2020.

All countries selected in this book, except for Venezuela, are characterized as "flawed democracies." "Flawed democracies" have free and fair elections and, even if there are some infringements (such as on media freedom), basic civil liberties are respected. However, there are significant weaknesses in other aspects of democracy, including problems in governance, an underdeveloped political culture, and low levels of political participation.

Recent rankings:

- Poland: flawed democracy (score = 6.85) (rank =50)[2]
- Hungary: flawed democracy (score = 6.56) (rank =55)[3]
- Philippines: flawed democracy (score = 6.56) (rank =55)[4]
- Brazil: flawed democracy (score = 6.92) (rank =49)[5]
- India: flawed democracy (score = 6.61) (rank =53)[6]

In 2012, Venezuela was rated a "hybrid democracy" – a system characterized by elections with substantial irregularities that often prevent them from being free and fair, government pressure on opposition parties and candidates, widespread corruption, and a weak rule of law. Ranking:

- Venezuela (2012): hybrid regime (score = 5.15) (rank =95)[7]

2. V-DEM electoral democracy index[8]

In the V-DEM electoral democracy index, all six countries rank somewhere between "closed autocracy" and "liberal democracy," rated as either "electoral democracy" or "electoral autocracy." "Electoral autocracies" hold de facto multiparty elections for the chief executive, but they fall short of democratic standards due to significant irregularities, limitations on party competition, and other violations of institutional requisites for democracies.

To be counted as "electoral democracies," countries not only have to hold de-facto free and fair and multiparty elections, but also have sufficient institutional guarantees of democracy, such as freedom of association, suffrage, clean elections, an elected executive, and freedom of expression.

---

[2] Economist, "Democracy Index 2020," *The Economist* (2020) at 10.
[3] Ibid., at 10.
[4] Ibid., at 10.
[5] Ibid., at 10.
[6] Ibid., at 10.
[7] The Economist Intelligence Unit, "Democracy Index 2012" at 6.
[8] V-Dem Institute, "Autocratization Turns Viral: Democracy Report 2021," www.v-dem.net/files/25/DR%202021.pdf.

V-DEM's electoral democracies index scores are below.

- Poland = 0.63 (rank 65)[9]
- Hungary = 0.47 (rank 96)[10]
- Philippines = 0.43 (rank 104)[11]
- Brazil = 0.69 (rank 56)[12]
- India = 0.45 (rank 101)[13]
- Venezuela = above 0.4 until 2013[14]

3. Freedom House (electoral democracy classification)[15]

Prior to the 2021 edition, Freedom in the World assigned the designation "electoral democracy" to countries that had met certain minimum standards for political rights and civil liberties. An electoral democracy designation required a score of 7 or better in the Electoral Process subcategory, an overall political rights score of 20 or better, and an overall civil liberties' score of 30 or better. In order to simplify the report's methodological outputs, Freedom House is no longer highlighting this designation, but the underlying scores remain publicly available.[16]

- Poland: electoral democracy[17]
    - Electoral processes 10/12 (7 required)
    - Political rights 30/40 (20 required)
    - Civil rights 48/60 (30 required)
- Hungary: electoral democracy[18]
    - Electoral processes 9/12 (7 required)
    - Political rights 26/40 (20 required)
    - Civil rights 43/60 (30 required)
- Philippines: electoral democracy[19]
    - Electoral processes 9/12 (7 required)

---

[9] Ibid., at 34.
[10] Ibid., at 35.
[11] Ibid., at 35.
[12] Ibid., at 34.
[13] Ibid., at 35.
[14] V-Dem, "Country Analysis," *V-Dem*, www.v-dem.net/en/analysis/CountryGraph (last accessed November 30, 2021).
[15] Freedom House, "Freedom in the World 2021: Democracy under Siege," www.freedomhouse.org/sites/default/files/2021-02/FIW2021_World_02252021_FINAL-web-upload.pdf.
[16] See Freedom House, "Freedom in the World Research Methodology," www.freedomhouse.org/reports/freedom-world/freedom-world-research-methodology.
[17] Score summaries for designation: www.en.wikipedia.org/wiki/Freedom_in_the_World#Country_ranking.
[18] Ibid.
[19] Ibid.

- ○ Political rights 25/40 (20 required)
- ○ Civil rights 31/60 (30 required)
- India: electoral democracy[20]
  - ○ Electoral processes 12/12 (7 required)
  - ○ Political rights 34/40 (20 required)
  - ○ Civil rights 33/60 (30 required)
- Brazil: electoral democracy[21]
  - ○ Electoral processes 10/12 (7 required)
  - ○ Political rights 31/40 (20 required)
  - ○ Civil rights 43/60 (30 required)
- Venezuela (2012): not an electoral democracy (was last classified as such in 2008).[22]
  - ○ Scores not publicised in 2012

4. Backsliding

To check the "backsliding" dimension (the fourth criterion in my list sketched in the first paragraph of this Annex), I have adjusted the Freedom House Rankings, which are now out of 100 but were previously out of 7 with 1 being the most free. The new scores out of 100 may be converted into scores out of 7 for a symmetric comparison. The scores out of 7 are assigned for both civil and political rights, so the best combined score would be 2 and the worst 14. To test the "backsliding" factor I have compared the ranking in the last "pre-populist" year in each of the case study countries with the 2021 ranking (for Venezuela: 2012 ranking) in (Table 1):

Table 1 *Democratic backsliding*

Country	Pre-Populist	Populist
Poland	2 (2014) – 2015 report	4 (2021)
Hungary	2 (2009) – 2010 report	6 (2021)
Brazil	4 (2017) – 2018 report	5 (2021)
India	5 (2013) – 2014 report	6 (2021)
Philippines	6 (2015) – 2016 report	7 (2021)
Venezuela	5 (1998) – 1999 report	10 (2012 report)

Source: Freedom House rankings

---

[20] Ibid.
[21] Ibid.
[22] Freedom House, "Freedom in the World 2008," (2008) at 885; Freedom House, "Freedom in the World 2009," *Freedom House* (2009) at 902.

REFERENCES

Aiyar, Swaminathan S. Anklesaria. "Despite Modi, India Has Not Yet Become a Hindu Authoritarian State." Policy Analysis No. 903. Washington, DC: The Cato Institute (November 24, 2020). www.jstor.org/stable/resrep28731.

Alemanno, Alberto. "Towards a European Health Union: Time to Level Up." *European Journal of Risk Regulation*, 11 (2020), 721–725.

Alfani, Guido. "Pandemics and the Asymmetric Shocks: Lessons from the History of Plagues." VoxEU/CEPR (April 9, 2020). www.voxeu.org/article/pandemics-and-asymmetric-shocks.

Amar, Akhil Reed. *America's Unwritten Constitution*. New York: Basic Books, 2012.

Amnesty International, "Hungary: Living under the Sword of Damocles: The Impact of the LEXNGO on Civil Society in Hungary." London, 2021.

"Status of the Hungarian Judiciary." Budapest: Amnesty International Hungary, 2021.

Applebaum, Anne. "The Coronavirus Called America's Bluff." *The Atlantic* (March 15, 2020). www.theatlantic.com/ideas/archive/2020/03/coronavirus-showed-america-wasnt-task/608023.

Arato, Andrew. "Populism, Constitutional Courts, and Civil Society." In Christine Landfried (ed.), *Judicial Power: How Constitutional Courts Affect Political Transformations* (Cambridge: Cambridge University Press 2019), pp. 318–341.

Arato, Andrew, Gábor Halmai, and János Kis (eds.). "Opinion on the Fundamental Law of Hungary (Amicus Brief)." In Gábor Attila Tóth (ed.), *Constitution for a Disunited Nation: On Hungary's 2011 Fundamental Law*. Budapest: CEU Press, 2012, pp. 455–489.

Atienza, Maria. "Emergency Powers and COVID-19: The Philippines as a Case Study." *Melbourne Forum on Constitution Building* (2020).

Bajpai, Anandita. "'Matters of the Heart': The Sentimental Indian Prime Minister on All India Radio." In Barbara Christophe, Christoph Kohl, Heike Liebau, and Achim Saupe (eds.), *The Politics of Authenticity and Populist Discourses*. Cham: Palgrave Macmillan, 2021, pp. 105–126.

Balcer, Andrzej, Piotr Buras, Grzegorz Gromadzki, and Eugeniusz Smolar. *"Polish Views of the EU: The Illusion of Consensus."* Warsaw: Stefan Batory Foundation, January 2017.
Barber, N. W. *The Principles of Constitutionalism.* Oxford: Oxford University Press, 2018.
Bene, Márton, and Zsolt Boda. "Hungary: Crisis as Usual – Populist Governance and the Pandemic." In Giuliano Bobba and Nicholas Hubé (eds.), *Populism and the Politicization of the COVID-19 Crisis in Europe.* Cham: Palgrave Macmillan, 2021, pp. 87–100.
Ben-Ghiat, Ruth. *Strongmen.* New York: W. W. Norton, 2020.
Bergmann, Eirikur. *Conspiracy and Populism: The Politics of Information.* Cham: Springer Nature, 2018.
Bevins, Vincent. "Where Conspiracy Reigns." *The Atlantic* (September 16, 2020). www.theatlantic.com/ideas/archive/2020/09/how-anti-communist-conspiracies-haunt-brazil/614665.
Bhatia, Gautam. "Mouse under the Throne: The Judicial Legacy of Sharad A. Bobde." *The Wire* (April 24, 2021). www.thewire.in/law/mouse-under-the-throne-the-judicial-legacy-of-sharad-a-bobde.
Bhuwana, Anuj. "The Indian Supreme Court in the Modi Era." In Tom Gerald Daly and Wojciech Sadurski (eds.), *Democracy 2020: Assessing Constitutional Decay, Breakdown, and Renewal Worldwide.* IACL-AIDC Global Roundtable E-book, December 2020, pp. 150–153.
Bickel, Alexander. *The Least Dangerous Branch: The Supreme Court and the Idea of Progress.* New Haven: Yale University Press, 1962.
Bieber, Florian. "Global Nationalism in Times of the COVID-19 Pandemic." *Nationalities Papers* (2020).
Bill, Stanley. "Counter-Elite Populism and Civil Society in Poland: PiS Strategies of Elite Replacement." *East European Politics and Societies,* 20 (2020), 1–23.
Blickle, Kristian. "Pandemics Change Cities: Municipal Spending and Voter Extremism in Germany, 1918–1933." *Federal Reserve Bank of New York Staff Reports* (2020).
Block, Elena, and Ralph Negrine. "The Populist Communication Style: Toward a Critical Framework." *International Journal of Communication,* 11 (2017), 178–197.
Blokker, Paul. "Populist Constitutionalism." *ResearchGate* (September 20, 2017), www.researchgate.net/publication/319938853_Populist_Constitutionalism.
Bodnár, Eszter. "Disarming the Guardians: The Transformation of the Hungarian Constitutional Court after 2010." In Martin Krygier, Adam Czarnota, and Wojciech Sadurski (eds.), *Anti-constitutional Populism* (in press).
Bollyky, Thomas J., and Chad P. Bown. "The Tragedy of Vaccine Nationalism." *Foreign Affairs* (September/October 2020). www.foreignaffairs.com/print/node/1126225.

Bonikowski, Bart. "Ethno-Nationalist Populism and the Mobilization of Collective Resentment." *British Journal of Sociology*, 68/Suppl. 1 (2017), 181–213.

"Nationalism in Settled Times." *Annual Review of Sociology*, 42 (2016), 427–449.

Bonikowski, Bart, and Paul DiMaggio. "Varieties of American Popular Nationalism." *American Sociological Review*, 81 (2016), 949–980.

Brandes, Tamar, and Yaniv Roznai. "Can COVID-19 Save Democracy from Populism?" In Tom Gerald Daly and Wojciech Sadurski (eds.), *Democracy 2020: Assessing Constitutional Decay, Breakdown, and Renewal Worldwide*, IACL-AIDC Global Roundtable E-book (December 2020), pp. 41–44.

Brodeur, Abel, Idaliya Grigoryeva, and Lamis Kattan. "Stay-at-Home Orders, Social Distancing and Trust." *Journal of Population Economics*, 34 (2021), 1321–1354.

Bustamante, Thomas, and Conrado Hubner Mendes. "Freedom without Responsibility: The Promise of Bolsonaro's COVID-Denial." *Jus Cogens*, 3 (2021), 181–207.

Bustamante, Thomas, and Emilio Peluso Neder Meyer. "Legislative Resistance to Illiberalism in a System of Coalitional Presidentialism: Will It Work in Brazil?" *The Theory and Practice of Legislation* (2021). DOI: 10.1080/20508840.2021.1942370.

Carothers, Thomas. "The End of the Transition Paradigm." *Journal of Democracy*, 13/1 (2002), 5–21.

Carothers, Thomas, and David Wong. "Authoritarian Weaknesses and the Pandemic." *Carnegie Endowment for International Peace* (August 11, 2020). www.carnegieendowment.org/2020/08/11/authoritarian-weaknesses-and-pandemic-pub-82452.

Casarões, Guilherme, and David Magalhães. "The Hydroxychloroquine Alliance: How Far-Right Leaders and Alt-Science Preachers Came Together to Promote a Miracle Drug." *Brazilian Journal of Public Administration*, 55/1 (2021), 197–214.

Castanho, Bruno Silva, Federico Vegetti, and Levente Littvay. "The Elite Is Up to Something: Exploring the Relation between Populism and Belief in Conspiracy Theories." *Swiss Political Science Review*, 23 (2017), 423–443.

Chafetz, Josh, and David E. Pozen. "How Constitutional Norms Break Down." *UCLA Law Review*, 65 (2018), 1430–1459.

Charron, Nicholas, Victor Lapuente, and Andrés Rodriguez-Pose. "Uncooperative Society, Uncooperative Politics or Both?" University of Gothenburg QOG Institute, *Working Paper* 12 (2020).

Chen, Dan. "Local Distrust and Regime Support: Sources and Effects of Political Trust in China." *Political Research Quarterly*, 70/2 (2017), 314–326.

Choudry, Sujit. "Will Democracy Die in Darkness? Calling Autocracy by Its Name." In Mark A. Graber, Sanford Levinson, and Mark Tushnet (eds.),

Constitutional Democracy in Crisis? (Oxford: Oxford University Press, 2018), pp. 571–584.
Christophe, Barbara, Christoph Kohl, Heike Liebau, and Achim Saupe. "Claims to Authenticity in Populist Discourses: General Introduction to the Volume." In Christoph Kohl, Barbara Christophe, Heike Liebau, and Achim Saupe (eds.), The Politics of Authenticity and Populist Discourses (Cham: Palgrave Macmillan, 2021), pp. 3–30.
Cohen, Jean L. "Populism and the Politics of Resentment." Jus Cogens, 1 (2019), 5–39.
Cohn, Samuel. "Pandemics: Waves of Disease, Waves of Hate from the Plague of Athens to A.I.D.S." Historical Research, 85 (2012), 535–555.
Colantone, Italo, and Piero Stanig. "The Trade Origins of Economic Nationalism: Import Competition and Voting Behavior in Western Europe." American Journal of Political Science, 62 (2018), 936–953.
Cooper, Glenda. "Populist Rhetoric and Media Misinformation in the 2016 UK Brexit Referendum." In Howard Tumber and Silvio Waisbord (eds.), The Routledge Companion to Media Disinformation and Populism (London: Routledge, 2021), pp. 397–410.
Corrales, Javier, and Michael Penfold-Becerra. "Venezuela: Crowding Out the Opposition." Journal of Democracy, 18/2 (2007), 99–113.
Cronert, Axel. "Democracy, State Capacity, and COVID-19 Related School Closures." APSA Working Paper (April 28, 2020). www.preprints.apsanet.org/engage/apsa/article-details/5e80bf4c6a2482001a4c1b9f.
Curato, Nicole, and Jonathan Corpus Ong. "Who Laughs at a Rape Joke? Illiberal Responsiveness in Rodrigo Duterte's Philippines." In Tanja Dreher and Anshuman Mondal (eds.), Ethical Responsiveness and the Politics of Difference. New York: Palgrave Macmillan, 2018, pp. 117–132.
Daley, Jim. "Venezuela Is Unraveling – So Is Its Science." Scientific American (February 15, 2019). www.scientificamerican.com/article/venezuela-is-unraveling-mdash-so-is-its-science.
De Búrca. Gráinne. "How British Was the Brexit Vote?" In Benjamin Martill and Uta Staiger (eds.), Brexit and Beyond: Rethinking the Futures of Europe. London: UCL Press, 2018, pp. 46–52.
Dixon, Rosalind, and David Landau. Abusive Constitutional Borrowing. Oxford: Oxford University Press, 2021.
European Commission. 2020 Rule of Law Report, Country Chapter on the Rule of Law Situation in Hungary. Brussels 30.09.2020, SWD (2020) 316 final.
European Commission for Democracy through Law. Opinion on the Fourth Amendment to the Fundamental Law of Hungary, adopted June 14–15, 2013. VC CDL-AD (2013)012.
  Opinion on the New Constitution of Hungary, adopted June 17–18. 2011. VC CDL-AD (2011) 016.

Evangelista, Rafael, and Fernanda Bruno. "WhatsApp and Political Instability in Brazil: Targeted Messages and Political Radicalisation." *Internet Policy Review*, 8/4 (2019), 1–23.

Feres Júnior, João, and Juliana Gagliardi. "Populism and the Media in Brazil: The Case of Jair Bolsonaro." In Christoph Kohl, Barbara Christophe, Heike Liebau, and Achim Saupe (eds.), *The Politics of Authenticity and Populist Discourses*. Cham: Palgrave Macmillan, 2021, pp. 83–104.

Fleck, Zoltán. "Judges under Attack in Hungary." *Verfassungsblog* (May 14, 2018). www.verfassungsblog.de/judges-under-attack-in-hungary.

Fleck Soares Brandao, Alexandre. "When Bolsonaro and the Judges Go Shopping: How Brazil's Legal Elites Opened the Door for Bolsonaro's Bad Populism." In Martin Krygier, Adam Czarnota, and Wojciech Sadurski (eds.), *Anticonstitutional Populism*. In press.

Frajman, Eduardo. "Broadcasting Populist Leadership: Hugo Chávez and *Aló Presidente*." *Journal of Latin American Studies*, 46 (2014), 501–526.

Frantz, Erica. "Voter Turnout and Opposition Performance in Competitive Authoritarian Elections." *Electoral Studies*, 54 (2018), 218–225.

Freedman, Laurence. "Muddled Messages as Britain Seeks to Stay Alert." *Lowy Interpreter* (May 14, 2020). www.lowyinstitute.org/the-interpreter/muddled-messages-britain-seeks-stay-alert.

Freedom House. "Countries and Territories." www.freedomhouse.org/countries/freedom-world/scores.

Freeman, Will. "Sidestepping the Constitution: Executive Aggrandizement in Latin America and East Central Europe." *Constitutional Studies*, 6 (2020), 35–58.

Frey, Carl Benedikt, Chinchih Chen, and Giorgio Presidente. "*Democracy, Culture, and Contagion: Political Regimes and Countries' Responsiveness to Covid-19.*" Oxford Martin School, Working Paper (May 13, 2020).

Galloway, Scott. *Post Corona: From Crisis to Opportunity*. London: Bantam Press, 2020.

Gardbaum, Stephen. "Are Strong Constitutional Courts Always a Good Thing for New Democracies?" *Columbia Journal of Transnational Law*, 53 (2015), 285–320.

Gauna, Anibal. "Populism, Heroism, and Revolution: Chávez's Cultural Performances in Venezuela, 1999–2012." *American Journal of Cultural Sociology*, 6/1 (2016), 37–59

Gdula, Maciej. *Nowy Autorytaryzm*. Warszawa: Wydawnictwo Krytyki Politycznej, 2018.

Gidron, Noam, and Peter A Hall. "The Politics of Social Status: Economic and Cultural Roots of the Populist Right." *British Journal of Sociology*, 68/Suppl. 1 (2017), 57–84.

Gingerich, Daniel, and Jan Vogler. "Pandemics and Political Development: The Electoral Legacy of the Black Death in Germany." *World Politics*, 73 (2021), 393–440.

Ginsburg, Tom. *Judicial Review in New Democracies*. Cambridge: Cambridge University Press, 2003.

Gloria, Glenda. "War of Words: Rodrigo Duterte's Violent Relationship with Language." *World Policy Institute*, 35/2 (2018), 9–13.

Golec de Zavala, Agnieszka. "Why Is Populism So Robustly Associated with Conspiratorial Thinking? Collective Narcissism and the Meaning Maintenance Model." In J. D. Sinnott and J. S. Rabin (eds.), *The Psychology of Political Behavior in a Time of Change*. Cham: Springer Nature, 2021.

Gonawela, A'ndre, Joyojeet Pal, Udit Thawani, Elmer van der Vlugt, Wim Out, and Priyank Chandra. "Speaking Their Mind: Populist Style and Antagonistic Messaging in the Tweets of Donald Trump, Narendra Modi, Nigel Farage, and Geert Wilders." *Computer Supported Cooperative Work*, 27 (2018), 293–326.

Góralczyk, Bogdan. "Axiological Disintegration of the EU? The Case of Hungary." *Yearbook of Polish European Studies*, 18 (2015), 81–109.

Greene, Alan. *Emergency Powers in a Time of Pandemic*. Bristol: Bristol University Press, 2021.

Grzymala-Busse, Anna. "Global Populisms and Their Impact." *Slavic Review*, 76/Suppl. S1 (2017), 3–8.

Guiso, Luigi, Helias Herrera, Massimo Morelli, and Tomasso Sonno. "Demand and Supply of Populism." *ResearchGate* (October 28, 2018). www.researchgate.net/publication/325472986.

Guriev, Sergei, and Elias Papaioannou. "The Political Economy of Populism" (February 21, 2020). www.ssrn.com/abstract=3542052.

Halmai, Gábor. "Populism or Authoritarianism? A Plaidoyer against Illiberal or Authoritarian Constitutionalism." In Martin Krygier, Adam Czarnota, and Wojciech Sadurski (eds.), *Anti-constitutional Populism*. In press.

"The Hungarian Approach to Constitutional Review: The End of Activism? The First Decade of the Hungarian Constitutional Court." In Wojciech Sadurski (ed.), *Constitutional Justice, East and West*. The Hague: Kluwer Law International, 2002, pp. 189–211.

Hameleers, Michael, Linda Bos, and Claes H. de Vreese. "'*They* Did It': The Effects of Emotionalized Blame Attribution in Populist Communication." *Communication Research*, 44 (2017), 870–900.

Harel, Alon, and Noam Kolt. "Populist Rhetoric, False Mirroring, and the Courts," *International Journal of Constitutional Law*, 18 (2020), 746–766.

Harteveld, Eelco. "Social Stigma and Support for the Populist Radical Right: An Experimental Study." *Scandinavian Political Studies*, 42 (2019), 296–307.

Hartleb, Florian. "Materializations of Populism in Today's Politics: Global Perspectives." In Christoph Kohl, Barbara Christophe, Heike Liebau, and Achim Saupe (eds.), *The Politics of Authenticity and Populist Discourses*. Cham: Palgrave Macmillan, 2021, pp. 31–52.

Hathaway, Oona A., Preston J. Lim, Alasdair Phillips-Robins, and Mark Stevens. "The COVID-19 Pandemic and International Law." Yale Law School, Public Law Research Paper (March 30, 2021), www.ssrn.com/abstract=3815164.

Hedges, Kristin, and Gideon Lasco, "Medical Populism and COVID-19 Testing." *Open Anthropological Research*, 1/1 (2021), 73–86.

Hendricks, Vincent, and Mads Vestergaard. *Reality Lost: Markets of Attention, Misinformation and Manipulation*. Cham: Springer Nature, 2019.

Heydarian, Richard Javad. "Subaltern Populism: Dutertismo and the War on Constitutional Democracy." In Martin Krygier, Adam Czarnota, and Wojciech Sadurski (eds.), *Anti-constitutional Populism*. In press.

Hiebert, Murray. "COVID-19 Threatens Democracy in Southeast Asia." *East Asia Forum* (May 25, 2020). www.eastasiaforum.org/2020/05/25/covid-19-threatens-democracy-in-southeast-asia.

Hochschild, Arlie Russell. *Strangers in Their Own Land*. New York and London The New Press, 2016.

Hofstadter, Richard. *"On the Unpopularity of Intellect."* In *Uncollected Essays, 1956–1965*. New York: Library of America, 2020, pp. 28–50.

"The Paranoid Style in American Politics." *Harper's* (November 1964), 77–86.

Holmes, Stephen. "How Democracies Perish." In Cass R Sunstein (ed.), *Can It Happen Here? Authoritarianism in America*. New York: HarperCollins, 2018, pp. 387–427.

Howard, Marc Morjé, and Philip G. Roessler. "Liberalizing Electoral Outcomes in Competitive Authoritarian Regimes." *American Journal of Political Science*, 50 (2006), 365–381.

Huang, Qingming, "The Pandemic and the Transformation of Liberal International Order." *Journal of Chinese Political Science*, 26/1 (2021), 1–26.

Human Rights Watch, "Brazil: Bolsonaro Sabotages Anti-Covid-19 Efforts." *Human Rights Watch* (April 10, 2020). www.hrw.org/news/2020/04/10/brazil-bolsonaro-sabotages-anti-covid-19-efforts.

"Venezuela: Events of 2020," *Human Rights Watch*. www.hrw.org/world-report/2021/country-chapters/venezuela.

Huq, Aziz Z., and Tom Ginsburg. "Democracy without Democrats." *Constitutional Studies*, 6 (2020), 165–187.

Huq, Aziz, and Tom Ginsburg. "How to Lose a Constitutional Democracy." *UCLA Law Review*, 65 (2018), 78–169.

Ibarra, Edcel John A. "The Philippine Supreme Court under Duterte: Reshaped, Unwilling to Annul, and Unable to Restrain." Social Science Research Council Democracy Papers (November 10, 2020). www.items.ssrc.org/dem

ocracy-papers/democratic-erosion/the-philippine-supreme-court-under-duterte-reshaped-unwilling-to-annul-and-unable-to-restrain.
Ignatieff, Michael. "The Reckoning: Evaluating Democratic Leadership." In Miguel Maduro and Paul Kahn (eds.), *Democracy in Times of Pandemic*. Cambridge: Cambridge University Press, 2020, pp. 89–103.
Innerarity, Daniel. "Understanding, Deciding, and Learning: The Key Political Challenges in the Pandemic." In Miguel Maduro and Paul Kahn (eds.), *Democracy in Times of Pandemic*. Cambridge: Cambridge University Press, 2020.
Issacharoff, Samuel. *Democracy Unmoored*. In press.
   Fragile Democracies. Cambridge: Cambridge University Press, 2015.
   "The Corruption of Popular Sovereignty." *International Journal of Constitutional Law*, 18 (2020), 1109–1135.
Jacint, Jordana, and Juan Carlos Triviño-Salazar. "Where Are the ECDC and the EU-Wide Responses in the COVID-19 Pandemic?" *The Lancet*; 395/10237 (May 23, 2020), 1611–1612.
Jaffrelot, Christophe, and Louise Tillin. "Populism in India." In Cristóbal Rovira Kaltwasser, Paul Taggart, Paulina Ochoa Espejo, and Pierre Ostiguy (eds.), *Oxford Handbook of Populism*. Oxford: Oxford University Press, 2017, pp. 179–194.
Kalmar, Ivan. "Islamophobia and Anti-antisemitism: The Case of Hungary and the 'Soros Plot.'" *Patterns of Prejudice*, 54 (2020), 182–198.
Karsai, Dániel. "The Curious and Alarming Story of the City of Göd." *Verfassungsblog* (May 15, 2020). www.verfassungsblog.de/the-curious-and-alarming-story-of-the-city-of-goed.
Katsambekis, Giorgos, Yannis Stavrakakis, Paula Biglieri, and Kurt Adam Sengul. "Populism and the Pandemic." *Populismus* (June 2020), www.researchgate.net/publication/342205771_Populism_and_the_Pandemic_A_Collaborative_Report.
Kazai, Viktor Z., "No One Has the Right to Be Homeless..." *Verfassungsblog* (June 13, 2019). www.verfassungsblog.de/no-one-has-the-right-to-be-homeless.
Keane, John. *The New Despotism*. Cambridge: Harvard University Press, 2020.
Kelemen, R. Daniel, Tomasso Pavone, and Cassandra Emmons. "The Perils of Passivity in the Rule of Law Crisis: A Response to von Bogdandy," *Verfassungsblog* (November 26, 2019). www.verfassungsblog.de/the-perils-of-passivity-in-the-rule-of-law-crisis-a-response-to-von-bogdandy.
Kenes, Bulent. "Viktor Orbán: Past to Present," European Center for Populism Studies, Leader Profile No. 1 (August 2020).
Kestenbaum, Jocelyn, "Coughing into the Crowd: Bolsonaro's Botched COVID-19 Response." *Just Security* (May 1, 2020), www.justsecurity.org/69960/coughing-into-the-crowd-bolsonaros-botched-covid-19-response.

Khaitan, Tarunabh. "Introduction: The World's Most Powerful Court on the Brink?" IACL-AIDC Blog (May 15, 2018). www.blog-iacl-aidc.org/blog/2018/5/17/introduction-the-worlds-most-powerful-court-on-the-brink.

"Killing a Constitution with a Thousand Cuts: Executive Aggrandizement and Party-State Fusion in India." *Law and Ethics of Human Rights*, 14 (2020), 49–95.

Khosla, Madhav, and Milan Vaishnav. "The Three Faces of the Indian State." *Journal of Democracy*, 32/1 (2021), 111–125.

Kis, János. "Introduction: From the 1989 Constitution to the 2011 Fundamental Law." In Gábor Attila Tóth (ed.), *Constitution for a Disunited Nation: On Hungary's 2011 Fundamental Law*. Budapest: CEU Press, 2012, pp. 1–21.

Klein, Ezr. "Francis Fukuyama: America is in 'one of the most severe political crises I have experienced'" (October 26, 2016). www.vox.com/2016/10/26/13352946/francis-fukuyama-ezra-klein.

Kleinfeld, Rachel, "Do Authoritarian or Democratic Countries Handle Pandemics Better?" *Carnegie Endowment for International Peace* (March 31, 2020). www.carnegieendowment.org/2020/03/31/do-authoritarian-or-democratic-countries-handle-pandemics-better-pub-81404.

Kohl, Christoph, Barbara Christophe, Heike Liebau, and Achim Saupe (eds.). *The Politics of Authenticity and Populist Discourses*. Cham: Palgrave Macmillan, 2021.

Koncewicz, Tomasz Tadeusz. "'Existential Judicial Review' in Retrospect, 'Subversive Jurisprudence' in Prospect." *Verfassungsblog* (October 7, 2018). www.verfassungsblog.de/existential-judicial-review-in-retrospect-subversive-jurisprudence-in-prospect-the-polish-constitutional-court-then-now-and-tomorrow.

Kornblath, Miriam. "The Politics of Constitution-Making: Constitutions and Democracy in Venezuela." *Journal of Latin American Studies*, 23 (1991), 61–89.

Körösenyi, András, Gábor Illés, and Attila Gyulai. *The Orbán Regime: Plebiscitary Leader Democracy in the Making*. London: Routledge, 2020.

Kövér, Ágnes. "Civil Society and COVID-19 in Hungary: The Complete Annexation of Civil Space." *Nonprofit Policy Forum*, 12/1 (2021), 93–126.

Kozicki, Katya, and Rick Pianaro. "From Hardball to Packing the Court: 'PEC do Pyjama' and the Attempt to Attack the Brazilian Supreme Court." In Tom Gerald Daly and Wojciech Sadurski (eds), *Democracy 2020: Assessing Constitutional Decay, Breakdown, and Renewal Worldwide*, IACL-AIDC Global Roundtable E-book (December 2020), pp. 59–62.

Krastev, Ivan. *Is It Tomorrow Yet?* London: Allen Lane, 2020.

Krastev, Ivan, and Stephen Holmes. *The Light That Failed*. New York: Pegasus Books, 2019.

Krygier, Martin. "The Challenge of Institutionalisation: Post-Communist 'Transitions,' Populism, and the Rule of Law." *European Constitutional Law Review*, 15 (2019), 544–573.

Krygier, Martin. "The Spirit of Constitutionalism." In Jakub Urbanik and Adam Bodnar (eds.), Περιμένοντας τους Βαρβάρους: *Law in the Days of Constitutional Crisis: Studies offered to Mirosław Wyrzykowski*. Warsaw: C. H. Beck, 2021, pp. 343–358.

Kucharczyk, Jacek. "The Pandemic as a Catalyst for Populist Authoritarianism in Poland." In Sophia Russak (ed.), *The Effect of Covid on EU Democracies*, European Policy Institutes Network, 2021, 27–28.

Kumar, Alok Prasanna. "'More Executive-Minded Than the Executive': The Supreme Court's Role in the Implementation of the NRC." *National Law School of India Review*, 31 (2019), 203–210

Kuo, Ming-Sung. "Against Instantaneous Democracy." *International Journal of Constitutional Law*, 17 (2019), 554–575.

Laclau, Ernesto. *On Populist Reason*. London: Verso, 2018.

Lamour, Christian. "Interviewing a Right-Wing Populist Leader during the 2019 EU Elections: Conflictual Situations and Equivocation beyond Borders." *Discourse and Communication*, 15 (2021), 59–73.

Lánczi, András. "The Renewed Social Contract: Hungary's Elections, 2018." *Hungarian Review*, 9/3 (2018). www.hungarianreview.com/article/20180525_the_renewed_social_contract_hungary_s_elections_2018.

Landau, David. "Abusive Constitutionalism." *University of California–Davis Law Review*, 47 (2013), 189–260.

Lee, Eunjung, and Marjorie Johnstone. "Resisting Politics of Authoritarian Populism during COVID-19, Reclaiming Democracy and Narrative Justice: Centering Critical Thinking in Social Work." *International Social Work*, 64 (2021), 716–730.

Levitsky, Steven, and Lucan Way. "The Myth of Democratic Recession." *Journal of Democracy*, 26/1 (2015), 45–58.

Levitsky, Steven, and Daniel Ziblatt. *How Democracies Die*. New York: Crown 2018.

Linz, Juan J., and Alfred Stepan. "Toward Consolidated Democracies." *Journal of Democracy*, 7/2 (1996), 14–33.

Lipiński, Artur. "Poland: 'If We Don't Elect the President, the Country Will Plunge into Chaos.'" In Giuliano Bobba and Nicholas Hubé (eds.), *Populism and the Politicization of the COVID-19 Crisis in Europe*. Cham: Palgrave Macmillan 2021, pp. 115–130.

Little, Mark, and Matthew Feldman. "Social Media and the Cordon Sanitaire." *Journal of Language and Politics*, 16 (2017), 510–522.

Lowy Institute. "Pandemic Performance Index." *Lowy Institute* (2021). https://interactives.lowyinstitute.org/features/covid-performance.

Lubbers, Marcel, and Marcel Coenders. "Nationalistic Attitudes and Voting for the Radical Right in Europe." *European Union Politics*, 18 (2017), 98118.

Lührmann, Anna. "Disrupting the Autocratization Sequence: Towards Democratic Resilience." *Democratization*, 28 (2021), 1017–1039.
Lührmann, Anna, and Staffan I. Lindberg. "A New Way of Measuring Shifts toward Autocracy." In *Post–Cold War Democratic Declines: The Third Wave of Autocratization*. Carnegie Europe (June 27, 2019), www.carnegieeurope.eu/2019/06/27/post-cold-war-democratic-declines-third-wave-of-autocratization-pub-79378.
Lust, Ellen, and David Waldner. "Unwelcome Change: Understanding, Evaluating and Extending Theories of Democratic Backsliding." *USAID* (2015). www.pdf.usaid.gov/pdf_docs/PBAAD635.pdf.
Maduro, Miguel, and Paul Kahn. "Introduction: A New Beginning." In Miguel Maduro and Paul Kahn (eds.) *Democracy in Times of Pandemic*. Cambridge, Cambridge University Press, 2020, pp. 1–18.
Mafei, Rafael, Thomas Bustamante, and Emilio Peluso Neder Meyer. "Brazil: From Antiestablishmentarianism to Bolsonarism." In András Sajo, Renata Uitz, and Stephen Holmes (eds.), *The Routledge Handbook on Illiberalism*. In press.
Magyar, Bálint. *Post-Communist Mafia State: The Case of Hungary*. Budapest: CEU Press, 2016.
Mansbridge, Jane, and Stephen Macedo. "Populism and Democratic Theory." *Annual Review of Law and Social Science*, 15 (2019), 59–77.
Mate, Manoj. "Constitutional Erosion and the Challenge to Secular Democracy in India." In Mark Graber, Sanford Levinson, and Mark Tushnet (eds.), *Constitutional Democracy in Crisis?* Oxford: Oxford University Press, 2018, pp. 377–394.
Mazzoleni, Gianpietro, and Roberta Bracciale, "Socially Mediated Populism: The Communicative Strategies of Political Leaders on Facebook." *Palgrave Communications*, 4 (2018). DOI: 10.1057/s41599-018-0104-x.
Mede, Niels, and Mike Schäfer. "Science-Related Populism: Conceptualizing Populist Demands toward Science." *Public Understanding of Science*, 29 (2020), 473–491.
Mendonça, Ricardo F., and Renato Duarte Caetano. "Populism as Parody: The Visual Self-Presentation of Jair Bolsonaro on Instagram." *The International Journal of Press/Politics*, 2 (2021), 210–235.
Meyer, Emilio, and Thomas Bustamate. "Authoritarianism without Emergency Powers: Brazil under COVID-19." *Verfassungsblog* (April 8, 2020). www.verfassungsblog.de/authoritarianism-without-emergency-powers-brazil-under-covid-19.
Meyer, Emilio Peluso Neder, and João Andrade Neto, "Courts Are Finally Standing Up to Bolsonaro." *Verfassungsblog* (August 9, 2021).
Miller, Joanne, Kyle Saunders, and Christina Farhart. "Conspiracy Endorsement as Motivated Reasoning: The Moderating Roles of Political Knowledge and Trust." *American Journal of Political Science*, 60 (2016), 824–844.

Minogue, Kenneth. "Populism as a Political Movement." In Ghita Ionescu and Ernest Gellner (eds.), *Populism: Its Meaning and National Characteristics*. London: Macmillan, 1969, pp. 197–211.

Mounk, Yascha. *The People vs. Democracy*. Cambridge: Harvard University Press, 2018.

Mudde, Cas. "Europe's Populist Surge." *Foreign Affairs*, 95/6 (November/ December 2016), 25–30.

Mukherjee, Gaurav. "Symposium: A Moment of Self-Reckoning for the Supreme Court of India? Reflections on the Judges' Press Conference." IACL-AIDC Blog (May 18, 2018). www.blog-iacl-aidc.org/blog/2018/5/17/a-moment-of-self-reckoning-for-the-supreme-court-of-india-reflections-on-the-judges-press-conference.

Mukherji, Rahul. "Covid vs. Democracy: India's Illiberal Remedy." *Journal of Democracy*, 31/4 (2020), 91–105.

Müller, Jan-Werner. *"Populism and Constitutionalism."* In Cristóbal Rovira Kaltwasser, Paul Taggart, Paulina Ochoa Espejo, and Pierre Ostiguy (eds.), *Oxford Handbook of Populism*. Oxford: Oxford University Press, 2017, pp. 590–606.

  "Protecting the Rule of Law (and Democracy!) in the EU: The Idea of a Copenhagen Commission." In Carlos Closa and Dimitry Kochenov (eds.), *Reinforcing Rule of Law Oversight in the European Union*. Cambridge: Cambridge University Press, 2016, pp. 206–224.

  What Is Populism? Philadelphia: University of Pennsylvania Press, 2016.

Novakova, Nataliya. "Civil Society in Central Europe: Threats and Ways Forward." GMF Policy Paper No. 21 (October 2020).

Panizza, Francisco. "Introduction: Populism and the Mirror of Democracy." In Francisco Panizza (ed.), *Populism and the Mirror of Democracy*. London: Verso, 2005, pp. 1–31.

Pardavi, Márta, and András Kádár. "Hungary Should Not Become Patient Zero," *Just Security* (April 22, 2020). www.justsecurity.org/69780/hungary-should-not-become-patient-zero.

Pasquino, Gianfranco. "Populism and Democracy." In Daniele Albertazzi and Duncan McDonnell (eds.), *Twenty-first Century Populism*. Hampshire: Palgrave Macmillan, 2008, pp. 15–29.

Pei, Minxin. "China's Coming Upheaval: Competition, the Coronavirus, and the Weakness of Xi Jinping." *Foreign Affairs*, 99/3 (May–June 2020), 82–95.

Pérez Hernáiz, Hugo Antonio. "The Uses of Conspiracy Theories for the Construction of a Political Religion in Venezuela." *International Journal of Humanities and Social Sciences*, 2 (2008), 970–981.

Plenta, Peter. "Conspiracy Theories as a Political Iinstrument: Utilization of Anti-Soros Narratives in Central Europe." *Contemporary Politics*, 26 (2020), 512–530.

Posner, Eric A. "The Dictator's Handbook, US Edition." In Cass R. Sunstein (ed.), *Can It Happen Here? Authoritarianism in America*. New York: HarperCollins, 2018, pp. 1–18.

Porterfield, Carlie. "Brazil's Bolsonaro Floats Conspiracy Theory That Coronavirus May Be 'Biological Warfare.'" *Forbes* (May 6, 2021). www.forbes.com/sites/carlieporterfield/2021/05/05/brazils-bolsonaro-floats-conspiracy-theory-that-coronavirus-may-be-biological-warfare/?sh=374800c32bb5

Przeworski, Adam. *Crises of Democracy*. Cambridge: Cambridge University Press, 2019.

Radnóti, Sándor. "A Sacred Symbol in a Secular Country: The Holy Crown." In Gábor Attila Tóth (ed.), *Constitution for a Disunited Nation: On Hungary's 2011 Fundamental Law*. Budapest, CEU Press, York, 2012, pp. 85–109.

Repucci, Sarah, and Amy Slipowitz. "Democracy under Lockdown." *Freedom House Special Report* (2020) 3. https://freedomhouse.org/sites/default/files/2020-10/COVID-19_Special_Report_Final_.pdf.

Rockwell, Rick. "Populism and Modern-Day Conspiracy Theories." *Global Americans* (May 17, 201). www.theglobalamericans.org/2015/05/populism-and-modern-day-conspiracy-theories.

Rodrik, Dani. "Has Globalization Gone Too Far?" *California Management Review*, 39 (Spring 1997), 29–53.

"Populism and the Economics of Globalization." *Journal of International Business Policy*, 1 (2018), 12–33.

"The Politics of Anger." *Project Syndicate* (March 9, 2016), www.project-syndicate.org/commentary/the-politics-of-anger-by-dani-rodrik-2016-03.

Rosenberg, Shawn W. "Democracy Devouring Itself: The Rise of the Incompetent Citizen and the Appeal of Right Wing Populism." *UC Irvine Previously Published Works* (2019), www.escholarship.org/uc/item/8806z01m.

Rovira Kaltwasser, Cristóbal. "Populism and the Question of How to Respond to It." In Cristóbal Rovira Kaltwasser, Paul Taggart, Paulina Ochoa Espejo, and Pierre Ostiguy (eds.), *Oxford Handbook of Populism*. Oxford: Oxford University Press, 2017, pp. 489–507.

Runciman, David. *How Democracy Ends*. London: Profile Books, 2018.

Rutzen, Douglas. "Authoritarianism Goes Global (II): Civil Society under Assault." *Journal of Democracy*, 26/4 (2015), 28–39.

Sadurski, Wojciech. *Poland's Constitutional Breakdown*. Oxford: Oxford University Press, 2019.

Sajó, András. *Ruling by Cheating*. Cambridge: Cambridge University Press, 2021.

Sánchez Urribarrí, Raul A. "Populism, Constitutional Democracy, and High Courts: Lessons from the Venezuelan Case." In Martin Krygier, Adam Czarnota, and Wojciech Sadurski (eds.), *Anti-Constitutional Populism*. In press.

Sandvik, Kristin Bergtora, Hans Petter Graver, and Peter Sharff Smith. "The Pomp of Popular Constitutional Outrage." *Verfassungsblog* (March 2, 2021). www.verfassungsblog.de/the-pomp-of-popular-constitutional-outrage.

Scheppele, Kim Lane. "Hungary: An Election in Question, Part 1." *New York Times* (February 28, 2014). www.krugman.blogs.nytimes.com/2014/02/28/hungary-an-election-in-question-part-1.

"Hungary: An Election in Question, Part 2." *New York Times* (February 28, 2014). www.krugman.blogs.nytimes.com/2014/02/28/hungary-an-election-in-question-part-2.

"Hungary: An Election in Question, Part 5." *New York Times* (February 28, 2014). https://krugman.blogs.nytimes.com/2014/02/28/hungary-an-election-in-question-part-5.

"The Opportunism of Populists and the Defense of Constitutional Liberalism." *German Law Journal*, 20 (2019), 314–331.

Scheppele, Kim Lane, and R. Daniel Kelemen. "Defending Democracy in EU Member States: Beyond Article 7 TEU." In Francesca Bignami (ed.), *EU Law in Populist Times: Crises and Prospects*. Cambridge: Cambridge University Press, 2020, pp. 413–456.

Scheppele, Kim Lane, and David Pozen. "Executive Overreach and Underreach in the Pandemic." In Miguel Maduro and Paul Kahn (eds.), *Democracy in Times of Pandemic*. Cambridge: Cambridge University Press, 2020, pp. 38–53.

Schroeder, Ralph. "The Populist Revolt against the West." *Comparative Sociology*, 20 (2021), 419–440.

Schulman, Ari. "The Coronavirus and the Right's Scientific Counterrevolution." *The New Republic* (June 15, 2020). www.newrepublic.com/article/158058/coronavirus-conservative-experts-scientific-counterrevolution.

Schultheis, Emily. "Viktor Orbán Has Declared War on Mayors." *Foreign Policy Magazine* (July 28, 2020). www.foreignpolicy.com/2020/07/28/viktor-Orbán-has-declared-a-war-on-mayors.

Serhan, Yasmeen. "Vaccine Nationalism Is Doomed to Fail." *The Atlantic* (December 8, 2020). www.amp.theatlantic.com/amp/article/617323.

Shapiro, Martin. *Courts*. Chicago: The University of Chicago Press, 1981.

Sharma, Chanchal Kumar, and Wilfried Swenden. "Modi-fying Indian Federalism? Centre-State Relations under Modi's Tenure as Prime Minister." *Indian Politics and Policy*, 1/1 (2018), 51–81.

Silva, Yago Matheus. "Bolsonaro and Social Media: A Critical Discourse Analysis of the Brazilian President's Populist Communication on Twitter." Master's Thesis, Uppsala Universitet, June 2020.

Singh, Pawan. "*Aadhaar* and Data Privacy: Biometric Identification and Anxieties of Recognition in India." *Information, Communication and Society*, 24 (2021), 978–993.

Sinpeng, Aim, Dimitar Gueorguiev, and Aries A. Arugay. "Strong Fans, Weak Campaigns: Social Media and Duterte in the 2016 Philippine Election." *Journal of East Asian Studies*, 20 (2020), 353–374.

Smith, Amy Erica. "Covid vs. Democracy: Brazil's Populist Playbook." *Journal of Democracy*, 31/4 (October 2020), 76–90.

Snyder, Timothy. *The Road to Unfreedom*. New York: Penguin Random House, 2018.

Somer, Murat, Jennifer L. McCoy, and Russell E. Luke. "Pernicious Polarization, Autocratization and Opposition Strategies." *Democratization*, 28 (2021), 929–948.

Sommer, Allison. "Did the Spanish Flu Pandemic Really Lead to the Rise of Nazism?" *Haaretz* (May 16, 2020). www.haaretz.com/us-news/.premium-did-the-spanish-flu-pandemic-really-lead-to-the-rise-of-nazism-1.8825631.

Spierings, Niels, and Andrej Zaslove. "Gender, Populist Attitudes and Voting: Explaining the Gender Gap in Voting for Populist Radical Rights and Populist Radical Left Parties." *West European Politics*, 40 (2017), 821–847.

Stanley, Ben. "Populism in Central and Eastern Europe." In Cristóbal Rovira Kaltwasser, Paul Taggart, Paulina Ochoa-Espejo, and Pierre Ostiguy (eds.), *The Oxford Handbook of Populism*. Oxford: Oxford University Press, 2017), pp. 140–160.

Steinhardt, Christoph. "How Is High Trust in China Possible? Comparing the Origins of Generalized Trust in Three Chinese Societies." *Political Studies*, 60/1 (2012), 434–454.

Suresh, Sandeep. "Gautam Bhatia. The Transformative Constitution: A Radical Biography in Nine Acts." *International Journal of Constitutional Law*, 18 (2020), 668–672.

Taibbi, Matt. *Insane Clown President: Dispatching from the 2016 Circus*. New York: Spiegel and Grau, 2017.

Toth, Tamas. "Target the Enemy: Explicit and Implicit Populism in the Rhetoric of the Hungarian Right." *Journal of Contemporary European Studies* (2020). DOI: 10.1080/14782804.2020.1757415.

Trinkunas, Harold. "Why Venezuela's Opposition Has Been Unable to Effectively Challenge Maduro." *Brookings* (January 8, 2018). www.brookings.edu/blog/order-from-chaos/2018/01/08/why-venezuelas-opposition-has-been-unable-to-effectively-challenge-maduro.

Truong, Mai. "Explaining Public Trust in Vietnam." *Asia Times* (October 7, 2020). www.asiatimes.com/2020/10/explaining-public-trust-in-vietnam.

"Vietnam's COVID-19 Success Is a Double-Edged Sword for the Communist Party." *The Diplomat* (August 6, 2020). www.thediplomat.com/2020/08/vietnams-covid-19-success-is-a-double-edged-sword-for-the-communist-party/.

Tumber, Howard, and Silvio Waisbord. "Media, Disinformation, and Populism." In Howard Tumber and Silvio Waisbord (eds.), *The Routledge Companion to Media Disinformation and Populism*. London: Routledge, 2021, pp. 13–25.

Tushnet, Mark. "Authoritarian Constitutionalism." *Cornell Law Review*, 100 (2015), 391–462.

"Comparing Right-Wing and Left-Wing Populism." In Mark Graber, Sanford Levinson, and Mark Tushnet (eds.), *Constitutional Democracy in Crisis?* Oxford: Oxford University Press, 2018, pp. 639–650.

Tushnet, Mark, and Bojan Bugarič. *Power to the People: Constitutionalism after Populism*. Oxford: Oxford University Press, 2021.

Uitz, Renáta. "Can You Tell When an Illiberal Democracy Is in the Making? An Appeal to Comparative Constitutional Scholarship from Hungary." *International Journal of Constitutional Law*, 13 (2015), 279–300.

Urbinati, Nadia. *Democracy Disfigured: Opinion, Truth, and the People*. Cambridge: Harvard University Press, 2014.

Me the People: How Populism Transforms Democracy. Cambridge: Harvard University Press, 2019.

V-Dem Institute. "Autocratization Turns Viral: Democracy Report 2021." The University of Gothenburg (March 2021).

Vaishnav, Milan. "Electoral Bonds: The Safeguards of Indian Democracy Are Crumbling." Carnegie Endowment for International Peace (November 25, 2019). www.carnegieendowment.org/2019/11/25/electoral-bonds-safeguards-of-indian-democracy-are-crumbling-pub-80428.

Vörös, Imre. "Hungary's Constitutional Evolution during the Last 25 Years." *Südeuropa*, 63 (2015), 173–200.

Waisbord, Silvio, and Adriana Amado. "Populist Communication by Digital Means: Presidential Twitter in Latin America." *Information, Communication and Society*, 20 (2017), 1330–1346.

Waldron, Jeremy. "The Core of the Case against Judicial Review." *Yale Law Journal*, 115 (2006), 1346–1406.

Walker, Neil. "The Crisis of Democratic Leadership in Times of Pandemic." In Miguel Maduro and Paul Kahn (eds.), *Democracy in Times of Pandemic*, Cambridge: Cambridge University Press, 2020), pp. 23–38.

Weyland, Kurt. "Populism's Threat to Democracy: Comparative Lessons for the United States." *Perspectives on Politics* (2020). DOI: 10.1017/S1537592719003955.

"The Threat from the Populist Left." *Journal of Democracy*, 24/3 (2013), 18–32.

White, Jonathan. "Emergency Europe after Covid-19." In Gerard Delanty (ed.), *Pandemics, Politics, and Society: Critical Perspectives on the Covid-19 Crisis*. Berlin: De Gruyter, 2021, pp. 75–92.

Wike, Richard, Katie Simmons, Bruce Stokes, and Janell Fetterolf. "Globally, Broad Support for Representative and Direct Democracy." *Pew Research Center* (October 6, 2017).

Wirz, Dominique. "Persuasion through Emotion? An Experimental Test of the Emotion-Eliciting Nature of Populist Communication." *International Journal of Communication*, 12 (2018), 1114–1138.

Wolff, Sarah, and Stella Ladi. "European Union Responses to the Covid-19 Pandemic: Adaptability in Times of Permanent Emergency." *Journal of European Integration*, 42/8 (2020), 1025–1040.

The World Bank, GovData360. "Civil Society Participation." *World Bank*

Zakaria, Fareed. *Ten Lessons for a Post-Pandemic World*. New York: W. W. Norton, 2020.

"The Rise of Illiberal Democracy." *Foreign Affairs*, 76/6 (November/December 1997), 22–43.

Zarefsky, David, and Dima Mohammed. "The Rhetorical Stance of Populism." In Ingeborg van der Geest, Henrike Jansen, and Bart van Klink, eds., *Vox Populi: Populism as a Rhetorical and Democratic Challenge*. Cheltenham: Edward Elgar Publishing, 2020, pp. 17–28.

ACKNOWLEDGMENTS

Martin Krygier and Jan Zielonka read the entire manuscript and provided me with invaluable friendly criticism. I am very grateful to them, as I am to Bojan Bugaric, who commented on several parts of the book, and to Eszter Bodnár, Thomas Bustamante, Gábor Halmai, Raul Sanchez-Urribarri, and Kim Lane Scheppele, who responded gracefully to my requests for information and opinion on this and that.

I thank Robert Clarke, Alexandre Fleck, Kirsty Gan, Pooja Khatri, and Katelin Schelks for their helpful input from the earliest stages of this project. Samuel Issacharoff let me read and permitted use of his as-yet-unpublished book manuscript; thank you, Sam. Two new books related to populism, by Mark Tushnet and Bojan Bugaric, and by Jean Cohen and Andrew Arato, came too late in the process for me to take them onboard as thoroughly as they deserve. But I am grateful to those colleagues for liaising with me on their work. Marianne Nield, Laura Blake, and the whole team at Cambridge University Press have been immensely encouraging and effective.

I acknowledge, with gratitude, the support by the Australian Research Council for a collaborative project of which I am a part, along with Adam Czarnota and Martin Krygier, and with Carolyn Evans as the project's Research Associate. I greatly value my main academic home, Sydney Law School, with its dean, Simon Bronitt, and my second academic home, Centre for Europe of the University of Warsaw, with its head, Kamil Zajączkowski, as well, of course, as my real home and the family in it.

INDEX

abortion, 109, 141, 183
Alfani, Guido, 175
Amar, Akhil Reed, 104
American Civil Liberties Union, 74
American Convention of Human Rights, 216
American Dream, 26–27
anti-colonialism, 42
anti-elitism, 32–34, 150
anti-globalization, 35, 37
anti-government coalitions, 210–212
Anti-Muslim Citizenship Act (India), 94
anti-populist strategies
  civil society, 214–218
  cordon sanitaire, 212–214
  electoral, 208–212
  incorporation, 214–218
anti-Semitism, 4
Anti-Terrorism Act of 2020 (Phillipenes), 68
Arato, Andrew, 118
Assad, Bashar al-, 7
authoritarian advantage, 176, 203

Balint, Magyar, 64
Barber, N. W., 58
Bathia, Gautha, 93
Ben-Ghiat, Ruth, 170
Bickel, Alexander, 106, 111
Biernat, Stanisław, 120
BJP, 97, *See* Modi, Narendra
  judiciary (attacks on), 92
  media (attacks on), 73
Blokker, Paul, 43
Bodnár, Eszter, 123, 136
Bolivar, Simon, 91, 160

Bolsonaro, Jair, 7, 161–162, 165, 186–187, 207, 214
  Congress, 66
  conspiracy theories, 147, 184
  Covid response, 134–135, 181, 187, 189, 191, 193–194, 203
  election law changes, 63
  election of, 125–126, 166
  judiciary (attacks on), 63, 116–117, 125, 134–135
  media (attacks on), 72–73, 168
  military, 60, 214
  NGOs, 76
  rhetoric, 60, 69, 159, 162
  social media, 170
Bonikowski, Bart, 11, 23
Brexit, 28, 42, 44, 106, 155
Budget Council
  of Hungary, 87–88
Bugarič, Bojan, 12, 48, 50

campaign finance, 65–66
Carothers, Thomas, 190, 193
Castro, Fidel, 146, 154
Central European University, 2, 137
centralization of power, 87
Chafetz, Josh, 80
Chávez, Hugo, 4, 53, 60
  conspiracy theories, 147, 149
  Constituent Assembly, 49
  constitutional amendment, 83–85
  executive aggrandizement, 61
  judiciary (attacks on), 91, 114–115, 123–124
  media (attacks on), 74, 114–115, 162
  rhetoric, 159–160, 166

INDEX

social media, 170
term limits, 43, 91
China, 21, 37, 176, 178, 184–185, 193, 197–198, 200
China trade shock, 37
Choudry, Sujit, 79
Christianity, 39–40, 96, 171
civil society, 9, 39, 57, 74, 76, 108, 190, 204, 215
clientelism, 207
climate change, 165
Cohen, Jean, 219
common sense, 103, 149, 165, 188, 190, 204
Communism, 85, 118, 214
conspiracy theories
　anti-elitism, 150
　Bhima Koregaon 16, 147
　causes of, 43, 148
　collective narcissism, 150–151
　communist plots, 147
　construction of, 148–149
　Covid-19, 147
　deep state, 214
　great replacement, 145–146
　polarization, 152
　Smolensk accident, 144–145, 151
Constitution
　of Hungary (1989), 85
　of India, 93, 95
　of Poland, 96
　of the Philippenes, 92
　of Venezuela (1961), 84
　of Venezuela (1999), 61, 83
constitutional amendments
　in Hungary, 85–86, 136
　in Poland, 96–97
　in Venezuela, 84, 91
constitutional courts, 116, 121–124, 130–132, 139
Copenhagen Commission, 217
cosmopolitanism, 1, 42
Council of Europe, 39, 44, 101, 215
coups, 4, 69, 78, 81, 115, 123
Court of Justice of the European Union, 133, 135, 216
court packing, 122
Covid responses
　importance of trust, 195–198
　international cooperation, 198–203
　seizure of power, 181–185
　transparency, 190–192
cult of personality, 6, 160–161

Data Protection Ombudsman (Hungary), 56
de Búrca, Gráinne, 45
de Zavala, Agnieszka Golec, 151
deep state, 33–34
democracy
　Christian, 40
　consolidated, 21
　illiberal, 8
democratic backsliding, 78, 222
democratic erosion, 9, 79
democratization, 20–21, 42, 80, 125, 165
discriminatory legalism, 5
disinformation, 134, 154, 156, 213
Dixon, Rosalind, 83, 99
Duda, Andrzej, 131
　2020 campaign, 61
　Covid response, 181
　judiciary (attacks on), 130–131
　norm breaking, 101, 114
　reelection, 180–181
Duterte, Rodrigo, 7, 60, 214
　Covid response, 181–183, 194–195, 197
　drug war, 68, 124
　executive aggrandizement, 92–95
　judiciary (attacks on), 92, 124–125
　media (attacks on), 168
　narcopoliticians, 69
　public safety, 60
　rhetoric, 76, 92, 162, 197
　social media, 170
Dworkin, Ronald, 220

echo chamber, 170
Ecuador, 46, 59, 83, 91
Effron, David, 157
Elections
　in Brazil (2018), 126
　in Hungary (2002), 60
　in Hungary (2010), 85

Elections (cont.)
  in Poland (2020), 181
  in Venezuela (2012), 115
  in Venezuela (2015), 180–181
Electoral Commission
  of Hungary, 57, 62, 65
  of India, 62
  of Poland, 61
Electoral Council
  of Venezuela, 61
Electoral Court
  of Brazil, 63, 135
electoral fraud, 60
  allegations of, 60, 63
Enabling Act (Hungary), 69, 178
Enlightenment, 4, 25, 219
equality
  gender, 151, 219
  political, 33
  racial, 219
establishment
  political, 19, 25, 28, 33, 150, 219
  scientific, 187, 189
European Central Bank, 202
European Commission, 153, 201, 216
European Court of Human Rights, 128, 132, 215
European Union, 28, 45, 200
  attacks on, 75, 96, 133, 167
  austerity measures, 46
  Covid response, 201–203
  refugee policy, 30
  role in responding to populism, 214–218

Facebook, 146, 169, 183–184
fake news, 135, 155, 165, 183, 205
fascism, 4
Fauci, Anthony, 187, 189
feminism, 42
Fidesz, 63, 66, 69–70, 88, 97, 164, *See* Orban, Viktor
Fieschi, Catherine, 156
Five Star Movement (Italy), 46, 50
Fleck, Alexandre, 125
France, 28, 46, 66, 175
free trade, 27, 35–36
Freedom House, 208, 224–225

Freeman, Will, 56
Fundamental Law (of Hungary), 86
  adoption of, 86
  contents of, 40–41, 87–88, 90, 97, 121
  drafting of, 69, 85
  funding of NGOs, 74–76

Gagliardi, Juliana, 166
Galloway, Scott, 48, 50
Garancsi, István, 3
Gdula, Maciej, 30
gerrymandering, 63
Gersdorf, Małgorzata, 130–131, 133
Gidron, Noam, 31
Ginsburg, Tom, 78, 98
Global Financial Crisis, 46, 200
globalization, 24–25, 28, 34–37, 46, 174, 198, 200–201, 203, 219
Greece, 46, 197
Grzymala-Busse, Anna, 103

Hall, Peter, 31
Hathaway, Oona, 201
Hernáiz, Hugo Pérez, 148
Hochschild, Arlie Russell, 25–27
Hofstadter, Richard, 147–148, 166, 186
Holmes, Stephen, 32, 156, 206
Human Rights Watch, 182–183
Huq, Aziz, 78, 98–99
hydroxychloroquine, 187

Ignatieff, Michael, 177
immigration, 29, 37, 40, 44, 46, 70, 145, 165, 184, 212
impeachment, 92, 104, 117, 124, 134
Inaugural Address (of Donald Trump), 32–33
institutions, undermining of
  electoral institutions, 59–66
  media (attacks on), 69–74
  NGOs, 74–77
  parliament, 66–69
International Criminal Court, 92
International Health Regulations (of 2005), 200
International Monetary Fund, 46
Iran, 21, 184

Issacharoff, Samuel, 13, 56, 99
Istanbul Convention, 39
Italy, 28, 46, 50, 163, 175, 185, 212

Jammu and Kashmir, 95
Jaya, Niraja Gopal, 94
Jews, 1, 4, 30, 146, 151, 164, 177
Jobbik, 164, 208
judicial independence, 57
judicial populism, 110–111
judicial resistance to populism, 132–138
Júnior, João Feres, 166
juristocracy, 138–139

Kaczyński, Jarosław, 4, 33, 96–97,
    143–144, 161, 164, 168, 173, 207
  conspiracy theories, 33, 60, 151, 153
  corruption, 5–6
  Covid response, 180
  judiciary (attacks on), 126, 141
  media (attacks on), 69, 168–169
  norm breaking, 114
  refugee politics, 29
  rhetoric, 31, 43, 54, 60, 162, 166
Kaczyński, Lech, 143–145, 152
Kahn, Paul, 176
Kaltwasser, Cristóbal Rovira, 11
Karácsony, Gergely, 193, 210
Kazai, Viktor, 137, 141
Khaitan, Tarunabh, 93, 95
Kirchner, Cristina Fernández de, 4, 147
Kis, János, 44, 86
Kövér, László, 69, 179
Krastev, Ivan, 156, 174, 200
Krygier, Martin, 51, 54, 102
Kumar, Alok Prasanna, 116
Kuo, Ming-Sung, 56
Kúria. See Supreme Court (of Hungary)

Lánczi, András, 161
Landau, David, 83, 99
Le Pen, Marine, 22, 173
Levitsky, Steven, 21–22, 105
LGBTQ rights, 90
Lindberg, Staffan I., 79
lockdowns, 20–21, 116, 182, 190
Lührmann, Anna, 79
Lust, Ellen, 23, 81

Macedo, Stephen, 11
Maduro, Miguel, 176
mafia state, 6
Magyar, Bálint, 164
mainstream media, 70, 168, 213
Manowska, Małgorzata, 131
Mansbridge, Jane, 11
mask mandates, 134
May, Theresa, 45
Media Council
  of Hungary, 70–71
  of Poland, 70
militant democracy, 214
military, 9, 33, 60, 76, 117, 123, 125,
    143–145, 179, 182, 214
Minogue, Kenneth, 158
misinformation, 134, 154, 201
Modi, Narendra, 42, 93, 147, 160, 162
  conspiracy theories, 147
  election law changes, 62
  executive aggrandizement, 94–95
  Hindu Nationalism, 60, 94–95, 147
  judiciary (attacks on), 107, 111–112,
    115–117
  media (attacks on), 73, 168
  NGOs, 75–76
  rhetoric, 73, 158, 162, 165
  social media, 183
Morales, Evo, 83, 91
Mounk, Yascha, 103
Müller, Jan-Werner, 10, 74, 217
multiculturalism, 28–29, 40, 42, 172, 212
Muslims, 1, 4, 30, 37, 93, 146–147, 164,
    166, 184
Myanmar, 117

National Council of the Judiciary
    (Poland), 96, 101, 113, 126,
    128–131, 135
nationalism, 24–25, 36–37, 42,
    198–199, 219
  economic, 36, 44
neo-Nazi, 77
Netanyahu, Benjamin, 107, 185,
    210–211
Nixon, Richard, 100
North African refugee crisis, 150
North Korea, 7, 21

Obama, Barack, 157
Orbán, Viktor, 3, 7, 122, 161, 173, 193, 207, 214
  anti-Semitism, 146, 164
  conspiracy theories, 145, 151–152, 214
  Covid response, 178–180, 182, 193
  illiberal democracy, 8
  judiciary (attacks on), 107, 121, 132, 136
  media (attacks on), 3, 70–72, 90, 160, 168, 193
  refugee policies, 30
oversight, institutional, 56

parliament
  of, 101
  of Hungary, 1, 3, 55, 62, 64, 67, 69–70, 86–87, 90, 122, 136
  of Poland, 52, 61, 113, 118–119, 126
  of Venezuela, 49, 84, 115, 182
  system, 17
PiS [Law and Justice Party], 5–6, 29–30, 33, 38–40, 43, 52, 97, 118
  climate change, 165
  corruption, 100
  intra-party fights, 95
  judiciary (attacks on), 106, 113, 119–120, 127, 129–131, 133
  legislative maneuvers, 102
  media (attacks on), 72
  parliamentary maneuvers, 67
Podemos, 46
Podgórecki, Adam, 155
polarization, 15, 85, 123, 152, 196, 212–213, 220
political constitutionalism, 138–139
political correctness, 162
political legitimacy, 59
Popper, Karl, 146
populism
  and conspiracy theories, 143–153, See conspiracy theories
  and Covid-19, 173
  and institutions, 48–51
    hollowing, 51–56
  and media, 168–171
  and truth, 153–157
  causes of

    anti-elitism, 34
    anti-modernism, 43
    illiberal impatience with institutions, 43–45
    nationalism, 34–38
    status anxiety, 25–29
    xenophobia, 29–30
  discursive concept of, 10–13
  diversity of, 17–20
  institutional concept of, 13–14
Posner, Eric, 100
Pozen, David, 80
propaganda, 1, 7, 30, 59, 71, 79, 107, 149, 164, 209
protectionism, 35–36
Przeworski, Adam, 20, 22, 35, 56, 109
Przyłębska, Julia, 120
public good, 12, 58, 105, 152, 174
public reason, 220

quarantine, 175, 181–182, 195

Radnóti, Sándor, 41
rationalism, 4
Rawls, John, 220
Reagan, Ronald, 27, 74
Recovery Plan (of the EU), 202
redistricting, 64
referenda, 42, 44, 84, 86, 95, 106, 114, 123
refugees, 25–26, 29, 36–37, 76–77, 159, 164, 184, 200, 219
Reporters Without Borders, 73
rhetoric (of populism), 157–163
  anti-LGBTQ, 40
  emotional appeals, 163–168
Rodrik, Dani, 35
Rosenberg, Shawn, 41
Rothschilds, the, 146
Roussef, Dilma, 146, 154
rule of law, 6, 8, 18, 45, 49, 97, 100, 138, 202, 215–218, 222–223
Runciman, David, 145, 150
Russia, 59, 80, 143, 145

Salvini, Matteo, 173, 184
Scheppele, Kim Lane, 14, 62, 65–66
Sejm. See Parliament (of Poland)

Selznick, Philip, 51
Sevel, Michael, 26–27
Shapiro, Martin, 108
Simicska, Lajos, 3
Snyder, Timothy, 145
social media, 42, 134, 147, 154, 165, 169–170, 183, 200–201, 213
social trust, 195–196
Socialist Party
 of Hungary, 3
Soros, George, 1–2, 4, 75, 145, 150–152, 157, 164–165
South Africa, 10, 85
Spain, 28, 46, 196
special legislative procedures
 in Hungary, 67–68
 in India, 67–68
 in Poland, 67
 in the Philippines, 68
Sri Lanka, 59, 208
Stalin, Joseph, 54, 61, 143, 148
state of emergency, 76, 179–181
Supreme Court
 of Brazil, 62–63, 125–126, 135
 of Hungary, 107, 132
 of India, 94, 111, 115–117, 134
 of Poland, 78, 114, 130–131
 of the Philippenes, 92–95, 125
 of the United States, 66, 100
 of Venezuela, 84, 91, 115
Syria, 7, 30, 72
Syriza, 46

Taibbi, Matt, 19
term limits, 43, 91–92, 114
Thatcher, Margaret, 74
transparency, 62, 65, 103, 190–192
Trianon Treaty, 64
Trump, Donald, 10, 22, 33, 50, 195, 212
 2016 election, 19
 Covid response, 184, 187–189, 191, 199, 203

judiciary (attacks on), 100
lies, 157
media (attacks on), 168
rhetoric, 32, 34, 159
Turkey, 10, 46, 59, 80, 178, 185
Tushnet, Mark, 12, 48, 50, 79, 104
Tusk, Donald, 143–144, 152, 165
Twitter, 169–170, 183

US presidential election
 of 2016, 19
unions
 decline of, 35
universities, 2, 9, 20, 37, 41, 129, 137, 168, 196, 219
unwritten norms, 102–103
Urbinati, Nadia, 9, 11, 33, 160, 168

vaccine nationalism, 198
vaccines, 198–199
Varga, András, 131–132, 138
V-Dem Institute, 9
Venice Commission, 87, 89–90
Vietnam, 21, 178, 185, 192, 197
Vörös, Imre, 88, 90

Waldner, David, 23, 81
war on drugs, 124, 154, 197
Watergate, 100
Wenliang Li, Dr, 190
Weyland, Kur, 53
WhatsApp, 170
Wong, David, 190, 193
World Bank, 46
World Health Organisation, 184, 188, 200–201, 203

xenophobia, 4, 19, 27, 29, 39, 184, 219

Zakharia, Fareed, 8
Ziblatt, David, 105
Zybertowicz, Andrzej, 167